LIFE TOGETHER

LIFE TOGETHER

Family, Sexuality and Community
in the New Testament and Today

STEPHEN C. BARTON

T&T CLARK
EDINBURGH & NEW YORK

T&T CLARK LTD

A Continuum imprint

59 George Street
Edinburgh EH2 2LQ
Scotland

www.tandtclark.co.uk

370 Lexington Avenue
New York 10017–6503
USA

www.continuumbooks.com

First published 2001

ISBN 0 567 08772 7

British Library Cataloguing-in-Publication Data
A catalogue record for this book is available from the British Library

Typeset by Waverley Typesetters, Galashiels
Printed and bound in Great Britain by Cromwell Press Ltd, Trowbridge, Wiltshire

To Robert Banks
teacher and friend
and
in loving memory of Julie

Contents

Preface

I should have been writing my doctoral thesis. Instead, I found myself attending lectures in the anthropology of religion and becoming engrossed in the literature of the social sciences. As things turned out, the courses of lectures and the reading were not all that unrelated to my doctoral research. They gave me some insight into society and culture and the complex interrelationship between culture, belief and sacred texts. They also laid the foundation for my ongoing curiosity regarding the social and symbolic dimensions of being human. Eventually this bore fruit in a thesis in New Testament Studies on *Discipleship and Family Ties in Mark and Matthew*. It bore fruit also in a preoccupation with the issues touched upon in the present collection of essays: the appropriation of Christian Scripture for illumination in our life together in matters of family, sexuality and community.

Most of the essays were written for particular occasions and in response to invitations. The first three, on the family, grew out of my doctoral research and also my participation in the Church of England Board for Social Responsibility Working Party on the Family which met between 1992 and 1995 and produced the report *Something to Celebrate: Valuing Families in Church and Society*. The first essay was written for a series in the *Expository Times* initiated by its editor Cyril Rodd. The second, on 'Biblical Hermeneutics and the Family', was presented at a Durham research seminar in 1994, coinciding with the United Nations International Year of the Family. The third was written for a special issue on 'The Family' of the North American journal *Interpretation*. In various ways each of these essays is concerned to show that Christian theology in general, and the Christian Scriptures in particular, have a vital contribution to make to contemporary wisdom about life together in families.

The same is true of the two essays about human sexuality. 'Is the Bible Good News for Human Sexuality?' was written by invitation for the inaugural number of the journal *Theology and Sexuality* and seeks to put questions about the interpretation of the Bible in the larger context of what it means to be the church and what kinds of readers we need to be to interpret wisely. Similarly, the essay on 'Thinking Theologically About Sexuality', first given as a public lecture in Durham Cathedral, grounds sexuality both in the Christian vision of God as a Trinity of love and in a doctrine of creation as God's play.

Then follow six essays under the broad rubric 'Community'. The first (Chapter 6) is a survey of the massive amount of work over the past three decades or so which attempts to delineate the social patterns of early Christian faith and life and the complex interplay between Christian faith and Graeco-Roman culture. The second (Chapter 7), delivered originally at a conference on biblical inter-pretation at King's College London in 1992, takes a critical look at attempts to use the sociology of sectarianism to describe early Christian sociality.

Chapter 8, on 'Women, Jesus and the Gospels', was written for a volume of essays edited by Richard Holloway and intended *inter alia* as a contribution to the Church of England debate in the early 1990s on the ordination of women to the priesthood. The essay is a call for a reading of the Gospels which is theological and ecclesial rather than 'purely' historical, in the belief that only so can the Gospels be interpreted in ways which are life-giving for women and men today.

Chapters 9 and 10 are a pair of essays which reflect on the nature of Christian community in the light of key New Testament texts: the Gospel of John and Paul's First Letter to the Corinthians. The former began life as a lecture to the Northumbria Community in July 1999, the latter as a lecture at the annual meeting of the Society for the Study of Christian Ethics in 1996 on the theme 'Christianity and Community'. Like several of the other essays in the collection, both of these are exercises in theologically engaged interpretation of Scripture with a view to the nurture of more godly patterns of Christian sociality today.

Since tolerance is accepted widely today as contributing to the common good, especially in pluralistic societies, I have included at the end of Part Two another essay on Paul, written originally for a conference at the Hebrew University in Jerusalem in April 1994 on the theme 'Tolerance and Its Limits in Early Judaism and Christianity'. One of my concerns in this essay is to question the usefulness of 'tolerance' as a category for understanding the moral world of early Judaism and Christianity and to ask what we lose if we neglect categories native to Paul's own way of seeing things.

Running through nearly all the essays is a concern with (what we commonly, but rather unfortunately, call) 'the use of the Bible': how may the ancient text of the Bible 'speak' to us today as Christian Scripture? To give an idea of my own response to this question, I have concluded the collection with an essay on the art of New Testament interpretation, given originally at the British New Testament Conference at Leeds University in 1997. Its central claim is that the Bible is the kind of text the truth of whose witness is discovered above all in the lives of individuals and communities seeking to share by grace in the life of the Trinity.

If this collection serves as an encouragement to such people, I shall be more than satisfied.

Acknowledgements

All the essays in this volume have appeared elsewhere in the past ten years, and are reprinted with permission. In a few cases, I have modified these earlier versions slightly, either to make corrections or to avoid unnecessary overlap. The details of previous publication are as follows:

Chapter 1: *New Occasions Teach New Duties?*, ed. C. S. Rodd (Edinburgh: T&T Clark, 1995), 159–72;

Chapter 2: *The Family in Theological Perspective*, ed. S. C. Barton (Edinburgh: T&T Clark, 1996), 3–23;

Chapter 3: *Interpretation* 52/2 (1998), 130–44;

Chapter 4: *Theology and Sexuality* 1 (1994), 42–54;

Chapter 5: *Religion and Sexuality*, ed. M. A. Hayes *et al.* (Sheffield: Sheffield Academic Press, 1998), 366–79;

Chapter 6: *Journal of Theological Studies* 43 (1992), 399–427;

Chapter 7: *The Open Text. New Directions for Biblical Studies?*, ed. F. Watson (London: SCM Press, 1993), 140–62;

Chapter 8: *Who Needs Feminism? Men Respond to Sexism in the Church*, ed. R. Holloway (London: SPCK, 1991), 32–58;

Chapter 9: *Christology, Controversy and Community. New Testament Essays in Honour of David R. Catchpole*, eds D. G. Horrell and C. Tuckett (Leiden: E. J. Brill, 2000), 279–301;

Chapter 10: *Studies in Christian Ethics* 10/1 (1997), 1–15;

Chapter 11: *Tolerance and Its Limits in Early Judaism and Christianity*, eds G. N. Stanton and G. G. Stroumsa (Cambridge: Cambridge University Press, 1998), 121–34;

Chapter 12: *Scottish Journal of Theology* 52/2 (1999), 179–208.

I have accumulated many debts in the course of writing these essays. Some of these are acknowledged in the footnotes. More generally, however, I would like to express my deep gratitude to my colleagues in the Department of Theology of the University of Durham, including the members of the New Testament Post-graduate Seminar where some of the pieces were given their first airing. For their companionship and fellowship in the gospel my gratitude goes also to the people of St John's Church, Neville's Cross, Durham. For their ongoing friendship, I wish to thank especially Walter Moberly, Richard and Clare Firth, Sue Martin, Nicholas Watkinson, Erin White and Graham English, and Jan MacGregor and George Hepburn. Most of all, I wish to thank my wife, Fiona, and our children, Anna, Thomas, Joseph and Miriam, for their ongoing love and nurture.

The book is dedicated to two people who taught me more than I can say about the meaning of friendship and the practice of Christian community.

Durham
July 2000

Part One

FAMILY AND SEXUALITY

1

Marriage and Family Life As Christian Concerns

I. Beginnings

Historically speaking, it is not at all surprising that marriage and family life have been Christian concerns from the very beginning. From Judaism, Christianity inherited sacred writings and an ethos in which genealogies, family relations and family law bulked large. From the Graeco-Roman world, Christianity inherited political ideals and patterns of social organization which accorded the patriarchal household a central role as the city state in microcosm. The New Testament and other early Christian writings bear witness to the pervasiveness of concerns related to marriage and the family. A list of examples would include: the teaching of Jesus prohibiting divorce; the sayings of Jesus about children; the 'hard' sayings in which Jesus summons followers to leave their families behind for his sake; stories of conversion by household; the practice of gathering for worship in 'house churches'; moral instruction for household members (the *Haustafeln*), including advice for spouses in 'mixed marriages'; and stories about the often disastrous effects of conversion upon family ties.[1]

The social sciences would lead us to expect to find marriage and family life high on the Christian agenda from the beginning, as well. From this perspective, the movement inaugurated by the charismatic leader Jesus was a new social world in the making, entry to which was a voluntary matter – one, not of ties of kinship or marriage, but of ties of a spiritual kind. This is epitomized in the

---

[1] I have explored this further in my book *Discipleship and Family Ties in Mark and Matthew* (Cambridge: Cambridge University Press, 1994).

saying of Jesus: 'Whoever does the will of God is my brother and
sister and mother' (Mk 3.35). But within this new social world,
urgent attention had to be given to the ordering of sexual relations,
gender roles, household patterns and communal authority. Mary
Douglas's anthropological studies point to the way in which a group
or society uses its members' physical bodies – in particular, the
boundaries and orifices of the body – as symbolic maps of the
larger and more complex social body.[2] It is understandable, therefore, that one of the ways in which Christianity established and
sought to maintain its own distinctive identity was by means of moral
rules governing who sleeps with whom, who eats with whom, and
who belongs to whom, i.e. rules about marriage and household
order. A rigorous marriage discipline enjoined upon men and
women alike, the advocacy and practice of celibacy in certain
quarters, and a strong but 'Christianized' household order were
potent (but by no means the only) ways of representing the new
life of the kingdom of God.[3] They were also ways of warding off the
accusation from outsiders that the Christian movement was socially
irresponsible and politically subversive.[4]

II. Marriage and family life as Christian concerns today

In addition to this distinctive inheritance, which has developed and
been elaborated in all kinds of ways throughout Christian history,[5]
many factors have contributed to making marriage and the family
lively Christian concerns still today. I draw particular attention to
the following.

[2] See Mary Douglas, *Purity and Danger* (London: Routledge & Kegan Paul, 1966),
and *Natural Symbols* (London: Barrie & Jenkins, 1973, 2nd edn).

[3] See further, O. Larry Yarbrough, *Not Like the Gentiles: Marriage Rules in the Letters
of Paul* (Chico: Scholars Press, 1985). That some early Christian women saw things
differently is well-demonstrated by Antoinette Clark Wire's study, *The Corinthian
Women Prophets* (Minneapolis: Fortress Press, 1990).

[4] This is the thrust of David L. Balch, *Let Wives Be Submissive: The Domestic Code in
I Peter* (Chico: Scholars Press, 1981).

[5] For useful historical surveys, see for example, Jack Goody, *The Development of
the Family and Marriage in Europe* (Cambridge: Cambridge University Press, 1983);
Ralph A. Houlbrooke, *The English Family 1450–1700* (London: Longman, 1984);
Peter Brown, *The Body and Society* (London: Faber & Faber, 1989); as well as the
essays on 'Church and Family' from a Christian feminist perspective by Rosemary
Radford Ruether in *New Blackfriars* 65 (January–May, 1984).

1. The impact of contemporary social trends in Britain[6]

The divorce rate in Britain is second only to Denmark in the European Community and stands at about 40 per cent of all marriages. The rate of remarriage is also high (although declining), one of the consequences of which is the growing number of step-relationships in families which are taking increasingly complex forms. The number of births out of wedlock continues to rise and the number of lone-parent families has more than doubled between 1971 and 1991. There are now 1.3 million lone-parent families containing 2.2 million children; and 90 per cent of these families are headed by a woman. Cohabitation, either prior to or as an alternative to marriage, has become widely accepted in society at large. The percentage of cohabitees doubled in the 1980s. In addition, demographic shifts due to changing economic circumstances and high rates of national unemployment have contributed significantly to family poverty and homelessness. Child poverty is now recognized as a major problem. These kinds of social trends are pervasive and affect the churches as well as the wider society. Hence the widespread interest in the United Nations' sponsored International Year of the Family in 1994. Hence also the proliferation of reports on the family coming from the social responsibility departments of most of the major Christian denominations.

2. The impact of the women's movement and feminism in its various forms

The critical analysis of marriage, childbearing and the family from the perspective of a feminist hermeneutic of suspicion has had a major impact, especially in the latter part of this century. We are more aware than ever before of the ways in which family, church and society have been organized along patriarchal lines, the effect of which has been to marginalize women in the public domain of politics and work and to subordinate them in the private domain of

[6] I am indebted for most of the information in this section to an unpublished paper entitled 'Family Trends and the Church' by Jonathan Bradshaw, Professor of Social Policy at the University of York. The paper was a contribution to the Working Party on the Family under the auspices of the Board for Social Responsibility of the Church of England. The report of the Working Party was published as *Something to Celebrate: Valuing Families in Church and Society* (London: Church House Publishing, 1995).

the family. Taking as a starting point women's own experience of
oppression, abuse and powerlessness, and the ways in which this
experience is reinforced by the way society distributes power and
opportunity along lines of gender difference, feminists have raised
major questions about all our social institutions, including marriage
and the family.[7]

In the continuing debate, Christian women and Christian
feminists have made important contributions. In a way without
parallel in human history, we are forced now to name sexism as a
sin and to struggle against it in all our family, church and social
relations. We are forced also to acknowledge the various ways in
which religious belief and 'biblical Christianity' have reinforced the
passivity of women in the face of abuse – by allowing them no voice
of their own, by inhibiting demonstrations of anger, and by
idealizing a notion of sacrifice which is self-destructive.[8] Speaking
at the broader cultural level, Rosemary Radford Ruether makes this
far-reaching recommendation for a way forward:

> What is needed is a redefinition of the relationship between home and
> work which would allow women to participate in the educational,
> cultural, political, and job opportunities of the public world, while
> integrating males into co-responsibility for parenting and homemaking.
> . . . We need a new culture of men and women, both as co-parents
> and partners in marriage and as co-workers in society, rather than a
> dichotomized culture that places them on opposite sides of the home –
> work division.[9]

3. Questions raised by advances in science and medicine

As is well known, the advent in the second half of this century of
mass-produced artificial contraceptives raised in a more acute way
than before questions about the nature and purpose of sexual

[7] The literature is growing apace. Two significant collections of essays are: Monica
Furlong, ed., *Mirror to the Church: Reflections on Sexism* (London: SPCK, 1988); and
Elisabeth Schüssler Fiorenza and Mary Shawn Copeland, eds, *Violence Against Women*
(London: SCM Press, 1994). See also Janet Martin Soskice, 'Women's Problems',
in A. Walker, ed., *Different Gospels* (London: SPCK, 1993), 194–203.

[8] See further Susan Brooks Thistlethwaite, 'Every Two Minutes: Battered Women
and Feminist Interpretation', in Letty M. Russell, ed., *Feminist Interpretation of the
Bible* (Oxford: Blackwell, 1985), 96–107.

[9] Rosemary Radford Ruether, 'Church and Family: Feminism, Church and Family
in the 1980s', *New Blackfriars* 65 (1984), 202–12 at 209–10, 211.

intercourse and the place of children in marriage.[10] The availability
of, and increasingly common recourse to, legal abortion has served
to reinforce these questions. In addition, recent developments in
biotechnology and scientific research have had a significant impact.
There is now a wide social and moral-theological debate taking place
about issues like *in vitro* fertilization, surrogate motherhood, genetic
engineering and the use of aborted foetal tissue for experimentation.[11] At the macro-social level, the debate over human fertility
control is related also to ecological concerns about overpopulation
and the protection of the environment.[12] In various and complex
ways, all of these issues bear on marriage and the family, and raise
moral and practical issues which it is important for Christians to
address. The kinds of issues I have in mind are, for example: What
is the relation of human beings to their own bodies? What are the
moral limits to technological intervention in the processes of nature?
To what extent are our values about biotechnology the product of
an unexamined liberal revolution which has turned us all into
private consumers of whatever technology has to offer, irrespective
of questions of moral truth?[13]

4. Our increased awareness of problems in family life

It is probably fair to say that the institutions of marriage and the
family are widely perceived to be in a state of crisis. Lord Jakobovitz
articulated this perception in a recent address when he said:

> I am not quite sure that we yet appreciate the depth of the crisis that
> currently besets the home, and the awesome price that we pay for the
> alarming breakdown of the family, on a scale that has made the family

[10] Of course, the use of artificial contraception goes back to antiquity and has
been a subject of moral debate throughout Christian history. See on this J. T.
Noonan, Jr, *Contraception: A History of its Treatment by the Catholic Theologians and
Canonists* (Cambridge, Mass.: Harvard University Press, 1965) and A. S. McLaren,
A History of Contraception (Oxford: Blackwell, 1992).
[11] See, for example, J. Mahoney, *Bioethics and Belief* (London: Sheed & Ward,
1984) and *The Making of Moral Theology* (Oxford: Oxford University Press, 1987);
also helpful are K. Boyd *et al.*, *Life Before Birth* (London: SPCK, 1986), and Kevin T.
Kelly, *Life and Love: Towards a Christian Dialogue on Bioethical Questions* (London:
Collins, 1987).
[12] See on this Edward P. Echlin, 'Population and Catholic Theology: Discovering
Fire Anew', *The Month* (January, 1992), 35–8.
[13] These are the questions addressed by Oliver O'Donovan's study of *in vitro*
fertilization: *Begotten or Made?* (Oxford: Oxford University Press, 1984).

a disaster area of modern times. Marriage is under siege, and married couples in their relationship to children with a loving home are almost beginning to be an endangered species. The price we pay is a crippling price in moral terms, in social terms, in economic terms . . .[14]

But our perceptions are shaped also by an increased awareness of problems that hitherto have remained largely hidden from public view. One of these is child sexual abuse. This phenomenon has been a subject of press reports for some time and was given special prominence with the 'Cleveland affair' of 1987.[15] Testimony to the fact that the problem touches the lives of Christian as well as non-Christian families is the recent founding of the organization Christian Survivors of Sexual Abuse, whose first national conference was held in 1993. A number of underlying issues need to be addressed, not least within the churches: Do we have a theology of children and a quality of care for children profound enough to protect them from being taken advantage of? To what extent do patriarchy and the dominant modes of gender construction in our society contribute to child sexual abuse? What is the nature of sexual intimacy and what are its limits? What does forgiveness mean and is it possible in cases of child abuse? In some of these areas, Christian reflection and action has only just begun.[16]

5. *The use of 'the family' in political debate*

Marriage and the family are contemporary concerns for Christians because of the way claims about the family relate to the larger political and cultural context. Here, it is important to recognize that the family has enormous symbolic potential which can be tapped in many ways. This symbolic potential derives from a number of factors.[17] Because it is a traditional social pattern, the family comes

[14] 'The Family – A Community of Giving', in Joanna Bogle, ed., *Families for Tomorrow* (Leominster: Fowler Wright Books, 1991), 5.

[15] See the account by social anthropologist Jean La Fontaine, *Child Sexual Abuse* (Oxford: Polity, 1990), esp. 1–13.

[16] See the excellent survey by Ann Loades in her John Coffin Memorial Lecture 1994, *Thinking About Child Sexual Abuse* (University of London, 1994), and the literature cited there. Also important are the essays in Joanne Carlson Brown and Carole R. Bohn, eds, *Christianity, Patriarchy and Abuse* (Cleveland: The Pilgrim Press, 1989).

[17] I am drawing here on my earlier essay 'Towards a Theology of the Family', *Crucible* (January–March, 1993), 4–13.

to stand for what is held to be traditional (and therefore valuable) on a wider front, including the fabric of society as a whole. As an intimate form of society it carries a high emotional voltage which makes it especially prone to rhetorical manipulation. This is exacerbated by the vulnerability of family members, especially the unwaged – mothers, children, the elderly, and the handicapped. Also, because it is ubiquitous, what is said about the family has the potential for affecting everyone in some way. Yet further, as a complex and dynamic social pattern, it is linked inextricably to a wide range of moral-political concerns such as the division of labour, questions of social security, the care of children, the disabled and the elderly, and so on. Finally, as a social pattern conventionally linked with religion and the church, it is a potent symbol of a higher order of things.

It is not surprising, therefore, to find that (a certain conception of) the family often becomes a political tool serving the interests of a larger agenda. For conservatives, this usually has to do with preserving or re-establishing a desired *status quo* of 'traditional family values', often linked to a free-market economic philosophy. For liberals, it has to do with social reform aimed at protecting individual rights. For fundamentalists, the family is a symbolic and practical bulwark against the moral ambiguities of secular modernity. For feminists, it is an instrument of the patriarchal oppression of women. And so on. My point here is not to evaluate these larger political interests, only to draw attention to (sometimes hidden) political dimensions of talk about the family which make it an important and legitimate focus of concern.

6. *Specifically Christian or ecclesiastical concerns*

Many developments in contemporary church life touch on marriage and the family in various ways, so it is worth mentioning a few here. In the Roman Catholic Church, the official ban on artificial contraception, taken further in *Humanae Vitae* and recently reiterated in *Veritatis Splendor*, represents in a very clear and uncompromising way a line of demarcation between the church as a moral community and the moral values of the modern world.[18]

---

[18] On the encyclicals see Janet E. Smith, *Humanae Vitae: A Generation Later* (New York: Catholic University of America, 1992); and Charles Yeats, ed., *Veritatis Splendor: A Response* (Canterbury: Canterbury Press, 1994).

This line of demarcation runs right through marriage and family life. At the same time, the dramatic decline in priestly vocations has reopened the question of priestly celibacy and the eligibility of married men for the priesthood. In the Church of England and the Anglican communion worldwide, the debate over the ordination of women to the priesthood has raised important theological and practical questions about gender construction and power relations directly relevant to marriage and the family. On another front, the increasingly common practice of cohabitation among Christian couples across the denominations has renewed the debate about the centrality of marriage in Christian sexual theology.[19] Not unrelated are concerns of a yet more general kind about how to respond to cultural and moral pluralism in contemporary society and how to respond also to what is perceived to be widespread moral breakdown in people's social relations. Here again, attitudes to marriage and the family have a pivotal role.

III. Ways forward

It is impossible to be comprehensive here about a subject which is so vast and the focus of enormous current interest.[20] Instead, I will try to suggest just a few possible ways forward in Christian thinking and practice with regard to marriage and the family.

1. We need to be as clear-sighted as we can about what is actually going on and why. I say this because the tendency to be sentimental about the intimate relations of marriage and family life, or to be nostalgic for what is often a highly idealized notion of how things were in times gone by, or (at the other end of the spectrum) to demonize traditional institutions as having no value whatsoever,

---

[19] See, for example, A. E. Harvey's two-part essay, 'Marriage, Sex and the Bible', *Theology* XCVI (1993), 364–72, 461–8, and the letters it provoked by Walter Moberly and Simon Barrington-Ward in the two subsequent numbers of the journal. See also Adrian Thatcher, *Liberating Sex: A Christian Sexual Theology* (London: SPCK, 1993).

[20] See, for example, Brigitte and Peter Berger, *The War Over the Family* (Harmondsworth: Penguin Books, 1984); Norman Dennis and George Erdos, *Families Without Father-hood* (London: IEA Health and Welfare Unit, 1992); Rodney Clapp, *Families at the Crossroads: Beyond Traditional and Modern Options* (Downers Grove: InterVarsity Press, 1993); Jon Davies, ed., *The Family: Is it Just Another Lifestyle Choice?* (London: IEA Health and Welfare Unit, 1993); Anne Borrowdale, *Reconstructing Family Values* (London: SPCK, 1994); and the literature cited in these works.

can be a strong temptation. One-eyed distortions of this kind do not help. Instead of contributing to the struggle for truthfulness about the family, all they do is to polarize opinion out of idolatrous allegiance to what we may call 'tribal interests' of one kind or another. It is important to add that in the modern world, those interests are often controlled or strongly influenced by the larger interests of the market and the media.

We can learn an important lesson from our Christian Scriptures in this connection. For what we find there is an intense and down-to-earth realism. The Bible knows about the beauty of human love and sexuality, and strongly affirms the goodness of creation. But it also knows about the dark side of human personality and relationships. It knows how men and women betray and maltreat each other. It knows about fratricide, rape, incest, adultery, and the ruthless exploitation of the poor by the rich. That is why the Bible (in both Testaments) contains so much instruction for marital and household relations – not as an expression of 'legalism', but as a way of giving due attention to basic issues of human society and sociality in the light, both of the human potential for good and of human frailty and sinfulness.[21]

2. We need to consider carefully to what extent our supposedly postmodern, postliberal world offers us an opportunity to rediscover a distinctively Christian lifestyle. This is the thesis of Rodney Clapp's recent book *Families at the Crossroads*, itself strongly indebted to the theological ethics of Stanley Hauerwas. Clapp says, for example:

> Now that there can no longer be simple, final appeals to 'objective', 'secular' or 'neutral' reason, Christians need not be ashamed of appealing to reasons based on the particular story of Israel and Jesus. Thus I will not assume that a Christian ethic of fidelity, for instance, must be stated in supposedly neutral, nonbiblical terms that would self-evidently make sense to 'any' sane person. I will not pretend that the Christian suspicion of sex outside marriage is vindicated by practical, secular appeals to how 'happy' or 'healthy' people are if they save their virginity until marriage. (The whole point is, what is true happiness, what is authentic health? And the answers depend on what story actually reveals truth and reality.) Ironically, the postmodern situation frees the Christian family to be Christian, to live distinctively and unabashedly out of its particular story.[22]

---

[21] For a sober account see Tikva Frymer-Kensky, 'Law and Philosophy: The Case of Sex in the Bible', *SEMEIA* 45 (1989), 89–102.
[22] *Families at the Crossroads*, 24.

While this kind of approach may be in danger of overreaction by rejecting what is good in the Enlightenment liberal heritage, there is also a refreshing robustness here about the particular truth-claims of the Christian tradition. The approach seeks to capitalize on the West's current preoccupation with cultural pluralism and epistemological relativism by using it to legitimate the recovery of a distinctive Christian lifestyle and set of virtues shaped by the Christian story as embodied in the community of the church.

Such an approach has considerable potential. It is an important corrective to certain forms of liberal individualism which have tended to undermine the institutions of marriage and the family by replacing covenantal relationships mediated by the church with contractual ones mediated by the secular state. It is also a corrective to the common tendency to idolize the private realm of the family as the place of meaning and value over against the public realm as the sphere of amoral reason and politics. Instead, it challenges us to rediscover our distinctive Christian vocation in every area of our lives, and to let our lives be guided, not by bourgeois, market-driven 'family values', but by the virtues into which we are inducted as members of the Christian church.[23]

3. Progress needs to be made in learning to listen to people whom (for want of a better word) we might call 'outsiders': single people, sexual minorities, the poor, the abused, children and the elderly. Of course, listening of a certain kind[24] has itself become an important professional skill in our society, in the various forms of counselling and psychotherapeutic practice. This has made a significant impact in areas like marriage enrichment, family therapy, sexual abuse counselling, and so on. None of this work is to be gainsaid or taken for granted. The kind of in-depth understanding it makes possible is reflected, for example, in Sue Walrond-Skinner's book *The Fulcrum and the Fire: Wrestling with Family Life.*[25]

---

[23] See further exploration along these lines in such works of Stanley Hauerwas as *A Community of Character* (Notre Dame: University of Notre Dame Press, 1981), and *After Christendom?* (Nashville: Abingdon Press, 1991).

[24] If this point were to be developed, it would be useful to distinguish different kinds of 'listening': the therapeutic listening of the counselling movement; the political listening involved in attending to people's experience as members of a particular group; and so on. I owe this observation to Bishop Peter Selby in conversation.

[25] London: Darton, Longman & Todd, 1993.

At the same time, it is important that listening does not become reduced to the hegemony of particular professional interest groups. For the happiness of marriage partners and of members of families depends to no small degree on people generally in their ability to listen. An important contribution of the church here should be that members of families learn in the fellowship skills of listening and attentiveness, shaped by the love and worship of God, which can then be used to good effect in other areas of life as well. Indeed, in the context of worship and discipleship, Christians are inducted into an understanding of listening as prayer and spirituality, thus giving it a profundity quite distinct from secular accounts.

Listening to 'outsiders' is particularly important, and is an insight for which we are indebted to liberation theology, in particular.[26] Its roots lie in the biblical story where God 'hears' the cry of the slaves in Egypt, and where God-in-Christ responds to the cries for help of the marginalized people of his day. Its effect is to radically 'de-centre' taken-for-granted power relations and to make possible new ways of doing things according to the values of the kingdom of God. Seen in this light, listening to single people is important for it helps us identify oppressive social patterns and assumptions – the romantic idealization of 'coupledom', for example, or the exclusivity and plain selfishness of much modern family life. Similarly, listening to sexual minorities is important because it helps us to confront our fears and ignorance about human sexuality and to see how those fears turn into prejudice and persecution.[27] Listening to abused women and children is important because it forces us to reckon with the poverty of our love relationships and the damage caused by power relations skewed by patriarchy.[28] Such listening is not a prelude to love. It is an act of love in itself. It is a quality of attention

---

[26] See, for example, Leonardo Boff, *Jesus Christ Liberator* (London: SPCK, 1980) and *Church: Charism and Power* (London: SCM Press, 1985).

[27] The work of the Institute for the Study of Christianity and Sexuality, based in London, is an important contribution to this listening process. It publishes a *Bulletin* on a regular basis and sponsors the journal *Theology and Sexuality* (Sheffield: Sheffield Academic Press).

[28] Note Ann Loades's comment, in *Thinking About Child Sexual Abuse*, 16–17: 'The slogan of "option for the poor" means in the first instance *listening* to them, so far as I know. Unheard voices include those of children, unsurprisingly, given the way they are so commonly perceived as the appendages of their mothers whose voices may also be unheard' (author's emphasis).

which contains the seed of transformed relationships, not least in marriages and family life.[29]

4. A related area where urgent progress is needed is that of the spirituality of the family.[30] In the Catholic tradition, the overall effect of priestly celibacy has been to restrict spirituality by making it a special concern of the clergy and the cloister. In consequence, lay spirituality generally and the spirituality of family life in particular has remained underdeveloped. Certainly, marriage is regarded as a sacrament, but most sacramental teaching has tended to focus on the other sacraments to the neglect, not only of marriage, but of the sacramentality of family life and domestic relations generally. In the Protestant tradition, a change to a more positive affirmation of marriage and the family took place, in reaction against clerical celibacy and the 'two-tier' system of holiness. But the sacramental understanding of marriage was played down and spirituality tended to shrink to matters of the personal holiness of the individual and certain acts of religious observance (like Bible reading and church going).

The result of all this is a loss of the sense of the home as the domestic church. The fact that this notion is strong in mainstream Christianity primarily in the Orthodox tradition, with its strong stress on the sacramentality of the material world, means that the family and the spirituality of ordinary domestic life has much to gain from developments in ecumenism.[31] At the same time, it is important to observe that inter-religious dialogue is also important in this regard, given the traditional importance of the home in Jewish spirituality, for example.[32] Lionel Blue expresses the ethos of Jewish domestic spirituality beautifully when he describes the effect on Jewish religion of the destruction of the Temple:

[29] See further the profound essay by Janet Martin Soskice, 'Love and Attention', in M. McGhee, ed., *Philosophy, Religion and the Spiritual Life* (Cambridge: Cambridge University Press, 1992), 59–72.

[30] I am indebted for some of what follows to Susan Dowell's incisive piece, 'Lay Spirituality and the Family', *The Way* 32 (1992), 104–12.

[31] On the Orthodox approach see Athenagoras Kokkinakis, *Parents and Priests as Servants of Redemption* (New York: Morehouse-Gorham, 1958) and Stanley S. Harakas, *Living the Liturgy* (Minneapolis: Light & Life Publishing Co., 1974). Attention should be drawn also to important developments in lay spirituality in 'para-church' Christianity. A leading theological contributor here is Robert J. Banks in, for example, *All the Business of Life* (Sydney: Albatross Books, 1987).

[32] A marvellous window onto this dimension of Judaism are the novels of the American rabbi Chaim Potok, published in England by Penguin Books.

The father became a priest, the mother a priestess, and the dining-room table an altar. The furniture of the Temple from the Holy of Holies itself came to rest beside the salt cellar, the mustard pot and the sauce bottle. The candles, the clothes, the white of the tablecloth brought the holiness and mystery of tremendous events into the surroundings of daily life. . . . Because of the new Occupier, the Jewish home became a meeting place for both natural and supernatural beings.[33]

Perhaps not surprisingly, it is lay women writers who have made significant recent contributions on the Christian side. Margaret Hebblethwaite has given a moving account of finding God in relation to motherhood;[34] as has Jane Williams, in an essay entitled significantly, 'Mothers, Chaos and Prayer', in which *inter alia* she makes a number of telling points about the ironies of so-called 'family services' which too often inhibit the worship of both adults and children, and bear little relation to what family life is really like for most people.[35]

Among the contributions which a lay family spirituality ought to offer is a pattern of moral and spiritual formation for which partners in marriage have a mutual responsibility to each other, and parents have a responsibility to their children.[36] It is in this context that important skills and virtues can be learned which have a funda-mental bearing on people's ability to enter into and sustain both intimate and non-intimate relationships. What I have in mind here is: learning to be angry in the face of injustice; learning to say sorry and to offer forgiveness; learning the art of hospitality as a means of showing solidarity towards strangers (including the 'strangers'

---

[33] Lionel Blue, *To Heaven with Scribes and Pharisees* (London: Darton, Longman & Todd, 1975), 38. The whole of ch. 4, on 'Holiness at the Kitchen Sink – the Jewish Home', is pertinent.

[34] Margaret Hebblethwaite, *Motherhood and God* (London: Geoffrey Chapman, 1984).

[35] Jane Williams, 'Mothers, Chaos and Prayer', in Furlong, ed., *Mirror to the Church*, 91–105.

[36] On the responsibilities of parents, Hauerwas makes the following important comment in *A Community of Character*, 166: 'It is not sufficient to welcome children, for we must also be willing to initiate them into what we think is true or good about human existence. For example, I think we should not admire religious or non-religious parents who are afraid to share their values or convictions with their children. It is a false and bad-faith position to think that if we do not teach them values our children will be free to "make up their own minds". [This refusal is] . . . a betrayal that derives from moral cowardice.'

in one's own family!); and learning the practice of mature friendship which outlives the vagaries of passion and provides the basis for loyalties which endure through thick and thin. Anger, forgiveness, hospitality and friendship appear to me to be four major areas where the riches of the Christian moral tradition deserve further exploration, not least for what they will contribute to justice, happiness and human flourishing in marriage and the family.

2

Biblical Hermeneutics and the Family

I. Introduction

Christian reflection on the family has always paid considerable attention to what the Bible says. Jesus cites Genesis in support of his prohibition of divorce (Mk 10.2–9 at vv. 6–8), and the fifth commandment in support of his protest against abuses of filial obligation related to the custom of Corban (Mk 7.1–13, at v. 10). The author of Ephesians quotes Genesis 2.24 as an authoritative scriptural warrant for husbands to love their wives as Christ loved the church (Eph 5.21–33 at v. 31).[1] The author of 1 Timothy likewise appeals to the story of Adam and Eve as a warrant for imposing silence on women in church and denying them a teaching ministry or authority over men (1 Tim 2.11–14).

Such examples could be multiplied from Christian history as a whole. Peter Brown has given us an authoritative account of attitudes to sexuality, marriage and family ties in the patristic period, and there too biblical interpretation is acknowledged as playing a vital role.[2] From a much later period, we could instance the English Puritans as a further case in point.[3] Their conception of the home as 'the spiritualization of the household' (to use Christopher Hill's

---

[1] For full discussion, see J. Paul Sampley, *'And the Two Shall Become One Flesh': A Study of Traditions in Ephesians 5.21–33* (Cambridge: Cambridge University Press, 1971), esp. ch. 7.

[2] Peter Brown, *The Body and Society: Men, Women and Sexual Renunciation in Early Christianity* (London: Faber & Faber, 1990).

[3] See further R. E. Clements, *Wisdom in Theology* (Carlisle: Paternoster Press, 1992), esp. 126–30. On the Puritans, Clements refers to Christopher Hill's *Society and Puritanism in Pre-Revolutionary England* (Harmondsworth: Penguin Books, 1986), 429–66.

phrase) was derived, at least in part, from their reading of the Bible. Of particular importance was the Book of Proverbs with its strong focus on the individual household, rather than the temple or the palace, as the primary sphere of moral formation and social duty. In a way which is interestingly analogous to this, the Puritans made the home a centre of Christian nurture and education, and saw themselves as developing an alternative to traditional patterns of piety fostered by the churches and the (suspect) ordained priesthood.

The central role accorded the Bible is no less true of Christian reflection today. Denominational church reports on human sexuality or marriage and the family invariably include a chapter early on which attempts to lay some biblical foundations.[4] A current series in the *Expository Times* entitled 'New Occasions Teach New Duties?', has as its first two contributions essays on, respectively, 'The Use of the Old Testament in Christian Ethics' and 'The Use of the New Testament in Christian Ethics'. The recent papal encyclical *Veritatis Splendor* builds its call for a reformation of Christian morality upon an exposition of the story of Jesus' encounter with the rich young man, in Matthew 19. Recent writing of a more systematic theological kind on the family also gives considerable prominence to the biblical material. For example, Adrian Thatcher in his book *Liberating Sex: A Christian Sexual Theology*, addresses as early as chapter 2, the question of 'The Place of the Bible in Christian Sexual Theology'.[5]

The prominence accorded the Bible is related to a number of factors. At a fundamental level, it has to do with the fact that Christianity is what George Lindbeck calls a 'textualized religion', where reality has an inscribed, 'it-is-written', quality about it.[6] A related factor is the history of Christian thought, in which the art of biblical interpretation has been a recurrent and dominant concern. There is a sense in which it is true to say that the history of the church *is* the history of the interpretation of the Bible. To put it another way: one of the main forms of Christian religious activity has always been scribal and exegetical. At the level of doctrine, the

---

[4] E.g. the Church of England document *Issues in Human Sexuality: A Statement by the House of Bishops* (London: Church House Publishing, 1991), ch. 2 of which is on 'Scripture and Human Sexuality'.

[5] London: SPCK, 1993.

[6] George Lindbeck, 'Barth and Textuality', *Theology Today* 43 (1986–7), 361–76 at p. 361.

warrant for such activity is the Christian doctrine of revelation, where the words of Scripture have a pivotal role as the unique and inspired testimony to the Word of God incarnate. More recently, the advent of historical criticism and the hegemony of this method of Bible reading in academic theology has made finding meaning in the Bible something of a problem. Now, for many readers, the Bible presents an unavoidable obstacle which has to be circumvented: a minefield of exegetical difficulties rather than a fount and wellspring of truth for life. The Bible is still important, but now for reasons more negative than positive.

More specifically in relation to Christian reflection on human social patterns like marriage and the family, the Bible bulks large precisely because it is the story of the revelation of God in and through God's relations with men and women in their common life. In this story, composed in a wide variety of literary genres, human relatedness through blood, marriage, household ties, land and cult provides the major idiom for exploring and experiencing relatedness with God.[7] The former Chief Rabbi, Lord Jakobovitz, expressed this conception of things in a recent address on the family, when he said:

> I belong to the people who first taught the human race that we were all originally descended from an identifiable father and an identifiable mother, that we all derive from a human pair, man and woman, out of whom the human race eventually evolved. I belong to a people that trace their origin to the idyllic couples of Abraham and Sarah, of Isaac and Rebecca, of Jacob and Rachel. In other words we are a people who were born at home, and therefore the entire focus of our national thinking is perhaps best expressed by the collective term by which we have been known since Biblical times: either 'the house of Israel' or 'the children of Israel'. We see ourselves as a family that has a house, a home, that constitute the fellowship, the brotherhood, the family unit of children of Israel.[8]

Of course, Jakobovits is talking of the Jewish Scriptures only. But the same idiom, transformed in interesting ways, continues into the New Testament as well. Jesus speaks of his followers belonging to households one hundredfold (Mk 10.28–30); the Acts of the

---

[7] See further Christopher J. H. Wright, *God's People in God's Land: Family, Land, and Property in the Old Testament* (Grand Rapids: Eerdmans, 1990).

[8] 'The Family – A Community of Giving', in Joanna Bogle, ed., *Families for Tomorrow* (Leominster: Fowler Wright Books, 1991), 5–7 at p. 5.

Apostles tells of conversion by household and the practice of hospitality among the early Christians; Paul uses familial imagery of his fellow believers and gives instruction on matters of marriage and household order; the letter to the Ephesians, already mentioned, uses biblical marriage symbolism to describe the relation between Christ and the church (Eph 5.21–33); and so on. Taken as a whole, then, the Bible is for Christians a book which reveals the true nature of human identity under God, an identity which is explored in the predominantly social-economic-political-religious idiom of marriage and the family.

However, what the Bible 'says' and how the Bible 'speaks' are not the same thing. The literal meaning of the text is not necessarily the true meaning or the meaning 'for us'. For the Bible to speak, acts of interpretation and discrimination on the part of the reader in his or her 'reading community', under the guidance of the Holy Spirit, are required. What I want to do in the remainder of this essay, therefore, is to take several specific and recent examples of acts of biblical interpretation which are used to underpin different kinds of Christian understandings of the family. My aim in so doing is to assess the strengths and weaknesses of these various interpretations with a view to fostering a more adequate use of the Bible in theological reflection in this area.

II. Case studies

1. As a first case study, I have chosen Adrian Thatcher's aforementioned book *Liberating Sex*, published in 1993. Chapter 2 of this book is a particularly clear attempt to define how to use the Bible in constructing a Christian sexual theology. The main argument is that 'a distinction must be made between a *biblical* sexual theology and a *Christian* sexual theology'.[9] This is because the biblical text is pervasively hierarchical and patriarchal in its assumptions about relationships between men and women, and anachronistic in its understanding of male and female homosexuality. Therefore, if the Bible is to contribute to theology, it has to be set firmly within a hermeneutical framework: that of Christian faith centred on Christ. 'What is required', says Thatcher, 'is a full, Christian sexual theology, as opposed to a mere biblical one, where that Love which God is and which is spread abroad in Christ is both our norm and gift.

---

[9] At p. 15 (author's emphasis).

This will give us a point of reference in making ethical judgements, and a framework for interpreting biblical material.'[10]

To make his point, Thatcher proceeds in two ways. The first is the negative one of criticizing both biblical texts for their sexism and church reports for their biblicism. The second is the constructive one of proposing what we might call a hermeneutic of retrieval. Here, a christological principle and a traditional doctrinal framework is advanced as the essential basis for renouncing 'sub-Christian', literalist readings of the Bible in favour of readings which testify to the revelation of the love of God in Christ: 'Sexual theology is Christian when it derives from a sharing in the vision and experience of God as love, made known in Jesus Christ. The role of the Bible in sexual theology must be that of testifying to that vision and experience.'[11]

In my view, this approach has much to commend it. It is genuinely theological in its focus on Christ as the norm for interpreting Scripture, a theological hermeneutic rooted in early Christian interpretation of the Hebrew Bible and given classic definition by Luther at the time of the Reformation. It also avoids being reductionist in the fashion of certain kinds of historical criticism which have no hermeneutical means for interpreting the Bible as Scripture. On the contrary, Thatcher argues quite properly that the framework he is adopting for interpreting the Bible is not alien, but is itself biblical and traditional. He says, for example:

> Christian faith is a sharing in divine love. Critical scholarship is one of the tools for identifying the patriarchy that mars this vision and experience of love. The interpretative task in relation to the Scriptures is to let their testimony point to Christ (John 5.39), the revelation of divine love in human, embodied, relational being. . . . This sharing in divine love is the basis for thinking about and having sex. The biblical themes of creation and re-creation, sin and redemption, brokenness and wholeness, estrangment and reconciliation, fill out the basic framework.[12]

Nevertheless, while endorsing Thatcher's basic approach, there are certain weaknesses which are worth teasing out. For instance, when it comes to treating the *text* of the Bible – as distinct from elucidating its broad *themes* – the overwhelming impression given is of the text

---

[10] Ibid. 22.
[11] Ibid. 28.
[12] Ibid. 27.

as a source of danger, threat and damage. Take his first example of
texts about husband–wife relations. Here, Thatcher's tactic is to
quote texts (such as Col 3.18; 1 Pet 3.1; Eph 5.22ff.) which support
the claim that New Testament teaching in this area is vitiated by
unquestioned assumptions about the propriety of relations of
domination, whether of husband over wife or of master over slave.
He concludes: 'If the teaching on marriage in the New Testament
letters is accepted, women are forever to be submissive to men and
the same teaching justifies owning slaves. It is inadmissable to appeal
to biblical teaching on marriage while at the same time rejecting
slavery since marriage and slavery are as indissolubly linked as a
man and woman are linked in marriage.'[13]

My problem with this is twofold. On the one hand, Thatcher is
not critical enough – or perhaps I should say, not properly critical.
When he wants to score a point, he resorts to the very proof-texting
methods used by his imagined literalist opponents. What he should
do is to seek first to understand these 'subordinationist' texts by
setting them carefully in their respective rhetorical and historical
contexts. This might help him to see, for example, that the
household code in 1 Peter springs from a specific, historically
conditioned apologetic concern: to defuse criticism by outsiders
that conversion to Christianity is socially irresponsible because it
subverts family loyalties and household duty.[14] In other words, the
issue is not hierarchy and patriarchy *per se*, but the defence of the
gospel and the maintenance of an effective witness to the rule of
God. Furthermore, a closer look at the changing status and roles
accorded women and slaves within the early 'house churches' would
help Thatcher to see that a process of deconstruction of patriarchal
norms had begun, and that hierarchy and patriarchy in the conventional sense were *not* taken for granted in the way he suggests.[15] But
all this requires a degree of attention to the text in its historical
context which Thatcher skates over.

His approach, by contrast, has the serious consequence of appear-
ing to trivialize the text. Large sections are so dangerous as to be

---

[13] Ibid. 16–17.

[14] See on this D. L. Balch, *Let Wives Be Submissive: The Domestic Code in I Peter*
(Chico: Scholars Press, 1981).

[15] On slavery see further Dale B. Martin, *Slavery as Salvation: The Metaphor of
Slavery in Pauline Christianity* (New Haven: Yale University Press, 1990). On women
see, from a vast literature, Antoinette Clark Wire, *The Corinthian Women Prophets*
(Minneapolis: Fortress Press, 1990).

dispensable – as in his devastating reference to 'the miserable subordinationism of some of the New Testament letters'.[16] If this is the case, why bother with the Bible at all? Is it not completely irretrievable, as Daphne Hampson argues, for instance?[17] And if the Bible is irretrievable, are not the broader themes and the christological testimony upon which Thatcher puts heavy weight irretrievable as well? Now, it is not necessarily the case that an all-or-nothing approach is the only viable one: and this, I think, is what Thatcher himself believes. But his deep ambivalence about the Bible is in danger of being the thin end of a large wedge which eventually cuts Christian theology off from its scriptural roots altogether.

In addition to this, it is possible to suspect that, in spite of Thatcher's avowed christological hermeneutic, there is another, virtually hidden hermeneutic at work in his treatment of these texts, as well. The tip of the iceberg appears in the statement: 'What is needed is a fresh approach to marriage and human relations generally which is not based on domination at all, *but on equality.*'[18] From a Christian theological viewpoint, we are justified in asking: Where has this norm of 'equality' come from? What is its genealogy? If it comes from post-Enlightenment, secular individualism, what justifies appeal to it as a basis for interpreting the testimony of Scripture to the will of God for human relations?

Such questions are not meant to disparage the legitimacy of the search for equality in man–woman relations today, nor to play down the human rights tradition in ethics. It is important nevertheless to observe that the goalposts have been shifted away from the Christian field, and that the distinctive Christian way of seeing things is in danger of being subverted. Unfortunately, this danger becomes alarmingly real when Thatcher quotes Ephesians 5.25 ('Husbands, love your wives, as Christ loved the church and gave himself up for it'), and then goes on to remark, 'This is no basis for love.'[19] At this point, it appears that Thatcher's own christological hermeneutic has been left behind in favour of a liberal Enlightenment notion of marriage as a contract between interested parties and a notion of family life as a constant juggling of individual rights. From a

---

[16] *Liberating Sex*, 21.
[17] See Daphne Hampson, *Theology and Feminism* (Oxford: Blackwell, 1990).
[18] *Liberating Sex*, 16–17 (my emphasis).
[19] Ibid. 16.

Christian theological understanding of love and marriage, such a
view, however fashionable today, is a long way from the truth.

2. A second case study worthy of notice for the attention it gives to
the Bible is Rodney Clapp's book *Families at the Crossroads*, also
published in 1993, but coming from the other side of the Atlantic,
and praised by Christian ethicist Stanley Hauerwas as 'quite simply
the best book we have on the family by a Christian theologian'![20]
Unlike Thatcher, Clapp does not distinguish explicitly between a
'biblical' theology and a 'Christian' theology, but some such
distinction is important for him all the same. This is because one of
Clapp's main concerns is to counteract a strong tendency he discerns
in American evangelical Protestantism to assume that the 'traditional' nuclear family is both 'natural' and 'biblical'. The disastrous
consequence of this, as he sees it, is to turn Christian values on
their head. Christianity gets defined in terms of (a particular
bourgeois conception of) 'the family', rather than the family being
understood in terms of Christianity. Or, in ecclesiological terms,
the family usurps the place of the church as the primary locus of
Christian nurture and self-understanding. Clapp epitomizes his
approach to biblical interpretation in this way:

> So the Bible itself is not a list of abstract, timeless formulas. It simply
> provides no detailed guidance or techniques, for all times and places,
> on disciplining children or seeking a mate or determining whether a
> wife should or should not work outside the home. Rather, the Bible is
> centrally and first of all the *story* of Israel and Jesus. Beyond that, it
> includes the poetry and prison letters of people who faithfully responded
> to that story in their own times and places. To create and live in a truly
> Christian family, the church in every generation and culture must read
> the biblical story anew. . . . What I offer, instead, is a reading of the
> biblical story with special relevance to the Western Christian family in
> the late twentieth and early twenty-first centuries. My aim is to discover
> what purposes and hopes our families should assume to remain faithful.
> Remaining faithful means witnessing to the living truth of the God
> revealed in Scripture. Witnessing means incarnating the family in
> peculiar shapes and rich practices *that can only be explained by resorting to
> the story of Israel and Jesus Christ.*[21]

---

[20] Rodney Clapp, *Families at the Crossroads: Beyond Traditional and Modern Options*
(Downers Grove: InterVarsity Press, 1993). The quotation comes from the back
cover.
[21] Ibid. 15–16 (author's emphasis).

Let us consider now how this works out in practice in what Clapp says theologically about the family. At one level, the Bible is used as a tool for deconstructing the widespread assumption among Clapp's evangelical readership that the 'traditional', nuclear family is the most natural and most biblical thing in the world.[22] Whereas the nuclear family is monogamous, the families of biblical times accept polygamy. Whereas the former sharply separates private and public worlds, in the latter these worlds substantially overlap. Whereas the one consists on average of 2.63 people, the average Hebrew household can range between 50 and 100 people. Whereas the modern family places a high premium on romantic love and sentimental bonds, biblical family life is bound above all by concerns of economic survival, property and inheritance.

Rhetorically speaking, Clapp is fighting his evangelical opponents on their own territory. He is using biblical data about ancient Israel to undermine the assumption that the traditional family is all that traditional, and argues to the contrary that it is a relatively modern, Victorian invention, which is quite unlike families in the Bible. This is a ground-clearing exercise on Clapp's part. What he wants to make space for is a theology of the family which involves, not an attempt to return to 'the biblical family', but an attempt to live in families in ways which flow from the biblical testimony to God-in-Christ: which means living in families in ways which are nurtured by the values of the kingdom and life together in the church. Kingdom and church first, family second: that is the order of priorities he is concerned to establish in order to dethrone the family as it is understood in the evangelical circles he is addressing.

In a chapter on 'Advanced Capitalism and the Lost Art of Christian Family',[23] Clapp goes on to argue that the modern family has been trivialized and subverted by capitalism and the economic-exchange model of society. Family life has become privatized, sentimentalized and oriented towards consumption; marriage has become a matter of secular, interpersonal contract rather than a religious, communally acknowledged covenant; and having children has become problematic because of the limitations they place on the autonomy and mobility of adults. Clapp's proposed solution to this problem is not, however, to reassert the central significance of

[22] Ibid. 27–47.
[23] Ibid. 48–66.

the family. That is the tendency of the religious Right, and it only exacerbates the problem by attempting to replace the late-twentieth-century family by the nineteenth-century bourgeois family in the guise of 'the biblical model'. Rather, Clapp seeks to go one step back by arguing that unless we start with the kingdom and the church we will have no basis upon which to decide how to live as Christians, whether in families or not.[24]

At this point, the Bible becomes important again. Previously, Clapp has used the Bible as a source of *historical information* about family forms in ancient Israel to undercut the claim that getting back to the traditional family is a getting back to the biblical family. Now he uses the Bible *theologically* to argue that, seen in the light of Christ, it is not the biological family which is 'the primary vehicle of God's grace and salvation', but the family of the church. In line with his methodological aim to develop a theology out of the story of Israel and Jesus, Clapp argues for example, that in Israel's covenantal theology, Israel's identity as the 'children of God' was above all a matter of election and obedience, even if ties of blood and kinship were important also. Turning to Jesus, Clapp emphasizes those Gospel traditions which firmly subordinate ties of natural kinship to the higher priority of obedience and discipleship in the light of the coming of the kingdom.[25] He then develops this strand of thought both with reference to the story of Mary the mother of Jesus, and with reference to Paul's transfer of kinship and household language to that solidarity which was of supreme importance for him – namely, the church.

So if, at an earlier point, Clapp has used historical interpretation of the Bible to dethrone the family, here he has used theological interpretation. In place of the family as the bastion against modernity and postmodernism, it is 'the church and its story' which give us a place to stand and which provide the resources for living together Christianly.[26] Among the consequences of this reordering of priorities around the kingdom and the church, Clapp has interesting things to say about the importance of the vocation to singleness, testimony to which is provided in the Bible not least

[24] Ibid. 67–88, on 'Church as First Family'.

[25] For further exploration of these Gospel texts, see Stephen C. Barton, *Discipleship and Family Ties in Mark and Matthew* (Cambridge: Cambridge University Press, 1994).

[26] *Families at the Crossroads*, 84ff.

by both Jesus and Paul. He also has interesting things to say about the nature of true fidelity and the importance of the ethic of hospitality to strangers, ideas of direct relevance to family life (and much else) but springing out of the biblical story of Israel and Jesus as mediated by and practised in the church.[27]

When we start to evaluate Clapp's work, what strikes us immediately is the remarkable absence of the sense of deep ambivalence and of the danger posed by the biblical text which so characterizes Adrian Thatcher's approach. Put in other words, where Thatcher's reading bears the marks of a hermeneutic of suspicion, Clapp's reading bears the marks of a hermeneutic of trust. Even though both authors interpret the Bible in the light of an explicit theological and christological framework, so that what is important is the words as witness to the Word, there is a sense in which Clapp is 'at home' with the Bible in a way which Thatcher is not.

The clue to this difference lies, I think, in the area of the sociology of knowledge. Thatcher writes in a way characteristic of liberal Anglicanism. His indebtedness to liberalism shows itself on the one hand in the way his agenda for a new sexual theology is heavily determined by issues of modernity such as patriarchy and homophobia. On the other hand, it comes through also in his modernist commitment to post-Enlightenment values such as equality between the sexes and individual human rights. Rodney Clapp writes from somewhere within the orbit of American evangelical Protestantism. His agenda is not a modernist one, however, but a postmodern one – something reflected in his book's subtitle, 'Beyond Traditional and Modern Options'. This allows him to capitalize upon the otherness and particularity of the biblical tradition, rather than being embarrassed or threatened by it. At the same time, his application of a christological hermeneutic and his strong ecclesiological orientation free him to explore the spirit of the text without being irresponsible with regard to the letter.

But I would want to express a number of reservations, nonetheless. My main one concerns Clapp's hermeneutical decision to make 'story' his primary category of biblical interpretation, as when he says: 'the Bible itself is not a list of abstract, timeless formulas. . . . Rather, the Bible is centrally and first of all the *story* of Israel

[27] Ibid. 89–148.

and Jesus. Beyond that, it includes the poetry and prison letters of
people who faithfully responded to that story in their own times
and places'.[28] Now, the strengths of the category 'story' as a kind of
organizing metaphor for biblical interpretation are evident: it does
justice to the massive amount of narrative material in the Bible; it
allows the Bible to be read as one book rather than being broken
up into disparate and conflicting parts; it fits in with the turn to
literary models in recent biblical scholarship; and it allows a high
degree of flexibility in the ways in which the text is theologically
and christologically appropriated.

The weakness, however, is that it is too general to be of any real
use. Or, to put it another way, it is so general that it says everything
and nothing at the same time. On the one hand, it represents a
refusal to engage with the detail of the text in all its complexity,
diversity and historicality. In that sense, it shares some of the
problems of its predecessor in the history of ideas, the 'salvation
history' approach to interpretation.[29] It also has the appearance of
taking seriously the Bible as literature without being at all literary-
critical. On the other hand, it represents a refusal to engage
with systematic theology, since truth is now a matter of somehow
'living within the story' rather than of the application of critical
reason to the claims about God and reality which the biblical text
conveys.

This does not necessarily mean that what he says about the family
is mistaken, only that it is not as well-grounded as it might be. In
the end, a lot hangs on the communitarian dimension of Clapp's
approach, i.e., a lot depends on the quality of life in the church if
the biblical story of Israel and Jesus is to function in a life-giving
way for people trying to live together in families. One wonders if, in
the end, Clapp has succeeded only in replacing one kind of tradi-
tionalist approach with another: instead of 'back to the Bible', he
invites us to get 'back to the church' (or, even more appealingly,
'back to the kingdom of God'!). Of course, from a Christian point
of view, none of these is a bad place to go. But Clapp's work provides
only the barest outline of what we should do when we get there, not
least in respect of marriage and the family. Adrian Thatcher's honest
grappling with issues like sexism, cohabitation, homophobia, gay

[28] Ibid. 15.
[29] I owe this and several other points in this paragraph to my colleague Dr Colin
Crowder in conversation.

and lesbian relationships, and so on, are strangely missing. If
Thatcher's broadly liberal approach at least takes seriously the need
for a new Christian casuistry, Clapp's narrative-communitarian
approach appears to leave that crucial dimension relatively un-
developed.[30]

3. My third and final case study again comes from 1993. It is clear
how many authors and publishers were gearing up for the International Year of the Family in 1994! The book is *The Fulcrum and the
Fire: Wrestling with Family Life*[31] written by Sue Walrond-Skinner who
is a family and marital therapist and also Adviser in Pastoral Care
and Counselling in the (Anglican) Diocese of Southwark. In the
course of a very wide-ranging and multi-disciplinary analysis of family
life, Walrond-Skinner devotes chapter 3, entitled 'Kingdom', to the
question of biblical perspectives.

Her argument may be summarized thus. First, there is a polemic
against what she calls 'the biblical approach to the family'. What
concerns Walrond-Skinner is Christian approaches to family life
which assume that the Bible tells us all we need to know about the
family, and that the family is all there is. She says, for example:

> There is a kind of double difficulty about the biblical approach to the
> family. It is both imperialist (family life is 'Christian in its essence';
> marriage is a 'Christian institution'; 'Christians should set a standard,
> God's standard, for everyone else to follow'); and exclusive as though
> there cannot and could never have been any other social institutions
> that fill the essential requirements of human aspiration within the will
> of God.[32]

Then she goes on to argue that the Bible in general (and the Old
Testament in particular) is vitiated in what it says about the family
by its pervasive patriarchalism. Nor is it safe to argue that monogamy
is 'the biblical ideal', since that particular way of ordering social
and sexual relations developed only gradually and in a way which
brought advantage only to the male household head. Women
remained subjugated and exploited.[33] Nevertheless, there are

---

[30] Of course, the same could not be said of Stanley Hauerwas, whose approach
to theological ethics underlies much of Clapp's work. Of Hauerwas's work, see
especially *A Community of Character* (Notre Dame: University of Notre Dame Press,
1981), part 3 of which contains essays on the family, sexual ethics, and abortion.

[31] London: Darton, Longman & Todd, 1993.

[32] *The Fulcrum and the Fire*, 28.

[33] Ibid. 30–4.

redeeming strands in the biblical tradition, such as the prophets' denunciation of relations of injustice and oppression. There are also pictures of loving relationships, such as Jacob's love for Rachel, the love between Naomi and Ruth, and between David and Jonathan, the love poetry of the Song of Songs, and so on. The principle and practice of hospitality to aliens is important too.

Over against this oppressive patriarchalism and transforming these faint glimmerings of light in the dark comes the 'startlingly different approach' of Jesus, with his 'revolutionary approach to personal and familiar relationships . . . [by which the] family as a central social and religious unit of Israelite society is now radically redefined'.[34] She continues:

> So far as we know, Jesus neither married nor founded a family himself and much of what he says about family and marriage severely challenges the *status quo* of a lineally descended conjugal, consanguineous household. On the contrary, the new command is to become a beloved community of equals brought into being not by the blood of parenthood nor the legality of marriage but by the grace of adoption.[35]

The argument is developed by pointing to strong evidence from the Gospels of the priority Jesus gave to the demands of the kingdom of God, demands which necessitated leaving families behind and which even split families apart. Jesus' teaching on divorce is interpreted as also reflecting kingdom values. What Jesus does is to prohibit a practice which allowed a man to control his wife by divorcing her on the slightest pretext, putting in its place God's original intention of the equality and unity of female and male.

Walrond-Skinner then presents two cameos of Jesus' revolutionary approach. The first is Jesus and the Samaritan woman of John 4. What is remarkable in this encounter is Jesus' lack of interest in 'the form of her personal relationships either past or present. . . . Not only is she not asked to repent or amend her living relationships, *it is the fact that they have been revealed and accepted by Jesus*, that enables her to believe and to tell others about her belief. She is accepted by Jesus just as she is and his acceptance kindles her apostolic zeal. Jesus' eye is on the kingdom, not on the outward form of things'.[36] The second cameo is Jesus' encounter with Martha

[34] Ibid. 36.
[35] Ibid. 37.
[36] Ibid. 42–3 (author's emphasis).

in John 11. This is emphatically *not* the 'domestic' Martha of Luke 10.38–42 and subsequent Christian tradition. Rather, it is the woman with whom Jesus explores profound spiritual and theological truths and who confesses him to be the Messiah – all this taking precedence over her natural, family concerns to do with the deceased Lazarus. Once again, therefore, kingdom values take priority over the family.

In a final section, Walrond-Skinner addresses the problem the church has had historically in getting the balance right between 'the primary claims of the kingdom and the subordinate claims of social and familial relationships'.[37] At certain times in history, sexuality and natural relationships generally are denigrated. At other times, especially when 'traditional values' are at risk in society at large, kingdom values are forgotten and an idol made of the family. Interestingly, Paul is upheld as someone who worked quite hard at getting the balance right:

> Much of what he teaches is good news . . . : the equality of marriage partners; the mutuality of marriage; the freedom of choice between marriage and celibacy; the acceptance that divorce is sometimes the right and necessary step to take; the valuing of the contributions of each person within the organic whole of the Body of Christ. And always his emphasis on the wider concerns and commitment to the community of Christ and to the primary claims made by membership of his Body and to the call of the kingdom. Moreover, Paul is always clear that the letter (or outer form) brings death and only the Spirit (or inner form) gives life.[38]

What are we to make of Walrond-Skinner's attempt to use the Bible theologically to reflect on marriage and family life? Her main goals appear to be of two kinds: on the one hand, to counter both Christianity's weighty heritage of biblical patriarchalism and its tendency to make an idol of (a particular form of) the family; on the other hand, to advance a theology of the kingdom of God which both relativizes the claims of the family and provides values which make new kinds of relationship possible. In my view, these are worthy goals, shared to a high degree by the two other writers we have looked at, and Walrond-Skinner goes some way to achieving them. But I have major reservations also.

[37] Ibid. 46.
[38] Ibid.

In the first instance, the overall structure of her argument seriously diminishes the effective contribution of the Old Testament to Christian moral theology. For in advancing what amounts to a kind of contamination theory, according to which the Old Testament in particular is polluted by patriarchalism, Walrond-Skinner makes the Old Testament as a whole almost unusable. Nor will it do to try to retrieve certain texts as passing the test of 'political correctness' on this issue. The fact that Jacob worked seven years more for Rachel, 'and the time seemed like only a few days to him, because he loved her' (Gen 29.20), does nothing to alter the fact that the marriage was a transaction between two men, Jacob and Laban. Nor are we told whether or not Jacob's strong feelings for Rachel were reciprocated. Again, to cite another of Walrond-Skinner's examples, the 'mutual love and self-sacrifice of Naomi and Ruth' does nothing to alter the fact that their indigence was caused by the deaths of their respective husbands, Elimelech and Mahlon, upon whom the women were completely dependent for their subsistence; and that salvation comes in the form of another significant male member of the clan, Boaz, to whom Ruth attaches herself upon the women's return to the land of Judah.

In short, what is needed here is another way of reading the Old Testament which allows it to speak as Christian Scripture. This will involve taking the text much more seriously than Walrond-Skinner does – by which I mean a willingness to read the text with historical sympathy and engage with it on its own terms, rather than pre-judging it according to political and moral notions which belong to another time and place. It is worth noting that the effect of Walrond-Skinner's approach, ironically, is to deprive us of most of what the Old Testament says which might be thought relevant to family life, not least the second table of the decalogue and the biblical laws relating to marriage and household management.[39]

This brings me to a second criticism. What is striking about Walrond-Skinner's interpretation of the Bible is the way it is skewed in an overwhelmingly 'personalist' direction. It is not coincidental that she can do little with the Old Testament, since so much of that tradition is devoted to building social, legal and religious *structures* to enable a people to live together in responsible freedom under

[39] For a much better way forward, see Christopher J. H. Wright, *Living as the People of God: The Relevance of Old Testament Ethics* (Leicester: InterVarsity Press, 1983); and, 'The Ethical Authority of the Old Testament: A Survey of Approaches', *Tyndale Bulletin* 43 (1992), 101–20, 203–31.

God. Instead, theologically speaking, a false polarization is introduced between law and grace and between structures and values;
and a kingdom of God theology is used, in effect, to draw a line
between the Testaments.

This polarization is reflected further in the way she talks of Jesus'
'revolutionary approach': for without the language of revolution it
is difficult to play down Christianity's damaging inheritance in the
way Walrond-Skinner wants to do. And if she is forced to isolate
Jesus and his kingdom-preaching from their biblical roots, she is
forced also to isolate them from what came after! Conscious of a
Jesus tradition apparently hostile to family ties, she says, for example:
'Indeed, it is hard to understand how "the family" as a structure has
ever become so inordinately preoccupying for Christians from the
way in which it is treated in the Gospels themselves.'[40] In short, if
the Old Testament got it wrong, so did the church; and all we are
left with is the Jesus of the Gospels and Paul.

But even Jesus and Paul are treated in curiously selective ways.
On Paul, no explicit mention is made of the 'household codes'
and their importance for Christian social ethics. Instead, 'outer
form' is disparaged and 'inner meaning' is exalted. When it comes
to Jesus, great emphasis is placed on the sayings of Jesus which
subordinate family life to the demands of the kingdom. But there
is no mention of the rhetorical, hyperbolic dimension of these 'hard
sayings', nor of the fact that these sayings stand themselves in
strong continuity with biblical and Jewish monotheism according
to which the demands of God must always take precedence over
everything and everyone else, even family.[41] There is no mention
either of traditions which show Jesus' respect for the obligations of
filial piety.

Interestingly, when it comes to case studies from the Gospels,
Walrond-Skinner leaves behind the Synoptic Gospels (where the
emphasis on 'the kingdom' is most pronounced) and turns to the
Fourth Gospel which is so distinctive in the way it structures its story
of Jesus around significant, one-to-one encounters between Jesus
and some other individual. Her exploration of Jesus' conversations
with, first, the Samaritan woman and then Martha allows her to
portray Jesus as someone not really interested in forms and
structures such as marriage and the family, but as someone who is

[40] *The Fulcrum and the Fire*, 36.
[41] See on this Barton, *Discipleship and Family Ties*, esp. ch. 2.

supremely interested in 'relationships' and 'values' and the quest of the individual for personal truth.[42] The representative status of the Samaritan woman and of Martha is passed over. In the end, one is left with the suspicion that Jesus the proclaimer of the kingdom has been transformed into Jesus the therapeutic counsellor, and that Jesus' concern for the repentance of Israel and the nations has been replaced by Jesus' concern for growth in personal self-discovery.

III. Conclusion

By way of conclusion, it may be worthwhile to reflect on two issues in biblical hermeneutics and the family that have arisen out of the preceding three case studies.

First, there is the issue of how to interpret the Bible in an age such as ours whose intellectual and moral horizons are strongly affected by the feminist critique of patriarchy. This is a very big question which is attracting increasing attention in biblical studies and in theological hermeneutics generally.[43] What I would say here is that a certain humility and circumspection are required if our reading is not to become 'single-issue' or 'tribal' in ways which are unhelpful.

A lot depends on what we are trying to achieve. If we are trying to expose patriarchal domination by exploring its historical roots in Western civilization, then it is legitimate and necessary to inquire into the role of sources of traditional authority like the Bible and interpreters of the Bible. But it would be a mistake if, in so doing, we came to the conclusion that the Bible is *only* about gender relations, or that it only speaks about gender relations in one way. It would also be a mistake to argue with the Bible as if the Bible has a mind of its own, ideologically committed to patriarchy or, for that matter, egalitarianism.

---

[42] Symptomatic is the following (from *The Fulcrum and the Fire*, 42): 'Jesus seems to be not at all interested in the form of her [the Samaritan woman's] personal relationships either past or present. Rather, he responds to this woman in her capacity to be transparently truthful herself.'

[43] Foundational works are Elisabeth Schüssler Fiorenza, *In Memory of Her: A Feminist Theological Reconstruction of Christian Origins* (London: SCM Press, 1983), and *Bread Not Stone* (Boston: Beacon Press, 1984) in the area of biblical interpretation; and, in systematic theology, Rosemary Radford Ruether, *Sexism and God-Talk* (London: SCM Press, 1983).

We have to reckon very often, instead, with ways in which, for good and ill, the Bible has been interpreted in particular reading communities. And we have to ask the question, What virtues and skills does a community of readers require in order to read the Bible in ways which are wise and life-giving (for families or whoever)?, and How might reading the Bible itself help to inculcate such virtues?[44] On this approach, attention is directed not only at the text but also at those who are doing the reading. If, however, we begin with the assumption that the Bible is only part of the problem instead of being also part of the solution, we are likely to adopt strategies which either trivialize the text or result in major amputations, usually at the cost of the Old Testament.

If it is essential to recognize the contribution of the reading community and the need for virtues and skills which make it possible to read the Bible well, it is also essential to recognize the importance of interpreting the Bible theologically and doxologically. In the context of theological reflection on the family, this means that we should read the Bible with a view to discerning more clearly how the biblical testimony to the love and justice of God *is* reflected and *ought to be* reflected in our life together in families.

If we do this, I think we will begin to see that marriage and family life are God-given ways – and, of course, not the only ways – of sharing in the life of the God who is love. We will see that God's desire for the nurture and growth to mature personhood of ourselves as God's creatures is a task and calling in which marriage and family life have an important role to play. We will see that the gift of procreation is one of God's ways of entrusting the future of his world to men and women, and that raising children is for us an act of trust that the future is in God's hands. We will see, yet further, that sharing as families in the life of God is a calling that requires the practical outworking of the values of the kingdom of God revealed in both the life of the nation of Israel and the life of the person of Christ. The values I have in mind are values like love, sacrifice, forgiveness, obedience, fidelity, friendship, neighbourliness and hospitality. But values are meaningless unless they are given shape and form in relationships and structures. That is why the fidelity of God is embodied in a covenant. It is

---

[44] See further Stephen E. Fowl and L. Gregory Jones, *Reading in Communion: Scripture and Ethics in Christian Life* (London: SPCK, 1991).

also why the institutions of marriage and the family are not to be disparaged. In the providence of God, and as the Bible testifies so amply, they are ways of giving shape and form to the life for which God has made us.

3

Living As Families in the Light of the New Testamnent

I. How do you read?

The wrong question to ask initially when reflecting on how to live as families in the light of the New Testament is, What does the New Testament say about the family? This is the wrong question, not because there are no texts that talk about the family in general and families in particular, but because it *forecloses prematurely* on the kind of wisdom to which the New Testament testifies and passes over the vital issue of the kinds of readers we need to be in order to understand God truly. Putting it in more general terms, in the rush to find out 'what the Bible says', there is a failure to consider how the Bible speaks and how we as readers may hear what God through the Spirit is saying to the church.[1]

Ironically, this mistake is made by both (so-called) 'simple, Bible-believing Christians' and scholarly biblical critics. The former *stretch* the relevant New Testament 'family passages' across the intervening centuries in order for them to function as scriptural proof texts for family life today; the latter do all in their power to emphasize how wide is the historical 'gap' separating the ancient 'documents' from life today. The former make the text speak, but at the expense of a fully informed historical imagination and at the risk of ethnocentric misinterpretation; the latter render the text almost voiceless for today, so keen are they to give primacy to the shaping of the text in and by its 'original historical context'.

---

[1] See further S. C. Barton, *Invitation to the Bible* (London: SPCK, 1997); and ch. 4 below. Also relevant are the wider issues discussed in D. H. Kelsey, *To Understand God Truly: What's Theological About a Theological School?* (Louisville: Westminster John Knox Press, 1992).

Although it is not recognized widely enough, these approaches
are two sides of the same coin, a coin minted in the Reformation,
with its appeal to 'Scripture alone' as the authority for Christian
living, and reminted in the Enlightenment, with its appeal to
universal reason in the form of scientific method and historical
criticism as the means of attaining the truth. Even so, it needs to be
acknowledged that each approach offers something important. The
one is a reminder that the Bible is the church's Scripture and that
the church's vocation is to live according to the judgement of the
Word of God in Scripture. The other is a reminder that the Word
of God is mediated with full historical particularity in lives and texts
from the ancient past.

Nevertheless, while both have something to offer, and while those
who think of themselves as 'Bible-believing Christians' and those
who think of themselves as religiously committed historical critics
would do well to listen to one another more attentively, it remains
the case that both suffer from a crippling *positivism*: the one from a
positivism of the text ('What does the Bible say about the family?'),
the other from a positivism of history ('What do the ancient sources
tell us about early Christian family life?'). Both kinds of positivism
are crippling because they cut the reader and the text off from
their lifeblood. That lifeblood is a reality which cannot be talked
about in positivist terms. Rather, it can only be talked about
theologically and ecclesially; and it can only be perceived by faith.
It is *the life of the triune God*, whose story is told in Scripture and
recapitulated in the sacraments and in the lives of saints and martyrs,
participation in which is the privilege of all Christian believers as
members of the Body of Christ.[2]

The implications of this alternative, theological and ecclesial,
perspective are profound. First, it means that whatever we say about
'living as families in the light of the New Testament' has to be
measured against the *greater reality* of the life of the Trinity to
which the New Testament bears authoritative witness. In other
words, living as Christian families today is not a matter of
reproducing the family life of New Testament times (even if it
were possible). Nor is it a matter of replicating the patterns of
authority contained in the New Testament 'household codes'.
Rather, it is a matter of *creative fidelity* to the witness of the text to

[2] See further S. E. Fowl and L. G. Jones, *Reading in Communion: Scripture and Ethics
in Christian Life* (London: SPCK, 1991); also D. Scott, 'Speaking to Form: Trinitarian-
Performative Scripture Reading', *Anglican Theological Review* 77 (1995), 137–59.

the triune life of God, a fidelity inspired by the Spirit and worked out in the fellowship of the church.[3]

Second, this alternative approach means that we cannot talk about the family in the light of the New Testament *taken on its own.* Rather, we have to take the New Testament in tandem with the Old Testament, since both Testaments together tell the story of God (as Father, Son and Holy Spirit) and both Testaments together tell the story of the people of God (as Israel and the church).[4] The danger of taking the New Testament on its own is that the faith-story of which we as families today are a part becomes truncated almost to the point of unintelligibility: incarnation without creation, redemption without sin, fulfilment without prophecy, grace without law, spirit without body, sonship of Abraham without Abraham, the church without Israel, and so on. To put it another way, there is a Marcionism implicit in the attempt to discover 'what the New Testament says about the family' which can lead to a serious impoverishment of what orthodox Christians might want to say.

Third, and related, is the importance of taking the New Testament in tandem with the church and (what became known in the patristic period as) the rule of faith (*regula fidei*), since what we as Christians want to say about family life is something *mediated to us* down the centuries through faith communities across the world seeking to live in the light of the New Testament. This is a way of acknowledging that the New Testament *is* the New Testament because of the Spirit's work in the church and that therefore we cannot hope fully to receive its message and respond appropriately unless we attend to how it has been read and lived out in previous generations and other places. There is a real sense, in other words, in which our reading of family life in the light of the New Testament has to be *catholic and ecumenical.* We must not keep our understanding of the family 'in the family' (whatever family or tribe 'we' happen to belong to)!

In consequence, fourthly, we cannot talk about what it means to be a family from a scriptural point of view without also asking *what it means to be the church.*[5] It is not only that the church mediates

[3] On creative fidelity in interpretation, see N. Lash's important essay, 'Performing the Scriptures', in his *Theology on the Way to Emmaus* (London: SCM Press, 1986) 37–46.

[4] Discussed further in Barton, *Invitation to the Bible*, 28–45.

[5] Good on this is S. Hauerwas, *A Community of Character* (Notre Dame: University of Notre Dame Press, 1981); also R. Clapp, *Families at the Crossroads: Beyond Traditional and Modern Options* (Downers Grove: InterVarsity Press, 1993).

Scripture to us by means of authoritative 'performance' past and present, but also that the church is itself the sacramental community which brings us into contact with God's triune life – is itself the 'true' family which (so long as it is faithful to its calling) shows us how to live as 'natural' families, communities and societies. Indeed, if Christians are right to talk of the family as one of the God-given 'orders of creation', then it may also be the case that what it means to be the church is illuminated by consideration of life together in families. We should keep a space for a certain reciprocity here.

Finally, what we say about family life will have a strong *eschatological* dimension. It will be oriented, like the New Testament itself, on what God's Spirit makes possible in the present as an anticipation of a new, heavenly reality yet to be revealed. It will therefore be something to do with hope, the overcoming of sin, oppression and despair, and growth towards full humanity. Whereas the proof-texting approach to the family tends to be rather static and the accompanying rhetoric a call to 'get back' to family patterns and fixed values long lost, a theological-ecclesial reading oriented on hope in a future which is in God's hands will be open much more to ongoing judgement and transformation. Likewise, whereas the historical-critical approach tends to lock the meaning of the text in the (reconstructed!) past, recognition of the eschatological dimension of the text helps us to see that historical criticism is not enough – that in the light of the coming of God the full meaning of life together in families past and present lies in the future.[6]

How should we proceed, then, in this present reflection on the family, in ways which take the ancient New Testament witness with full theological-ecclesial seriousness? There is no simple answer to this question, nor should we expect there to be one. To talk about 'living as families' is to talk about a complex reality in which we are all enmeshed in various ways;[7] and to talk about families 'in the light of the New Testament' is a complex and multi-faceted business, as we have seen above. What I propose to do in what follows, therefore, is to discuss in a theological-ecclesial way texts

[6] Compare on this G. Loughlin, 'Living in Christ: Story, Resurrection and Salvation', in G. D'Costa, ed., *Resurrection Reconsidered* (Oxford: Oneworld, 1996), 118–34.

[7] See further *Something to Celebrate: Valuing Families in Church and Society* (Report of the Church of England Board for Social Responsibility Working Party on the Family; London: Church House Publishing, 1995).

which may be felt to speak or have been found to speak in significant ways, either directly or indirectly, to family life today.

II. Trends in interpretation

Before doing so, however, it is worth making some observations about trends in interpretation in recent scholarly discussion of the New Testament. This will help to show further why a theological-ecclesial approach has become a matter of urgency and why it would represent a significant advance in Christian understanding. There are two trends in particular to which I wish to draw attention.

The first is the use of philological and historical or social-scientific analysis to show how different the contemporary family is from the world of the family in the first century. The literature is burgeoning and readily available, so all that is needed here is a brief outline of the customary observations made:[8] (i) There is no word in Hebrew, Greek or Latin for 'the (nuclear) family' as we understand it. This is because the social reality in antiquity was that of extended families, clans and tribes. (ii) The family or household was constituted by both persons (related to one another in a wide variety of ways, such as descent, marriage, patronage, friendship, business, ownership, etc.) and property. It was not limited to the intimate (and romantic) ties between husband and wife and parents and immediate offspring characteristic of modernity in the West. (iii) As a microcosm of the patriarchal city state, the family was a patriarchal institution. Men ruled in the public domain and over their households and women's authority was confined largely within doors. (iv) Honour and shame were pivotal social values and were related closely to gender definition. Women were a potential source of shame, and it was the role of the male household head to guard the family's honour by protecting the women's sexual virtue. (v) Authority in the household was hierarchical and distinctly non-egalitarian, and the institution of slavery was taken for granted.

Such findings are a major contribution to the art of reading the New Testament with historical depth and imagination. They help

---

[8] Representative works are: B. J. Malina, *The New Testament World: Insights from Cultural Anthropology* (London: SCM Press, 1983); C. Osiek, 'The Family in Early Christianity: "Family Values" Revisited', *Catholic Biblical Quarterly* 58 (1996), 1–24; H. Moxnes, ed., *Constructing Early Christian Families* (London: Routledge, 1997); C. Osiek and D. L. Balch, *Families in the New Testament World* (Louisville: Westminster John Knox Press, 1997).

us to see that our relation to the world of the New Testament is one
of continuity *and* discontinuity. That is an important corrective to
attempts to interpret the text which are blind to questions of
historical distance and particularity or which overstate historical
distance and particularity.

What is disheartening, however, is the extent to which historical
investigation appears to *exhaust* the inquiry – the way in which 'hard'
and rather positivist historical inquiry has marginalized 'soft'
theological-ecclesial reflection. Now, all that is left is the tentative
drawing of a few theological 'implications' in a final paragraph once
the historical work is done. As Christian Scripture, the text is
rendered mute. So, for example, Carolyn Osiek's in many ways fine
presidential address of 1995 to the Catholic Biblical Association of
America, entitled 'The Family in Early Christianity', ends in the
following disappointingly minimalist way with little more than a
few, mainly sociological, commonplaces:

> If biblical scholars can make any contribution to the present debate
> about 'family values', perhaps it can be to bring an awareness that the
> mid-twentieth century nuclear family is not normative, that the golden
> age of biblical families was not all it is cracked up to be, but that the
> family is a very strong social structure, strong precisely because it is so
> flexible. . . . The family must look outward and be part of something
> greater than itself. Only then will it achieve its end of fostering the
> most basic qualities of faith, hope, and love. These are the family values
> worth striving for.[9]

Most noticeably in this kind of discussion, the witness of the New
Testament to the *corporate and institutional dimensions* of Christian
discipleship is relativized severely. In effect, the ground is cleared,
and what we are left with is a set of lofty, Christian-sounding, universal
values, like 'faith, hope and love', whose relevance to the family
and whose embodiment in social structures are not spelt out.
Prevented from talking about the institutions of marriage and the
family – now deemed by some to be hangovers from the past – we
are left to talk in largely personalist and therapeutic vein about
'meaningful relationships'. At precisely this point, the ideological
character of historical criticism as an instrument of Enlightenment
rationalism and individualism becomes clear. But all too often the
damage has been done and the potential contribution of the New

[9] At p. 24.

Testament to the practice of godly sociality in family and society is short-circuited.

The second trend in scholarly accounts of 'the New Testament and the family' is to point up a 'tension' in the canonical texts between those which are 'for' the family and those which are 'against' it.[10] Sometimes this is expressed in terms of a contrast between the 'radical' discipleship sayings of Jesus in the Gospels (especially the Synoptics) and the more 'conservative' teaching about church and household order in the Epistles. Sometimes it is seen as a tension present within both the Gospels and the Epistles. Sometimes it is seen as a tension between Paul and the post-Pauline tradition, or between Paul and his opponents. Sometimes, yet again, it is seen as a tension between Palestinian Christianity and Hellenistic Christianity.

Once again, this attention to the full diversity of strands of tradition relevant to the family is an important gain, even if it is hardly new, given the intense interest in these very texts and traditions from the ascetically minded Church Fathers onwards.[11] It is undeniably the case both that allegiance to Jesus and the Christian Way was a threat to household ties by giving access to a new, eschatological family *and* that such an allegiance could serve to strengthen and even reinvigorate household ties through, for example, the conversion of whole households and the meetings of Christians hosted by household heads. As Osiek teasingly puts it: 'Which is more biblical, "Wives be submissive to your husbands as to the Lord" (Eph 5.21) or "Whoever loves father or mother or son or daughter more than me is not worthy of me" (Matt 10.37)?'[12]

What tends to happen in the absence of a clear theological-ecclesial hermeneutic, however, is either that we are left with the debilitating conclusion that the New Testament is 'ambivalent' about the family, or alternatively, one side of the tension is emphasized at the expense of the other. Typically, those who want to portray the institutionalization of Christianity as a step down the slippery slope of 'routinization' and 'patriarchalization' play up Jesus' individuality

---

[10] See, for example, S. C. Barton, *Discipleship and Family Ties in Mark and Matthew* (Cambridge: Cambridge University Press, 1994); P. N. Harvey, 'Christianity Against and For the Family', *Studies in Christian Ethics* 9/1 (1996), 34–9; J. M. G. Barclay, 'The Family as the Bearer of Religion in Judaism and Early Christianity', in *Constructing Early Christian Families*, 66–80.

[11] See on this, P. Brown, *The Body and Society: Men, Women and Sexual Renunciation in Early Christianity* (London: Faber & Faber, 1989).

[12] 'The Family in Early Christianity', 2.

and anti-familial radicalism,[13] while those who want to reassert the moral authority of social institutions like the family play up the household codes of the Epistles. Either way, by being left with an overwhelming sense of the ambivalence of the tradition, the New Testament as Scripture is rendered mute once more with respect to the family and related social institutions. The only thing left is the competing values of the interpreters, values which may be related only tenuously to the Christian faith tradition.[14]

So we need a better way of reflecting on and living out the New Testament. This will be one which takes the task of philological and historical investigation with full seriousness, but at the same time allows the text to function *as Scripture* by locating our work as interpreters in a wider context of divine and human action.

III. 'The Word became flesh and dwelt among us' (Jn 1.14a)

The Christian doctrine of the Incarnation is an overwhelming affirmation of the redeemability of creation and the goodness of the body and bodily relatedness. As such, it offers a powerful and truly countercultural alternative to the strong tendency in modernity to escape from the body and bodily relatedness, either by the denial of the body in favour of the spirit or by the exaltation of the body to the exclusion of the spirit. Put in terms of the family, which is the fundamental social form of bodily relatedness and the fecundity of the body, the Incarnation is an affirmation of *what we are given* in creation, a refusal to accept that the life of the spirit is achieved either by exalting the family or by demeaning it. As the revelation of the glory of God in human flesh, the Incarnation is creation (the material world, the body, the family) *redeemed and transfigured* – an emphasis particularly strong in Catholic and Orthodox theology.[15]

At the present time, such a word is truly 'gospel'. It is judgement on modernity's alienation from the natural and the human and it

[13] See, for example, E. S. Fiorenza, *In Memory of Her: A Feminist Theological Reconstruction of Christian Origins* (London: SCM Press, 1983).

[14] For evaluation of specific case studies of biblical interpretation in this area see ch. 2 above.

[15] Of interest here are the *Letter to Families from Pope John Paul II* (Boston: St Paul Books, 1994), and the essays by Kallistos Ware and Andrew Louth in S. Coakley, ed., *Religion and the Body* (Cambridge: Cambridge University Press, 1997), 90–110 and 111–30 respectively.

is salvation for men, women and children seeking to live together purposefully and harmoniously. In this context, it is not helpful to appeal in a simplistic way to texts which appear to set Christianity 'against' the family, or to observe with ironic detachment that there is in the New Testament a 'fundamental tension' about the family. Such detachment can only be afforded by people who have themselves an investment in the *status quo*.

Even feminism, with its praiseworthy protest against modernity's denigration of (female) body in favour of (male) spirit, has not gone far enough. By sharing in modernity's ambivalence about the family, feminism's deep insight into the necessarily embodied nature of personal and social reality has been compromised. The dysfunctional or patriarchal or abusive family has become the dominant image, as if this is what family life *must* be like; and this has left feminism in collusion with modernity's anti-family dualism. This point has been made convincingly by Linda Woodhead, in her essay in the special number of *Concilium* on 'The Family'.[16] Her conclusion is worth quoting at length:

> Christianity and feminism both display ambiguous attitudes to modernity. On the one hand they both question and resist many of modernity's most cherished convictions. On the other, they both accept a great deal of the modern ethos, often oblivious to how much it compromises their own foundational beliefs. . . . [F]eminism has been enormously helpful to Christianity in recalling it to a belief in the importance of the bodily and in showing how much it had compromised itself by collaborating with modernity's spiritualization of the human. . . . [C]hristianity may now be in a position to return the favour by showing feminism that its uncritical acceptance of some key aspects of the modern ethos has prevented it from acknowledging the importance of the family. In so doing, Christianity could help feminism come to a full acceptance of the implications of its belief in the importance of the body for the first time. No less significant, it could help reassure the millions of women who are sustained and fulfilled through love of husband and children that there really is no reason why they should continue to feel traitors to the feminist cause.[17]

In the light of this kind of analysis, what is needed now is an affirmation of flesh, the body, bodily relatedness, marriage, and the family (nuclear and extended) which offers a life-giving,

[16] L. Woodhead, 'Faith, Feminism and the Family', in L. S. Cahill and D. Mieth, eds, *The Family* (*Concilium* 1995/4; London: SCM Press, 1995), 43–52.

[17] Ibid. 50–1.

countercultural alternative. One such affirmation is found, I am suggesting, in Christian reflection on the Johannine testimony to the incarnation of the divine Word.

For example, it is by no means insignificant that the incarnate Word begins his public ministry by being present with his mother at a wedding (Jn 2.1–11). This has long been recognized and affirmed in the Christian liturgical tradition of the marriage rite, in which the Wedding at Cana is taken as the customary Gospel lection.[18] But perhaps this is a case where scholarly exegesis has suffered by being kept separate from *Christian worship*. The focus of the exegete is so singlemindedly on the reconstruction of the (putative) 'signs source' or the History of Religions 'parallels' (to the multiplication of wine) with the cult of Dionysus that the revelation of God's glory *at a wedding* is given short shrift by a kind of scholarly 'spiritualizing' of the text. The spiritual (or better, symbolic) dimension is there, certainly;[19] but that should not blind us to the anthropological and ritual dimensions. And even if the exegete is correct in arguing that the symbolic-christological meaning of the story is the Johannine meaning also, the witness of the Christian liturgical tradition both Eastern and Western should open us up to the possibility that the Johannine meaning is not the only possible true meaning. Ironically, perhaps, we may need to take the text more literally than the exegete allows.

Equally significant is the fact that the end of Jesus' ministry also has a strong familial dimension (Jn 19.26–27). Sometimes it seems, however, as if the historical quest for the identity of the 'beloved disciple' is in danger of obscuring the main issue. What is of first importance is this further manifestation of Jesus' love. This love is not for 'the world' in the abstract. It is a love which is quite concrete. Here, it focuses on his mother: 'When Jesus saw his mother . . .' (Jn 19.26). As her loving son, the dying Jesus does not leave her on her own, like an orphan (cf. Jn 14.18). Rather, Jesus fulfils his filial duty by arranging her reception into the household of the beloved disciple. Nor should we assume that the evangelist has in mind only Mary's entry into a 'spiritual' family

[18] See K. Stevenson, *Nuptial Blessing: A Study of Christian Marriage Rites* (New York: Oxford University Press, 1983), 10.

[19] Excellent is M. Hengel, 'The Interpretation of the Wine-Miracle at Cana: John 2.1–11', in L. D. Hurst and N. T. Wright, eds, *The Glory of Christ in the New Testament* (Oxford: Clarendon Press, 1987), 83–112.

founded at the foot of the cross.[20] At the literal level, the story is about the transfer of this (presumably widowed) woman, Jesus' mother, from one household to another in view of her son's imminent departure in death and her need for ongoing support.

In sum, we may say that the revelation of the divine glory in the Incarnation and the Passion is not a denial of the body and bodily relatedness in the form of human institutions, like marriage and family ties: it is their transfiguration in the light of the greater reality of the triune life of God.

IV. 'Who are my mother and my brothers?' (Mk 3.33)

This powerful rhetorical question, posed by Jesus to the crowd on learning that his mother and brothers were 'outside' calling for him (Mk 3.31–35), speaks still both in relation to modernity and postmodernity.

One tendency in *modernity*, not least in Christian circles, has been to make the family – the nuclear family, in particular – the *sole measure* of human relationships in general. Related to this has been the widespread acceptance of the view that the family is the last bastion of morality and goodness in human society, a 'haven in a heartless world'. This brings with it a number of consequences and corollaries. There is a pressure within families to put the family first, to the exclusion of neighbourliness and wider social concerns. There is a pressure for men and women to conform to their 'traditional' roles of, respectively, breadwinner and nurturer. Children in modernity, as we are learning to our cost, tend to be either idolized or abused. Single people and sexual minorities are marginalized. And the church becomes an extension of the life of the family, to the point that worship is moulded around the (strikingly named) 'family service' and people who do not fit the model feel excluded.[21] In sum, where human relationships should be ordered according to the life of the triune God made known in Christ, they are ordered around (a particular form of) the family.[22]

[20] The symbolic dimension is given a fine exposition in I. de la Potterie, *The Hour of Jesus* (Slough: St Paul Publications, 1989), 132–52, but the literal dimension is marginalized, even though the admission is made (p. 133) that the Church Fathers, both Greek and Latin, took this aspect seriously.

[21] See on this the two essays by Peter Selby and Michael Vasey in Barton, ed., *The Family in Theological Perspective*, 151–68 and 169–86 respectively.

[22] See further, Harvey, 'Christianity Against and For the Family', and Linda Woodhead's response, 'Christianity For and Against the Family', in *Studies in Christian Ethics* 9/1 (1996), 34–9 and 40–6 respectively.

48

In this context, the question 'Who are my mothers and my brothers?' is dynamite. This is one of a surprisingly large number of texts in the Gospels which make it abundantly clear both that Jesus' relations with his natural kin were fraught and that discipleship of Jesus was a priority that relativized family ties and generated fierce – even mortal – familial opposition (cf. Mk 1.16–20; 6.1–6a; 10.28–31; 13.9–13; etc.).[23] Indeed, as our text goes on to show, discipleship of Jesus brought participation in a new, eschatological family: 'Here [in the crowd] are my mother and my brothers! Whoever does the will of God is my brother, and sister, and mother' (Mk 3.34–35).

How does this speak to modernity? To say that it speaks 'against' the family is to go too far. Exegetically, such a view fails to account for the rhetorical, hyperbolic aspect of Jesus' sayings, both here and elsewhere, whereby Jesus seeks to shock and challenge his listeners' taken-for-granted ways of seeing things. It also overlooks sayings which manifestly support family ties (e.g. Mk 7.9–13; 10.1–12). Psychologically and sociologically, it is counterintuitive and even, in some contexts, irresponsible. Theologically, it contradicts the goodness of God in creation and the redemption of creation through the Incarnation, referred to already.

What it *does* say to us, however, is that the family is *not an end in itself* and that modernity's 'idolatry of the family' stands under judgement. It says to us that belonging to Jesus and the 'new' family of Jesus – theologically speaking, the church – is the prior, more profound (because eschatological) reality to which human beings are called and in terms of which human relationships, including familial relationships, are to be judged.[24] It says to us that children are important, not just for their parents' fulfilment, but because they are loved by God who in Jesus took them in his arms and blessed them (Mk 9.36–37; 10.13–16) and who entrusts them to parents and the church for their nurture and growth into mature human beings.

[23] For discussion of all the relevant texts in the first two Gospels, see Barton, *Discipleship and Family Ties*; for the New Testament as a whole, most recent is Osiek and Balch, *Families in the New Testament World*, 103–55.

[24] Compare Hauerwas, *Community of Character*, 174: 'The family is not just something we do because we are in the habit, nor is it something we must do to fulfil a moral purpose. Rather marriage and the family, like the life of singleness, becomes a vocation for the upbuilding of a particular kind of community. . . . [T]he family, in order to be a viable moral enterprise, requires community beyond itself.'

But Jesus' question resonates powerfully and disturbingly in a *postmodern* context as well. For in postmodernity, the question of personal identity – who I belong to, how I trace my genealogy, what narrative I own as mine, what name I accept, and so on – is plural, plastic and negotiable in ways previously unknown. A case in point is the complex of issues raised by developments in human fertilization and embryology. Michael Banner puts the point well:

> We have in recent times multiplied significantly the occasions on which the question 'who are my mother and my brothers?', taken quite literally, could have a use. . . . The various practices of donation of gametes have brought into being a whole class of foundlings, for whom this question, 'who are my mother and my brothers?' has immediate use and purpose, expressing that radical dissociation and alienation which has been wished upon them by the utopian dreamers of our times. And these children, the offspring of anonymous donors or of surrogates, may yet be joined by others, born from eggs harvested from the dead or the unborn. . . .[25]

This disturbing statement brings home the importance of Jesus' words for the postmodern family and for postmodern society. And what Banner highlights in his essay is how lost we are if we neglect the vocation of the family to live as part of the larger community of the church and engage, as part of that larger community, in serving society by witnessing to the truth. That, for Banner, is the force of the saying 'Whoever *does the will of God* is my brother, and sister, and mother' (Mk 3.35); and, as resources for discerning how the family may witness to the truth, he appeals to the social ethics of Bonhoeffer, monasticism according to the Benedictine Rule, and the moral theology of John Paul II, especially his encyclical of 1981, *Familiaris Consortio*.

Such resources help us to see that human identity in a post-modern society need not be at the mercy of an amoral pluralism and an unbridled scientism. Families are called to witness otherwise: to the fact that our true personal identity and our deepest interpersonal kinship (within and beyond families) is found within the solidarity of the church doing the will and work of God in the power of the Spirit of God.

[25] M. Banner, '"Who are my mother and my brothers?": Marx, Bonhoeffer and Benedict and the Redemption of the Family', *Studies in Christian Ethics* 9/1 (1996), 1–22 at p. 1.

V. 'Likewise you wives, be submissive to your husbands' (1 Pet 3.1)

If the Bible is 'good news' for families it is *not* because it is politically correct! From the viewpoint of political correctness, the Bible is a 'problem text' of irredeemable proportions. This is so, not least with respect to what have become known as the 'household rules (or codes)' (*Haustafeln*) of the New Testament. These rules are a recurrent feature of the moral teaching of the epistolary texts in particular (cf. Col 3.18 – 4.1; Eph 5.22 – 6.9; 1 Pet 2.18 – 3.7; also 1 Tim 2.8–15; 6.1–2; Tit 2.1–10). They are found also in early post-New Testament texts (e.g. Didache 4.9–11; Barnabas 19.5–7; Ignatius, *Polycarp* 4.1 – 5.2).[26]

Following a fairly regular pattern, with strong precedents in standard discussions from Greek antiquity on of matters of 'household management' (*oikonomia*),[27] the rules set out how relations within households are to be ordered, as between husbands and wives, parents and children, and masters and slaves. Generally, the three sets of relations are addressed in that order, and the subordinate in each pair is addressed first. What is of evident concern is the importance of preserving orderly relations and the proper social hierarchy in the households of Christians (or in households which have Christian members). That hierarchy consists in the subordination of wives to husbands, children to parents, and slaves to masters. It is a hierarchy which is pervasively patriarchal, as feminist scholarship in particular has drawn to our attention. It is also a hierarchy which assumes a class structure in which the institution of slavery is morally acceptable.

All this is a world away from contemporary Western society (even if it may be closer, in some respects, to non-Western cultures). We may characterize the contrast as between inequality in social relations then and egalitarianism now; the obligation then to know your place over against the obligation today to exercise your rights (as men or women or children); and the expectation in antiquity to conform to patterns laid down in traditions held as venerable over against the expectation today to experiment and choose from

[26] See further, J. D. G. Dunn, 'The Household Rules in the New Testament', in S. C. Barton, ed., *The Family in Theological Perspective*, 43–63 for a valuable survey and evaluation. The relevant texts are laid out on pp. 44–6.

[27] Especially valuable on this is D. L. Balch, *Let Wives Be Submissive* (Chico: Scholars Press, 1981).

the range of options currently 'on the market'. In the face of this undeniable distance between contemporary social values and the world of the text, what are we to do with the New Testament household rules?

One important step is to remember that this kind of issue is not new. In an earlier generation, for example, Rudolf Bultmann attempted to deal with the questions of interpretation raised, not by the problem of 'political correctness', but by the problem of (for want of a better phrase) 'cosmological correctness': how to enable 'modern man' to be confronted by the true 'scandal' of the gospel in a way that did not demand assent to the outmoded cosmology and mythology of the biblical writings. His solution was to deny that the truth of the gospel is bound indissolubly to an ancient world view, and to provide a method of interpretation (which became known as 'demythologization') that allowed the deeper meanings behind the biblical mythology to come to expression. These deeper meanings have to do with an understanding of human existence; and in the existentialist philosophy of his day, Bultmann found ready to hand the categories of interpretation that made possible the 'translation' of biblical myth into terms intelligible to modern man.[28]

The adequacy of Bultmann's approach need not detain us here; but it does provide pointers to possible ways forward in dealing with other kinds of 'problem texts'. For Bultmann recognized that the way to deal with problem texts is not to excise them or censor them, but to interpret them *in a larger philosophical and theological framework*: to see them in all their historical particularity as witness to the incomprehensibility and otherness of a God whose reality no words are able to convey in ways true for all time. Related to this, Bultmann showed that responsible interpretation involves ongoing acts of engagement between the reader and the text in openness to God's justifying grace in Christ. The true meaning of the text is never static, therefore. For the true meaning resides in the transcendent, living Word of God to whom the words of the text bear frail witness.

[28] See R. Bultmann, 'New Testament and Mythology', in Hans Werner Bartsch, ed., *Kerygma and Myth: A Theological Debate* (London: SPCK, 1972), 1–44, and the essays in response collected therein; also, A. C. Thiselton, *The Two Horizons: New Testament Hermeneutics and Philosophical Description* (Grand Rapids: Eerdmans, 1980) chs 8–10.

Having recognized that the 'problem' of the household rules is endemic to New Testament interpretation as a whole and that a theological-ecclesial framework of understanding is essential, we need to ask, What is the fundamental subject matter of these rules? Could it be that the essential issue is not the laying down of a divinely ordained pattern of hierarchical family relations (including slaves!) under male 'headship', but rather something to do with the *relationship between church and culture* – specifically, with how as families (or households) to be the church, how the *already given* structures of personal and social existence are to be renewed in the light of membership of the Body of Christ?

Seen in this way, the household rules continue to speak as Scripture in a number of ways. Above all, they show that the revelation of the grace of God in the death and resurrection of Christ and the coming of the eschatological Spirit forced the early church to re-examine fundamental questions of personal identity, social obligation, and power and authority. Noteworthy in the Epistles, for instance, is the way in which theological and christological affirmation is followed by reflection on how to live.[29] In the light of Christ, things could never be the same again. Christian believers could not be *complacent* about even the most 'sacred', taken-for-granted aspects of their individual and social lives, including life in families.

The household rules are, at least in part,[30] an outworking of this process of critical, theological re-examination. Now, the measure of relations between husbands and wives is *Christian existence 'in the Lord'* (Col 3.18). Husbands – and this in a patriarchal society – are to love (not abuse) their wives, and the measure of that love is laid down as Christ's self-giving love for the church (Eph 5.25–27). Wives, especially those married to unbelievers, are to 'be subject' to their husbands, not out of servility and weakness, but for the higher good of 'gaining' their unbelieving husbands for Christ (1 Pet 3.1–2).

---

[29] On the theological framework of Paul's ethics, for example, see R. B. Hays, *The Moral Vision of the New Testament* (San Francisco: HarperCollins, 1996), 16–59.

[30] Other factors may well have influenced the formation of these Christian(ized) household rules. The so-called 'delay of the parousia' is one possibility, although direct evidence is weak. A more likely additional concern was apologetic: to encourage believers to conform (as far as possible) to wider social norms in order to allay the suspicion of unbelievers that conversion to Christ threatened to undermine the family and the state (cf. 1 Pet 2.12; 3.15–16). On the latter, see especially Balch, *Let Wives Be Submissive*, 63–116.

Children are to obey their parents 'in the Lord', and fathers are not to abuse their authority by 'provoking' their children, but are to bring them up 'in the Lord' (Eph 6.1–4). Similarly, relations between masters and slaves are framed in terms of their mutual belonging to a 'master in heaven' (Col 4.1). In other words, what we are witnessing in these texts is the criticism and transformation of Jewish and pagan household ties in the light of Christ.

This is not best seen as the 'grafting of Christianity onto the pattern of family life',[31] as if the two entities are alien to each other. Such an interpretation gives the unfortunate impression that believers were not members of families already and that involvement in family life was a retrograde step, a second-best dirtying of their spiritual hands. Rather, it is the transformation of the family *from within*, in the light of Christ. Speaking of the moral stance represented by 1 Peter, Miroslav Wolf puts the matter well:

> Notice the significance of the new birth for Christian social identity. Christians . . . are not outsiders who either seek to become insiders or maintain strenuously the status of outsiders. Christians are the *insiders* who have diverted from their culture by being born again. They are by definition those who are not what they used to be, those who do not live like they used to live. Christian difference is therefore not an insertion of something new into the old from outside, but a bursting out of the new *precisely within the proper space of the old.*[32]

If this is so, then the attempt to reject the household rules wholesale by those who consider them inegalitarian, oppressive and out of date, may be as inappropriate a response as the attempt to impose the household rules wholesale by those who consider them to be the church's last hope in the face of contemporary moral indiscipline and social disintegration. Neither the 'liberal-radical' nor the 'conservative' response will do. Both are too 'sectarian', too totalitarian in their desire, either to wipe the slate clean and start somewhere else or to wipe the slate clean and return to 'what the Bible says'.[33]

Understood in their historical context and evaluated in terms of Christ and the church, the household rules help us to see instead

---

[31] See Barclay, 'The Family as Bearer of Religion', 77.

[32] M. Wolf, 'Soft Difference: Theological Reflections on the Relation Between Church and Culture in 1 Peter', *Ex Auditu* 10 (1994), 15–30 at 18–19.

[33] On Stephen Toulmin's analysis of the 'myth of the clean slate' as a characteristic of modernity see Wolf, 'Soft Difference', 23.

that what is required is something more modest, realistic, local, and concrete, but no less demanding. What is required is day-by-day participation in the life of the family and other social and political networks in ways which witness with full integrity to our true, eschatological identity as members together in a *new* household, the 'household of God'. That we today are likely – indeed *obliged* – to do so in ways which do not reproduce the domestic pattern of those early Christian household rules does not mean that they no longer have anything to say. What is required is *creative fidelity*: where fidelity involves recognizable continuity with our scriptural faith tradition, and creativity is an openness to the Spirit to inspire us to interpret that tradition in ways which are life-giving for families, church and society.

VI. '. . . as we also have forgiven our debtors' (Matt 6.12)

In conclusion, a word about what we might call 'good practice'. That good practice is *forgiveness* and its corollary, confession.[34] Forgiveness lies at the heart of a holy society. It is central to the piety and cult of Israel in its covenant relationship with God (cf. the Psalter). It is central to the teaching of Jesus about what prayer and practice sustain life together in the Christian family of the church (Matt 6.9–15; 18.21–22), and it was the prayer on his lips at the crucifixion (Lk 23.34, 43). It is what the Holy Spirit empowers the church to offer as agent and representative of the heavenly Father (Jn 20.21–23). It lies at the very heart of Christian celebration of the death and resurrection of Christ in the sacraments of baptism (Acts 2.38) and eucharist (Matt 26.28). So, in learning from the story of Israel and in participating in the life of the church, the family is called upon to be a community of forgiveness also.

This means that men will have to acknowledge and confess their violence (both active and passive) against women, and women their complicity; parents their abuse and desertion of children and the elderly; corporations their failure to establish pay and work structures which do not threaten family life; governments their complicity in policies which undermine communities while presupposing a return to 'basic family values'; and the church its

---

[34] Excellent on this is L. G. Jones, *Embodying Forgiveness: A Theological Analysis* (Grand Rapids: Eerdmans, 1995).

failure to serve as a good model for just relations in the family. All this needs further exploration.[35]

Even more, it requires responding at ever deeper levels to the forgiveness offered to us by God at the cost of his Son, an offer continually renewed by the Spirit in the reading of the Scriptures, in the sacramental life of the church, and in the lives of the holy. Just as forgiveness is the way by which we come into right relations with God, so it is the practice by which we come into right relations with our neighbours. Those neighbours include, not least, the people we live with.

---

[35] Helpful on the different levels of offence which require the practice of forgiveness in different ways is A. Borrowdale, 'Right Relations: Forgiveness and Family Life', in Barton, ed., *The Family in Theological Perspective*, 203–17.

4

Is the Bible Good News for Human Sexuality? Reflections on Method in Biblical Interpretation

I. Introduction

There can be little doubt that there is more disagreement than ever before over the question of the relevance of the Bible for understanding human sexuality. As in so many areas of Christian belief and practice, the consensus has broken down and is fiercely contested. For many, the Bible remains the touchstone and authoritative guide for how men and women are to understand and practise their sexuality and how life together in family, church and society is to be conducted.[1] For many others, the Bible has little or no authority because it belongs so obviously to a bygone age and its teaching is neither credible nor helpful.[2] Others, yet again, find themselves somewhere in the middle, caught between feelings of loyalty to the Bible and what it stands for on the one hand, and on the other, a firm conviction that modern people do not and cannot take the Bible seriously any more, especially when it is interpreted literally.[3]

---

[1] See, for example, Lewis Smedes, *Mere Morality* (Grand Rapids: Eerdmans, 1983); also, John R. W. Stott, *Issues Facing Christians Today* (London: Marshall, Morgan & Scott, 1984), esp. part 4 on 'Sexual Issues'.

[2] This stance is particularly clear in Daphne Hampson's *Theology and Feminism* (Oxford: Blackwell, 1990). In her discussion of the Bible in ch. 3, she says, for example: 'That the bible is deeply patriarchal may be taken as read. . . . The text is the product of a sexist, indeed misogynist, culture: the presuppositions of a patriarchal world are written into it. Moreover, such texts are the more dangerous in that they affect us at a subconscious level. . . . There is, one must conclude, little that can be done. Yet these texts are read as sacred texts' (pp. 85, 92).

[3] See, for example, John Shelby Spong, *Living in Sin? A Bishop Rethinks Human Sexuality* (San Francisco: Harper & Row, 1988), esp. part 2 on 'The Bible'.

One of the issues which often lies behind these disagreements is that of interpretation: What is the Bible for?, What does the Bible mean?, and Is the Bible true? The aim of this essay is to discuss issues of method in interpretation with a view to showing that the original question is wrongly put. Instead of asking, Is the Bible good news for human sexuality?, the question we should be asking is much more of the kind, What sort of people ought we to be and become so that we are enabled to read the Bible in ways which are life-giving in the area of gender and sexuality? In other words, I wish to suggest that it is not the Bible that should be the main bone of contention. Rather, the focus ought to be on the readers: who it is that is reading the Bible, and what it might mean for us to read the Bible well and wisely.

II. The right place to start

Knowing the right place to start is the critical issue, often overlooked. One very common approach is to start with the Bible. Ironically, given their mutual antagonism, this tends to be the approach of both conservative fundamentalists and liberal historical critics. Both groups, faced with the question, Is the Bible good news for human sexuality?, assume that the obvious and correct thing to do is to go 'back to the Bible', find the relevant texts, and see what they have to say. Many reports issued by church bodies and ecclesiastical authorities likewise begin with opening chapters on 'what the Bible teaches',[4] the obvious intention being to lay the firm foundations for what follows on interpretation and application. Here, the implicit assumption, of course, is that interpretation and application follow the laying of the biblical foundations rather than influencing it from the start! It is as if the answers to this and any other question can be 'read off' the text in a relatively straightforward way, either by 'stretching' history (in the case of the fundamentalist) or by asserting historical distance (in the case of the historical critic), with the matter of application following on subsequently. The problem with this kind of approach is highlighted well by Nicholas Lash in his

---

[4] See, for example, the document from the House of Bishops of the General Synod of the Church of England, entitled *Issues in Human Sexuality* (London: Church House Publishing, 1991). After a short Introduction, the first major section addresses the biblical material, under the heading 'Scripture and Human Sexuality' (pp. 5–18).

critique of what he memorably depicts as the 'relay-race' model of the relation between biblical criticism and systematic theology:

> When the New Testament scholar has done his job, produced his completed package of 'original meanings', he hands this over to the systematic theologian, whose responsibility it is to transpose the meanings received into forms intelligible within the conditions of our contemporary culture. Systematic theologians who subscribe to this model are sometimes irritated by the fact that, because the work of New Testament interpretation is never finished, the baton never reaches them. The New Testament scholar appears to be 'running on the spot'; he never arrives at the point at which the baton could be handed over. The New Testament scholar, for his part, either ignores what the systematic theologian is doing (it is not his business: he is only running the *first* leg of the race) or disapproves of the fact that the baton is continually being wrenched prematurely from his hands.[5]

Nevertheless, in some ways, starting with the Bible seems a common-sense and unobjectionable way of proceding. Obviously, an important ingredient of any Christian attempt to answer 'the question of human sexuality' will be to try to find the relevant biblical material and see what it says. Given that there are two horizons in biblical interpretation, the horizon of the text and the horizon of the reader,[6] why not start with that of the text? But there are problems lying not too far beneath the surface of this apparently common-sense, 'objective' approach.

1. First, there is the problem of what model of the Bible and Bible reading is being presupposed. To put it in the form of a question, What is involved in using the Bible as a source of information or instruction? Is the Bible understood best as a source, something to go back to or dig into? Operating on the assumption that this is so, the conservative fundamentalist quarries the Bible for the appropriate proof texts, ascertains the plain (i.e. literal) sense of the text and seeks then to apply it in (what is believed to be) a straightforward, rational way to everyday life. Operating on basically the same assumption, the liberal historical critic also quarries the Bible, ascertains the plain (i.e. historico-philological) sense of the text and then, if he or she is religiously disposed, tries

---

[5] N. Lash, *Theology on the Way to Emmaus* (London: SCM Press, 1986), 79.
[6] See A. C. Thiselton, *The Two Horizons: New Testament Hermeneutics and Philosophical Description* (Grand Rapids: Eerdmans, 1980).

to weigh up rationally whether it is applicable or not, taking its historically conditioned character into account.

But what if the Bible is something more than a source to be quarried and analysed in the privacy either of the believer's 'quiet time' or of the academician's study? What if interpreting the Bible is not best understood in these decidedly positivist terms as a kind of archaeological dig for historical facts or revelatory propositions? What if the Bible is more like the text of a Shakespearean play or the score of a Beethoven symphony, where true interpretation involves corporate performance and practical enactment, and where the meaning of the text or score will vary to some degree from one performance to another depending on the identity of the performers and the circumstances of the performance? A number of writers have begun to explore this alternative model of interpreting the Bible.[7] Its advantage is that it brings the reading of the Bible back into the process of community formation, celebration and mission, and places responsibility on the community to read the text in ways which are transforming and life-giving.

2. Related to the first problem is the problem of the 'Little Jack Horner' approach to the Bible. How adequate are approaches to the Bible which select out the 'purple passages' about gender and sexuality, or focus in a proof-texting way on those texts which support a particular understanding? This approach is very common, perhaps the most common. In an area of debate which is closely related to human sexuality, that of the status and role of women in Christian faith, think of the enormous attention devoted to New Testament texts like Galatians 3.28 ('neither male nor female . . . in Christ Jesus'), or 1 Corinthians 11.2–16 ('the head of a woman is her husband'), or 1 Timothy 2.8–15 ('Let a woman learn in silence with all submissiveness . . .'). Even on single verses and single words within verses the scholarly and other literature can be enormous.[8]

---

[7] See N. Lash, *Theology on the Way to Emmaus*, 37–46; Frances Young, *The Art of Performance* (London: Darton, Longman & Todd, 1990); also Sandra M. Schneiders, *The Revelatory Text* (San Francisco: HarperCollins, 1991), 149–50.

[8] To take but one example, a recent article by Joseph Fitzmyer on the meaning of the word *kephalē* ('head', according to the RSV and REB) in 1 Cor 11.3 lists over twenty previous studies, most of which have been published since the early 1970s and the list does not even include works in languages other than English! See Joseph A. Fitzmyer, '*Kephalē* in I Corinthians 11.3', *Interpretation* 47 (1993), 52–9 with bibliography of other studies in n. 2.

There seems to be something fundamentally inadequate about this. For instance, there is the danger of trivializing the text, as if all that matters is whether or not selected texts (can be made to) speak for or against a particular conception of human sexuality.[9] I am not at all wishing to deny the general point that issues of human sexuality are important.[10] What I wish to question is the wisdom of so focusing the sexuality debate on Bible reading and interpretation that such issues become the dominant, sometimes almost exclusive agenda, and the Bible becomes little more than a battleground for competing special interest groups. Instead of being 'a lamp unto our feet and a light unto our path', the Bible is trivialized and at the same time the issue of human sexuality is trivialized as well. Our reading of the Bible becomes distracted from what might be regarded as more central, or at least equally legitimate, concerns – to do, for example, with faith in God and the pursuit of righteousness and justice. At the same time, the issues of gender and sexuality are marginalized: limited to matters of exegesis, an exercise for which, in any case, only very few are equipped.

Then there is the danger that the Bible will not be allowed to speak as *one book*, but become fractured and fragmented instead into many isolated or even opposing parts. So, for example, the account of the creation of the man and the woman in Genesis 1 is played off against the account in Genesis 2–3, the celebration of sexual love in the Song of Songs is played off against the disciplinary emphasis of the Pentateuch, Jesus' attitude to 'prostitutes and sinners' is played off against Paul's, Paul the liberationist is played off against the apparent authoritarianism of the Pastoral Epistles, or more generally, the Old Testament is played off against the New.

Now I do not wish to deny that there are often very significant differences between one part of the Bible and another, not least on issues of gender and sexuality. Nor do I wish to encourage a simplistic harmonizing of one Bible passage with another. What I am concerned to point out, however, is the potential of these kinds of interpretative strategy paradoxically to cut off the scriptural

---

[9] The way in which the same texts can be interpreted in diametrically opposed ways by people with (academically speaking) the same kinds of credentials is illustrated well in Willard M. Swartley, *Slavery, Sabbath War and Women: Case Issues in Biblical Interpretation* (Scottdale: Herald Press, 1983).

[10] Hence my early essay, 'Homosexuality and the Church of England: Perspectives from the Social Sciences', *Theology* 92 (1989), 175–81.

branch on which they rest. For in the end, the Bible can be dispensed with altogether. Those who 'flatten out' the text of the Bible by a process of harmonization so that it is always saying the same thing, undermine the Bible by making it monolithic, static and ultimately uninteresting. Those who divide up the Bible by setting one text over against another also undermine it, this time by divesting it of coherence and authority. What is needed instead is a way of reading the Bible which transcends these reductionist alternatives and allows the Bible to function as life-giving, revelatory Scripture for the church.[11]

Also, there is the danger that the text becomes captive to tribal interests of one kind or another, whether conservative fundamentalism, liberal biblical criticism, feminism, gay liberation, or whatever. When this happens, the meaning of the text and even more the truth of the text tend to get confused with the question whether or not the text can be used to support the identity and self-understanding of the group concerned. Katherine Boone has shown how this happens in the way the Bible is used in Protestant Fundamentalism.[12] Anthony Thiselton, on the other hand, has also shown how this happens in the interpretation of the Bible by some feminists.[13] And, lest the historical critics think that their approach escapes this tendency towards tribalism, Stanley Hauerwas and Steve Long have argued with some force that historical criticism tends to serve the narrow interests of modern liberal individualism, and that the natives of this tribe are to be found most commonly in university departments of theology and religion![14]

The corollary of all this is a tendency towards scapegoating. So, for example, the Bible becomes the scapegoat for the anxieties of feminists and gay liberationists, or feminists and gays become the scapegoat for the anxieties of the loyalists, or the historical critics adopt an approach along the lines of 'a plague on both your houses' and withdraw to the apparently neutral and 'scientific' activity of the quest for the historical Jesus (or Mary or whoever).

---

[11] See further Daniel L. Migliore, *Faith Seeking Understanding* (Grand Rapids: Eerdmans, 1991), 40–55.

[12] Kathleen C. Boone, *The Bible Tells Them So* (London: SCM Press, 1990).

[13] Anthony C. Thiselton, *New Horizons in Hermeneutics* (San Francisco: HarperCollins, 1992), esp. ch. 12.

[14] Stanley Hauerwas and Steve Long, 'Interpreting the Bible as a Political Act', *Religion and Intellectual Life* 6 (1989), 134–42.

3. Then there is the issue, What constitutes an appropriate set of expectations to bring to the biblical text? For some, it is essential to approach the text in a spirit of absolute trust, itself based upon a 'high' view of the Bible as the word of God. For others, it is necessary to approach the text from a stance of systematic suspicion, on the assumption that the Bible is either outdated (so the modernist) or a weapon of oppression (so certain kinds of feminist). But it is rarely acknowledged that both the loyalist position and the revisionist (or rejectionist) positions are two sides of the same coin, according to which the main issue is whether or not the Bible can be trusted. The Enlightenment tendency to put God in the dock for cross-examination is transferred here to the Bible. Now it is the Bible which is placed in the dock, with some quoting proof texts in its defence, and others quoting proof texts on behalf of the pro-secution. Instead of allowing ourselves to be judged by Scripture as in some fundamental theological sense 'the book of God' – a stance advocated *inter alios* by Karl Barth and Dietrich Bonhoeffer – we become its judges. Instead of learning in community the kinds of skill and wisdom necessary to faithful interpretation and trans-forming enactment, we reify and absolutize the text either as a book to be obeyed or as a book to be dismissed.

4. Yet another problem is that of assuming that the text has only one meaning, the literal meaning, and that this is to be ascertained rationally using common sense in one form or another – that is, the common sense of the proverbial man or woman on the Clapham omnibus or the common sense arising out of the application of historical criticism. On this view, once the meaning of the text has been established, it is a matter simply of 'applying' it to the modern world, or of disregarding it as irrelevant to the modern world. But why assume that the meaning of the biblical text is univocal? It is one thing to resist the idea that 'anything goes' and that there are no limits to what a text may mean. It is another to go to the opposite extreme of saying that the text has one true meaning only (which usually happens to be the meaning my group holds to).

However, there is a more moderate position in between the extremes, with strong precedent in the Bible itself as well as in the exegesis of the early church and the Middle Ages. According to this view, and taking its hermeneutical cue from Paul's statement in 2 Corinthians 3.6 that 'the letter kills but the spirit makes alive', a text may have meanings over and above that intended by the original author, meanings which the author was unable to see or which the author did not anticipate.[15] It is the character of the reading community, itself influenced by the history of the reception of the text in previous generations, which will determine in large measure in which direction the process of interpretation goes.[16] Once again, we are made to see the importance of the communal and practical dimensions of interpreting what the Bible says (and does not say) about gender and sexuality.

5. Finally, there is the problem which arises from a failure to address the difference between the meaning of a text and whether or not it is true. It is one thing to establish what the biblical text says. It is quite another to determine whether and how the text 'speaks'. To put it bluntly, questions like, Was Jesus a feminist? – even if it could somehow be shown that the question was not meaningless (on the grounds of anachronism) and that, on the balance of historical probabilities, Jesus was a feminist – invite the rather deflating riposte, So what? What difference does it make to women suffering sexual abuse and political and economic oppression today to know that there happen to be historians who believe that Jesus was a feminist? Unless we have a broader theological and ecclesiological framework of understanding, experience and practice which enable us to see that Jesus' positive regard for the marginalized expresses something truthful about the inclusive nature of human salvation in Christ and about all humankind as made in the image of God, then the supposed attitude of the historical Jesus is of hardly more than (so-called) antiquarian interest.

To put it another way, unless we have an understanding of who Jesus is for us now and of how to be Christ-like in the way we as women and men conduct our relations, whether or not Jesus was a feminist (or gay liberationist or whatever) can be of only passing interest. This implies, in turn, that we cannot leave the task of wise readings of the Bible in the hands of historians, even historians who are Christian believers.[17] This is not to deny that the biblical

---

[15] See the illuminating essay by the Reformation historian David C. Steinmetz, 'The Superiority of Pre-Critical Exegesis', *Ex Auditu* 1 (1985), 74–82.

[16] See Stephen E. Fowl and L. Gregory Jones, *Reading in Communion: Scripture and Ethics in Christian Life* (London: SPCK, 1991).

[17] If I may venture a collegial comment at this point, it is, in my view, a weakness of J. D. G. Dunn's influential and otherwise very valuable approach to the art of biblical interpretation that, in practice, he places too one-sided an emphasis on

text has a historical dimension which the methods of critical historiography will help to elucidate. Nor is it to deny the significance of the historian's contribution to a more nuanced and less anachronistic appraisal of (say) attitudes to gender and sexuality in ancient Israel or in the early church.[18] It is however to assert that historical tools are not adequate on their own to the task of discerning the truth or otherwise of the biblical testimony, including the biblical testimony about human sexuality in relation to God and to one's fellow humans.

The same point needs to be made about the more recent 'literary turn' in biblical interpretation, including feminist biblical interpretation.[19] For while the methods of literary criticism in its various forms undoubtedly open up dimensions of the text and its power to communicate which might not otherwise be so evident to us, such tools on their own are not adequate to the task of discerning whether or not what the text says is true. Literary criticism helps us appreciate how the text speaks, but is mute when we come to ask, Is what it says true? For the question of the truth of the Bible is above all a theological, ecclesial and practical question. As Robert Morgan puts it: 'all Scripture has a literal meaning, but it does not all have a Christian theological meaning'.[20]

---

historical criticism and reconstruction and does not acknowledge sufficiently the essential contribution to the interpretative process of both the tradition of faith which the reader brings to the text and the impact of the reader's own experience and community. See, for example, his essay, 'The Task of New Testament Interpretation' in his *The Living Word* (London: SCM Press, 1987), 3–24, where 'normative significance in all matters of interpretation' is assigned to the meaning intended by the original author (p. 22). Cf. also his essay 'The New Testament as History' in Andrew Walker, ed., *Different Gospels: Christian Orthodoxy and Modern Theologies* (London: SPCK, 1993), 43–53.

[18] See, for example, Sarah B. Pomeroy, *Goddesses, Whores, Wives, and Slaves* (New York: Schocken Books, 1975); Peter Brown, *The Body and Society: Men, Women and Sexual Renunciation in Early Christianity* (London: Faber & Faber, 1989); L. William Countryman, *Dirt, Greed and Sex* (London: SCM Press, 1989).

[19] See, for example, Phyllis Trible, *Texts of Terror: Literary-Feminist Readings of Biblical Narratives* (Minneapolis: Fortress Press, 1984).

[20] Robert Morgan, 'Feminist Theological Interpretation of the New Testament', in Janet M. Soskice, ed., *After Eve: Women, Theology and the Christian Tradition* (London: Collins Marshall Pickering, 1990), 26. See also Adrian Thatcher, *Liberating Sex: A Christian Sexual Theology* (London: SPCK, 1993), 15ff., where the distinction is drawn between a *biblical* sexual theology and a *Christian* sexual theology.

III. Starting somewhere else

If there is any force in the objections I have raised to approaches
which start with the Bible, is there an alternative way of answering
the question, Is the Bible good news for human sexuality? I think
that there is, and the alternative takes the form I stated at the
beginning. It is that we start somewhere else. If we start with 'what
the Bible says', the possibilities for disagreement are almost endless,
and the answers we come up with – especially if they disturb beliefs
and practices which we take for granted – can usually be postponed
or kept at arm's length.

It is probably true to say, for example, that the attempt to resolve
the ongoing and often highly charged debate over 'gay rights' and
the legitimacy of the ministry of 'practising' gay priests by appeal to
scriptural texts and exegetical inquiry has not proven conclusive
and cannot do so.[21] It is not clear that the 'homosexuality' referred
to in the Bible is what is meant by 'homosexuality' today. The texts
themselves are opaque at crucial points and do not permit exegetical
certainty. At the same time, it is possible to argue that it is not always
the apparently most obvious texts which should count the most.
Should our judgement in matters of sexuality be based on the
story of Sodom in Genesis 19, or on the list of sexual prohibitions
in 1 Corinthians 6.9–10, or on the (at first sight irrelevant) parable
of the Good Samaritan in Luke 10?

So, while by no means ignoring exegetical inquiry, we need to
start instead with questions of a different kind, such as: What is our
experience as men and women in church and society today? and,
What kind of people do we need to be in order to interpret wisely
what the Bible says, in a way which is life-giving in the realm of
gender and sexuality? The point is powerfully made by Janet Martin
Soskice in her recent essay, 'Women's Problems':

> What we must also ask ourselves as Christians, women as well as men, is,
> Has our Church made things any better, or have we colluded in silencing
> the already half-voiced, and in making the problems of women, 'just

---

[21] The literature is enormous. Representative of various positions are the follow-
ing studies: John Boswell, *Christianity, Social Tolerance, and Homosexuality* (Chicago:
Chicago University Press, 1980); Robin Scroggs, *The New Testament and Homosexuality*
(Minneapolis: Fortress Press, 1983); Michael Vasey, *Evangelical Christians and Gay
Rights* (Nottingham: Grove Books, 1991); David F. Wright, 'Homosexuals or
Prostitutes? The Meaning of ARSENOKOITAI (1 Cor. 6.9, 1 Tim. 1.10)', *Vigiliae
Christianae* 38 (1984), 124–53.

women's problems'? Bodies are being broken day after day on linked wheels of poverty, prostitution, sexual abuse and domestic violence. How can we map these sufferings on the broken and risen body of Christ?[22]

This approach has a number of significant benefits. For a start, it avoids the biblicism, both of a loyalist and of a critical kind, implicit in accepting the original question on its own terms. Now, it is no longer the Bible which is in the dock but we who ask the question or of whom the question is asked. Also, it makes possible the recognition that the Bible is the book of the church and that adequate interpretation of the Bible will be interpretation which is played out, crafted and honed in the practice, mission and perhaps especially in the suffering of the church in the world. Instead of remaining suspended at the theoretical level of either dogmatic literalist assertion or positivist historical inquiry, the issue of whether or not the Bible is good news becomes an invitation and a summons to show that it can be so by the way we live and the kinds of community we build.

Finally, I mention two consequences of this kind of approach. One consequence is that the way the Bible is interpreted by being lived out will be affected by considerations of context. In other words, the communities for whom the Bible is Scripture will have the demanding task of working out in practice how the Bible is and continues to be good news. They will do this each in their own way. But it will not be a case of 'anything goes'. The church, as in a fundamental sense the privileged interpreter of the Bible, provides traditions of interpretation, social embodiment and liturgical action within which to work and upon which to build.

In addition, there are the important lines of insight and guidance provided by individuals, groups and movements outside the community of faith.[23] Indeed, in the area of gender relations in particular, it may for various significant reasons be the case that communities of faith have at least as much to learn about the will of God from outsiders or from those on the margins of the church as

---

[22] Janet Martin Soskice, 'Women's Problems', in Andrew Walker, *Different Gospels*, 194–203.

[23] Cf. Fowl and Jones, *Reading in Communion*, 111: '[I]f the people of God hope to read and enact the Scriptures faithfully in the various contexts in which we find ourselves, we will need to listen to (if not always follow) the words of the outsiders we encounter'.

from those within the church. This point is well made by Ann Loades in her Scott Holland lectures: 'The person who did more than anyone else to clarify the troublesome use in her White Anglo-Saxon Protestant culture of selective and uncontextualized quotation from Pauline Epistles that had helped to bring women to the pass in which they were was Virginia Woolf.'[24]

A second and related consequence of this approach is that individual groups and communities will have to accept responsibility for the way they interpret and 'perform' what the Bible says about gender and sexuality. This will involve making decisions (either explicitly or implicitly, consciously or unconsciously) of a theological and ethical kind – questions about who Christ is for us, who we are in the light of Christ, and what kind of people we want to be in relation to God-in-Christ and to our neighbours. Here, it will undoubtedly be the case that the communities who do this most wisely will be the ones whose members are trained in the Christian virtues and who therefore have the traditions, skills and practice necessary to the task.[25]

The question, Is the Bible good news for human sexuality? is, in other words, not best taken as a question first and foremost to put to the Bible. Rather, it constitutes a challenge to the church at the fundamental level of practical spirituality. It is those who know in what just and loving Christian practice consists who will be best equipped to read the Bible in a life-giving and liberating way. It is those who are themselves transformed and being transformed according to the image of Christ who will be best able to 'perform' the Scriptures in ways which bring life and Christlike transformation to human sexuality.[26]

[24] Ann Loades, *Searching for Lost Coins* (London: SPCK, 1987), 64. See also the valuable collection of essays by feminists of a very wide variety of faith perspectives and religious backgrounds, *Womanspirit Rising*, edited by Carol P. Christ and Judith Plaskow (San Francisco: Harper & Row, 1979).

[25] For further discussion along these lines see Stanley Hauerwas, *The Peaceable Kingdom* (London: SCM Press, 1984).

[26] I would like to acknowledge the helpful comments on this essay which I received from Professor Ann Loades, Dr Walter Moberly and Professor Denys Turner.

5

'Glorify God in Your Body' (1 Cor 6.20): Thinking Theologically About Sexuality

I. Prolegomena

1. Sexual discourse in context

Sexuality is such a basic aspect of human being that it is important now and then (but not too often) to talk about it publicly and to try to develop an adequate discourse about it. I say 'not too often', because I do not think we should talk about it too much, as if it is something which is constantly 'up for grabs'. The danger is that we cheapen, demystify and destabilize an aspect of life which has been regarded traditionally and with good reason as *holy ground* – as that place where intimate interpersonal meanings and desires are communicated in profound ways with enormous social and religious corollaries and consequences.[1]

Nevertheless, there is a big job to be done in developing both a more adequate discourse, and the *qualities of character and community* needed to sustain it, and so far we have not been very good at it. Rabbi Lionel Blue comes close to the mark for many, perhaps, when he says (in a rather Freudian way): 'I think that sexuality is quite a problem in the religions. Religion is very good about truth on the higher slopes, but it's not been very honest about the forests below. It's been an enormous muddle.'[2] Or perhaps, as I am inclined sometimes to think, our *memories* have become so short and untutored and our sense of history so weak that we have forgotten the wisdom about sexuality learned over time in preceding generations.

---

[1] Another way to put this would be to observe that the idea of something being understood as 'taboo' has an overwhelmingly pejorative connotation these days.

[2] *The Independent*, 26 July 1989.

Airing the matter responsibly *in public* may help us to rescue sexuality from the realm of the purely private and individual, the realm of personal preference without accountability, and the realm of what is for many a paralysing ignorance, shame and guilt. It may help us also to make some important *connections* in our understanding, between our individual, physical bodies and the corporate bodies of family, church and society – making it possible for us to see that the personal is also the moral, the religious and the political.

This implies, of course, that the public domain we are talking about and talking in is *not a vacant space*.[3] It is, rather, the space marked out and criss-crossed by traditions, communities, rituals, institutions, economics, and the like. So what we learn to think and say about sexuality and about how to behave as sexuate human beings constitutes an important part of what we want to think and say about life together in general.[4] This is the insight embodied in the traditional Christian claim that a true understanding of human sexuality is inseparable both from a true understanding of the sacrament of lifelong marriage[5] and from a true understanding of what it means to be the church for the world. In doctrinal terms, *sexuality and ecclesiology go hand in hand.*[6]

2. *Fallacies and pitfalls*

But there are a number of fallacies and pitfalls to be aware of in talking about human sexuality. First, there is the danger of assuming that there is an essential thing called 'sexuality'. In fact, as biology, history and the social sciences have helped us to see more clearly perhaps than ever before, there is more than one way of

[3] Helpful here are the comments of Brenda Almond on 'the myth of neutrality' in her essay 'Seven Moral Myths' in C. S. Rodd, ed., *New Occasions Teach New Duties? Christian Ethics for Today* (Edinburgh: T&T Clark, 1995), 75–83 (esp. 79–80).

[4] This is the basic thesis also of Stanley Hauerwas's excellent essay 'Sex in Public: Toward a Christian Ethic of Sex' in his book *A Community of Character* (Notre Dame: University of Notre Dame Press, 1981), 175–95.

[5] See further Gilbert Meilander's survey essay on 'Sexuality' in D. J. Atkinson and D. H. Field, eds, *New Dictionary of Christian Ethics and Pastoral Theology* (Leicester: InterVarsity Press, 1995), 71–8.

[6] See further Stanley Hauerwas's chapter on 'The Politics of Sex: How Marriage is a Subversive Act', in his book *After Christendom?* (Sydney: Anzea, 1991), 113–31. Very helpful also along these lines is Linda Woodhead, 'Sex in a Wider Context', in Jon Davies and Gerard Loughlin, eds, *Sex These Days: Essays on Theology, Sexuality and Society* (Sheffield: Sheffield Academic Press, 1997), 98–120.

understanding 'sexuality' and more than one way of being sexual.[7] So we need to keep an eye out for *persuasive definition* in talk about sexuality, where sexuality is spoken of as if it is all there is, or where an inappropriate power relation is built into the terms in which the discussion is set up.[8]

Think, for example, of how in machismo cultures (and most Hollywood movies) the sexuality of women is defined in terms of the sexuality of men, and the sexuality of the gay and lesbian minority is defined in terms of the sexuality of the heterosexual majority. Or think of the ways that in our Barbie Doll and Batman culture the sexuality of children is defined in terms of the sexuality of adults. Think also of the ways in which, historically speaking and still today, the sexuality of blacks, Jews and other marginal groups viewed as suspect has been defined in terms of the sexuality of whites.[9] As the French philosopher Michel Foucault has shown us in his studies of the history of sexuality,[10] the temptation to define sexuality in ways which reflect a deeper and more sinister concern to maintain illegitimate control is one that groups and societies succumb to all too often. We need, therefore, to find ways of talking about sex which are wise enough and courteous enough to allow us to hear each other clearly, honestly and on equal terms.

This does not mean that we come to our thinking about sex as a *tabula rasa* without any prior sense of right and wrong, honour and shame, propriety and impropriety. For that kind of attitude – presupposing as it does that we are free spirits rather than embodied selves – would undermine considerably the very communities of character and memory that help to make us who we are as sexual beings with rich, sexuate imaginaries.[11] But it does mean that we leave *necessary space* both for human freedom and for divine freedom:

[7] See further Elaine Graham, *Making the Difference: Gender, Personhood and Theology* (London: Mowbray, 1995), the main elements of which are summarized conveniently in her essay 'Gender, Personhood and Theology', *Scottish Journal of Theology* 48 (1995), 341–58.

[8] Important here is Judith Butler, *Gender Trouble: Feminism and the Subversion of Identity* (New York and London: Routledge, 1990).

[9] See further, Elsa Tamez, ed., *Against Machismo* (Oak Park: Meyer Stone Books, 1987).

[10] See, for example, Michel Foucault, *The History of Sexuality: Volume One: An Introduction* (London: Penguin Books, 1981).

[11] Important on sexuate imaginaries, drawing on Luce Irigaray, is Graham Ward's essay 'In the Name of the Father and of the Mother', *Journal of Literature and Theology* 8/3 (1994), 311–27.

human freedom to see things in new ways and make new choices in sexual behaviour, and divine freedom to bestow grace in the realm of sexuality in ways quite beyond our previous experience and expectation.

A second danger is that of confusing sexuality with sex, especially when (as in our Western culture) 'sex' has the connotation of inter-course – as in to 'have sex'. This is unhelpful because it narrows down a very complex and many-sided, physical-psychological-social-religious-political aspect of being human to questions about the 'how-when-where-why-with-whom' of sexual intercourse.[12] These latter questions are important, but they need to be set in the larger context of the meaning of the body and *the meaning of being human*.[13] To put it another way, human sexuality is not just about sexual *technique*, even if that is the impression given by so much output on the subject in the contemporary media.

By tolerating this catastrophic *narrowing* of the meaning of sexuality, we perpetuate the false assumption that being sexual involves being in a genital sexual relationship – an assumption which excludes many people, including those whose life circumstances prevent them having a sexual partner, those who have committed themselves to a life of singleness and celibacy, those who suffer certain kinds of disability, and so on. It is worth remembering that some of the most profound reflections on the nature of sexuality have come from just such people – not least, in the Christian tradition, celibate men and women.

Then there is the danger of not taking sufficient account of the *context* in which our discussion about sexuality is taking place. This has a personal-psychological dimension to it, related in part to our particular stages of emotional development as individuals, in part also to our proneness to transfer our own sexual anxieties on to those who might represent the 'darker side' of our unacknowledged sexual feelings. But our context also includes the social and cultural backgrounds from which we come, along with the ways in which gender relations are constructed there. This is one of the important issues which the social sciences along with feminism have drawn to

[12] Good on this is Linda Woodhead, 'Sex in a Wider Context', 99–101 (speaking about 'Sex in the Context of One: The Privatization of Sex These Days').

[13] Compare Roger Scruton's conclusion to his essay 'Sex', in his *An Intelligent Person's Guide to Philosophy* (London: Duckworth, 1996), 127–39 (138–9): 'Sexual morality returns us, then, to the great conundrum . . . : the conundrum of the subject, and his relation to the world of space and time.'

our attention.[14] For what it means to be a man or a woman is not just a matter of whether our sex at birth is male or female. It has to do also with the gender definitions and constructions which have been given to us as we grow up in particular families and communities: and all of this affects our sexuality and how we understand it.

The values of the wider society play a big part too. They shape us whether we like it or not. Historically speaking, it could be argued that in European humanism the patristic and medieval concern to integrate earthly love and heavenly love has been reversed.[15] Love of God has been reduced to love of neighbour, and love of neighbour reduced to sexual love of a quite individualistic kind. The consequence is that today we seem to be in a situation of crisis.

I have in mind, for instance, our massive cultural and economic investment in romantic love as *the* model for human intimacy. This makes it possible for sexual desire to be harnessed to the economic process by the commodification of sex and the sexualization of commodities. You only have to watch the television advertisements for coffee or chocolate or clothes or cars to see what I mean.[16] It is as if the only language we understand is the language of unfulfilled desire, where sexuality is the master symbol and the products of consumer capitalism the means of fulfilment. And all of this is a process of *seduction* on a massive scale. The constant invitation is to surrender moral responsibility in favour of hedonism in the private domain and cynicism in the public domain.

If human sexuality has to do with *how we communicate desire for 'the other' through our bodiliness* – which is the closest I come to a definition of sexuality in this essay[17] – it is important that we understand this kind of communication as much as possible. Especially in our own highly sexualized social context, where there is a tendency for

[14] In addition to Elaine Graham's *Making the Difference*, see also Jeffrey Weeks, *Sexuality* (London: Routledge, 1989) and *Sex, Politics and Society* (London: Longman, 2nd edn, 1989).
[15] See on this Charles Taylor, *Sources of the Self: The Making of the Modern Identity* (Cambridge: Cambridge University Press, 1989).
[16] Entertaining and informative here is Roland Barthes, *Mythologies* (London: Granada, 1973).
[17] For an insightful phenomenology of sexuality and sexual desire see further Roger Scruton, 'Sex', which summarizes his much more substantial work *Sexual Desire: A Philosophical Investigation* (London: Weidenfeld & Nicolson, 1986). For a profound theological account, see Rowan Williams, *The Body's Grace: The 10th Michael Harding Memorial Address* (London: Lesbian and Gay Christian Movement, 1989).

personal freedom to be idolized at the expense of social cohesion, we have to find a way through between the Scylla of prudery and denial, often based upon fear, and the Charybdis of promiscuity and excess, the reflection of immaturity, dependence and irresponsibility.

Another danger in talking about sexuality – which, no doubt, I have fallen into already – is that of being too serious, in a way that inhibits a sense of perspective and an ethic of humility in an area which is both ambiguous, mysterious and fraught with risk.[18] That is why a BBC comedy series like 'The Vicar of Dibley' is so popular. It pokes a sharp pin into over-heavy balloons of religion and sexuality. Rowan Williams, Bishop of Monmouth, puts the point this way:

> Most people know that sexual intimacy is in some ways frightening for them; most know that it is simply the place where they begin to be taught whatever maturity they have. Most of us know that the whole business is irredeemably comic, surrounded by so many odd chances and so many opportunities for making a fool of yourself; plenty know that it is the place where they are liable to be most profoundly damaged or helpless. Culture in general and religion in particular have devoted energy to the doomed task of getting it right.[19]

Finally, there is the danger of *complacency*. I mean by this assuming that religion has too much to say, or has said all that needs to be said, or has nothing worth saying in relation to human sexuality. For some, religion just makes people neurotic about sexuality – and Susan Howatch has made a fortune exploring these neuroses in her novels about life in the cloisters of Starbridge Cathedral. For others, religion properly regulates human sexuality, and makes it precious and meaningful. For others, yet again, religion is the root cause of all manner of 'licensed insanities' in the area of sexuality, and therefore something to grow out of and dispense with as quickly as possible.

So it is important to examine critically what the Christian tradition has to say in order to see what wisdom the tradition has to offer. It is important also to bring that tradition into critical, two-way conversation with contemporary knowledge and experience, in

---

[18] Marvellous on the place of humour in (Jewish) religion generally is Lionel Blue, *To Heaven with Scribes and Pharisees* (London: Darton, Longman & Todd, 1975), 66–75.

[19] *The Body's Grace*, 2.

order to develop – or, indeed, to *recover* – Christian understandings
of sexuality relevant for today. Theological reflection is a search
for Christian wisdom. This wisdom is a gift of God. It is discerned
most clearly when the two horizons of the faith tradition and contemporary experience are brought together in the life of the
worshipping community and in openness to the guidance of the
Holy Spirit. Our attempts to articulate what is true about human
bodiliness and desire for the other has to be part of our more
fundamental attempt to articulate and embody our desire for God
and God's desire for us.

II. A theological proposal

1. Beginning with God as Trinity

Christian faith is a response to a story which has been found to
reveal God. Faith is what we do when we set our own stories trustfully
within the context of the story of God. That story comes to us in the
Bible, with the story of the Incarnation at its heart. It comes to us
also in the Christian tradition, and in the life and worship of the
church serving God in the world. So the question of what sexuality
is about and what it means to become a mature, embodied human
being is not just our story. It is God's story as well – the story of how
God desires us in creation and makes us desirable in redemption
and sanctification.[20]

Our thinking about sexuality has to begin at a surprising place,
therefore. It has to *begin with God*: the Christian vision of God as a
Trinity of love, where the love between the Persons of the Trinity is
characterized by desire for union with the other, a love characterized
also by faithfulness, mutual indwelling, interdependence and trust,
and flowing over in the creation and redemption of the world. In
other words, *the trinitarian sociality of God is the basis for true creaturely
sociality.*[21] The desire we have for union (or should we say, unity?)
with the other – whether the union of solidarity, or of friendship,
or of intimacy, or of sexual intercourse – is a desire which expresses
the divine nature in us and in accordance with which we have been

---

[20] On the narrative character of Christian ethics in general, see further Stanley
Hauerwas, *A Community of Character* (Notre Dame: University of Notre Dame Press,
1981).

[21] I am indebted at this point to the thought of Daniel W. Hardy. See his collected
essays *God's Ways with the World* (Edinburgh: T&T Clark, 1996).

created. If God is love, as the First Epistle of John affirms (1 Jn 4.16), then there is *eros* in God, and God's love shows us what *eros* means and how it is to be directed.

Some, like Anders Nygren,[22] have wanted to draw a sharp distinction between *eros* and *agape*, as between sensual love and spiritual, sacrificial love. However, while the distinction is important to a point, the result of making it too sharp is a damaging split between aesthetics and spirituality, the beautiful and the good, human love and divine love.[23] The Tübingen Lutheran theologian Jürgen Moltmann makes this point when he comments on the interpretation of the Song of Songs:

> A significant example of the way the one, single love has been split up into two different forms is the transferred, mystical interpretation of the Song of Solomon and its literal, erotic interpretation. Does this wonderful love song really have a place in a religious book? People who were bothered by this, interpreted the poem allegorically, claiming that it referred to the soul's love for God. By so doing they abstracted sensual love from the love of God and banished it to 'the lower instincts', so that the transcendental love for God might be pure, spiritual, and confined to 'the heart'. But if the Bible is called – and rightly called – 'the book of life', then the life-giving experiences of love belong to this book, and in that case it is inadmissible to withdraw from this immanent experience of love its transcendent depths by abstracting from it a higher love. God – the quickening Spirit – can be experienced in the experience of human love. Even if his name is not explicitly mentioned in the Song of Solomon, his shining splendour radiates from every phrase with which the experience of love is described, for this experience is a 'flame of the Lord' (8.6). That is why the old Benedictine hymn maintains: '*Ubi caritas et amor, ibi Deus est*' – where love is, there is God.[24]

This means that in our thinking about sexuality – about the desire for self-transcendence in union with the other which is the natural expression of our embodied humanity – it is important to recall that it is grounded in God and is an outworking of the life of God. *So our sexuality is sacred.* It is not something to be abused or trivialized either by denial or by promiscuity. It bears the stamp of the divine nature. It is a means for us to glorify God and to share that glory with our fellow human beings.

[22] Anders Nygren, *Agape and Eros* (New York: Harper & Row, 1969).
[23] The same concern is expressed by Philip Sheldrake, *Befriending Our Desires* (London: Darton, Longman & Todd, 1994), 25–9.
[24] *The Spirit of Life: A Universal Affirmation* (London: SCM Press, 1992), 260.

2. Creation as God's play grounded on grace

This brings us to the other part of the Christian story on which I want to focus: that of *creation* understood in a particular way. According to Moltmann, himself indebted to Johan Huizinga, 'the creation is God's play, a play of his groundless and inscrutable wisdom. It is the realm in which God displays his glory'.[25] Now, if that is so, if the God who is the ground of our being is a God who plays with loving freedom, then there are important implications for how we understand human sexuality.

Above all, a theology of *creation as God's play* is an invitation to allow ourselves to be caught up into the sense of the delight of God in us as the objects of God's love and desire. Our bodiliness, sexuality and sexual differentiation are expressions of God's play in creating the world: 'male and female God created them'. Given the repeated affirmation in Genesis 1–2 of the *goodness* of what God made, this tradition represents the strongest possible affirmation of human sexuality. As such, it is a corrective to attempts to deny the body by being prudish. It is also a corrective to other attempts to deny the body by casual sex or sexual perversion or sexual abuse.

Furthermore, if our sexuality is an expression of God's play in creation, then we have here a corrective to narrowly instrumental approaches to sexuality which claim that sexuality and sexual intercourse are for the purpose only, or first and foremost, of *procreation*. Within a theology of play, sexuality may be understood more broadly than this, and in a way that is not limited to the imperative of human reproduction.

That imperative still needs to be taken with utmost seriousness, especially in the context of marriage, as one of the main purposes of marriage – and it continues to be sustained, especially within the long and venerable tradition of Catholic and Orthodox forms of Christianity.[26] For the bringing of *children* into the world is one of the ways we participate in God's ongoing and gracious playfulness

[25] Jürgen Moltmann, *Theology and Joy* (London: SCM Press, 1973), 41; also his *God in Creation: An Ecological Doctrine of Creation* (London: SCM Press, 1985), 310–12; cf. Johan Huizinga, *Homo Ludens: A Study of the Play Element in Culture* (Boston: Beacon Press, 1955).

[26] See, for example, *The Catechism of the Catholic Church* (London: Geoffrey Chapman, 1994), p. 370, s. 1652: 'By its very nature the institution of marriage and married love is ordered to the procreation and education of the offspring and it is in them that it finds its crowning glory.'

in creating and sustaining the world. Indeed, in view of certain contemporary trends, it needs to be said that the place given to children in reflection on sexuality and sexual mores is an important touchstone of its adequacy from a Christian moral-theological point of view.[27]

But sexuality is about more than procreation, not least because sexuality is about more than sexual intercourse, as I said earlier. As part of our creatureliness, sexuality can be understood as being for the sake of sheer joy, a way of communicating through the body the human discovery of *meaning in relationship*. So Bishop Richard Holloway of Edinburgh is right, I think, when he says:

> It is our nature and destiny . . . to share in the divine nature. We seek that unity and relationship, that connectedness or wholeness, which is the life of God. Sexuality is a figure or symbol of our ultimate destiny with God, because it is a search for the other. We feel that it is not good for us to be alone. We feel mysteriously incomplete, so all our life is a searching for a remembered unity we have never yet known. Sexuality is one of the modes of our search; it is both a symptom of our incompleteness and a sign of our fulfilment. For the Christian, therefore, there are two ingredients in sexual experience. One is clearly a participation in the joy of God. We need not be afraid to rejoice in the pleasures of our bodily nature, but we must remember that these pleasures are the sign and seal of unity, relatedness, bondedness. For the Christian, sex should be part of a covenant between two persons, because it is a reflection or earthly representation of the covenant or marriage within the Godhead, and it is a reflection of the covenant or marriage between God and his people and Christ and his Church.[28]

This reference to the Christian idea of *covenant* relationships is worth more attention. For another contribution of a theology of play is that it creates space (in an area sometimes taken over by the language of coercion) for bringing onto centre stage the *language of grace*. Instead of seeing sexuality as something to be denied or casualized out of fear, it becomes now a potential source of liveliness and joy: for it is an outworking of grace – a *being present to another for the sake of the other,* as God is present to us.[29]

[27] See further Maureen Junker-Kenny and Norbert Mette, eds, *Little Children Suffer* [= *Concilium* 1996/2] (London: SCM Press, 1996). On the 'dark side' of this see Ann Loades, *Thinking About Child Sexual Abuse: The John Coffin Memorial Lecture 1994* (London: University of London, 1994).

[28] Richard Holloway, *Anger, Sex, Doubt and Death* (London: SPCK, 1992), 34–5.

[29] For a moving evocation of the covenantal nature of Christian marriage, see Dan Hardy's 'Sermon at a Marriage' in his *God's Ways with the World*, 396–400.

This does not mean that anything goes or that rules of some kind may not be helpful or that a kind of sexual etiquette has no place. On the contrary, it is often the case that such rules or etiquette make the 'deep play' of human sexuality possible in a way which is not destructive or perverted. A strong argument for the Christian ideal of the covenant of lifelong, monogamous, heterosexual marriage is that such a publically acknowledged relationship provides a framework which allows mature sexual relationships to develop.[30]

What I want to emphasize here, however, is how much is gained if the rules, the framework and the etiquette are understood, not as a form of domination or coercion, but as an expression of *a theology of play grounded on grace*. For now the framework – in particular the disciplined commitment of the Christian marriage covenant or the disciplined commitment of the vocation to celibacy – can be seen as life-giving and life-enhancing, allowing the time and space for deeper sexual awareness and for greater freedom and maturity in sexual relations to develop.[31] It need not be the institutionalizing of fear that some claim. Nor need it be a licence for permanently unbalanced relations whose outworking finds expression in violence and sexual perversion of one kind or another.

This leads to me to observe, further, that there seems to be a sense in which sexual *perversion* arises when sexuality loses its connection with creation as God's play grounded on grace. Pornography, for instance, is a perversion of sexuality because it is so distancing, so one-sided, so deterministic, and, in the final analysis, so humourless. Instead of human sexuality being one of the joyous ways we, as embodied selves, create meanings with one another and grow in relatedness to one another, it becomes debased to the relation of the *voyeur*. Power in the relation is *all on one side*. The same may be said of rape, as well.[32]

[30] Cf. Hauerwas's comment, in *After Christendom?*, 125. '[I]n order to talk sensibly about sex you must have available determinative practices that place such discussions in a purposive framework'.

[31] On the importance of taking time see Williams, *The Body's Grace*, 5: 'I can only fully discover the body's grace in *taking time*, the time needed for a mutual recognition that my partner and I are not simply passive instruments to each other. Such things are learned in the fabric of a whole relation of converse and cooperation. . . . Properly understood, sexual faithfulness is not an avoidance of risk, but the creation of a context in which grace can abound because there is a commitment not to run away from the perception of another.'

[32] A useful philosophical essay on what constitutes sexual perversion comes in Thomas Nagel's *Mortal Questions* (Cambridge: Cambridge University Press, 1979), 39–52.

If there is something in this, then a theology of creation as God's play may help. For in a theology of play, the emphasis is on sexuality as a *process of communication between embodied selves* where the end in view is joy, healing, affirmation and the development of human possibility – in a phrase, sexuality is a process of communicating what Rowan Williams has called '*the body's grace*'.[33] This is a world away from perverted sexuality where instead of grace, there is only *determinism* of one kind or another: of macho power, where a certain interpretation of male sexuality is everything; of the undisciplined sexual drive where bodily needs just must be satisfied; of an economic system which has made sexuality captive to the interests of commercial gain; or the determinism of religious systems which reduce sexuality to sin or its near neighbour, guilt.

A theology of play points us in a different direction. It points us to a God who in the playfulness of divine grace has made us as embodied persons, who desires us with a holy desire, and who therefore *makes us desirable and able to desire one another*. It is that desirability and ability to desire another which come from God as grace, and which we are able to communicate through our bodies in a great variety of ways. Nor is sexuality limited to our relations with one another. It has a *mystical* dimension whereby it is able to become fundamental to our relations with God as well.[34] That is why the Song of Songs has always been interpreted both as a celebration of love between a woman and a man, and also as a celebration of the relation of mutual desire between God and the people of God.

III. Conclusion

In writing to the Christians in the house churches in Corinth, the apostle Paul addresses questions to do with sexuality and sexual morality more than once. The heart of his teaching is directed against those who thought that true reality was entirely 'spiritual' and had nothing to do with – required, indeed, an *escape* from – human embodiment, and therefore that what you did with your body was a matter of no consequence. In response, Paul gives the positive command: 'Glorify God in your body' (1 Cor 6.20).

---

[33] See his lecture of that title (above n. 17).

[34] See further the section on 'Sexuality and Spirituality' in Adrian Thatcher and Elizabeth Stuart, eds, *Christian Perspectives on Sexuality and Gender* (Grand Rapids: Eerdmans, 1996), 211–27; also Sheldrake, *Befriending Our Desires*.

Contrary to much popular opinion, Paul's approach to sexuality is not primarily negative and 'legalistic' – although rules and discipline certainly do have a place in his attempt to reorder desire according to the truth of the gospel. Rather, Paul's overall concern is the constructive one of building up the community so as to bring healing and transformation in people's lives and thereby bring glory to God. Paul does not focus on sexual matters just for their own sake, but for the contribution they make to the larger task of creating an ordered, holy and life-giving society. In other words, his sexual ethics are a part of his *social* ethics.[35] His thinking about sexuality is part of his thinking about what it means to be both Christian households and the eschatological 'household' of the church of God.

This focus in early Christianity on the physical body as a 'natural symbol' of the social body is instructive.[36] For Paul's writings reflect a notion of the positive function of the body in representing what it means to be a member of 'the body of Christ'. Modern sexual ethics has tended to move in the opposite direction: from a concern with social duty and the social good to a concern with individual choice and personal authenticity.

But the pendulum has swung too far. Perhaps our quest for personal freedom and individual choice in sexual and other matters has brought us to the point where we do not know any longer who we really are and *what our 'freedom' is for*. Instead of being 'members one of another', we have learned too well to 'do our own thing'. In consequence, the social values and structures which make our freedom possible are themselves under threat.[37]

If that is so, then perhaps we need to rediscover understandings of sexuality which have become lost or obscured. Saint Paul's advice, 'Glorify God in your body', has much to commend it. For it puts sexuality in its rightful place – namely, how we build one another

[35] Helpful here is Lisa Sowle Cahill, 'Sex and Gender Ethics as New Testament Social Ethics', in John Rogerson, ed., *The Bible in Ethics* (Sheffield: Sheffield Academic Press, 1995), 272–95.

[36] The idea of 'natural symbols' is explored brilliantly by anthropologist Mary Douglas in her books *Purity and Danger* (London: Routledge & Kegan Paul, 1966), and *Natural Symbols: Explorations in Cosmology* (London: Barrie & Jenkins, 1973).

[37] In relation to the institution of the family see Jon Davies, 'A Preferential Option for the Family', in S. C. Barton, ed., *The Family in Theological Perspective* (Edinburgh: T&T Clark, 1996), 219–36. On a wider front see Gertrude Himmelfarb, *The De-Moralization of Society: From Victorian Virtues to Modern Values* (London: IEA Health and Welfare Unit, 1995).

up as embodied selves, called to be members of the body of Christ, in relationships of love, to the glory of God. This, of course, is where traditional Christianity would wish to place a doctrine of marriage and the procreation of children, and properly so. It is also the place for the rich traditions of Christian reflection on the vocation to celibacy. Yet further, it is the place for the equally rich traditions about the institution of friendship.[38]

My fundamental point, however, is that we cannot think adequately about sexuality unless we know *how to build community and how to be the church*.[39] For sexuality is God's good gift – but not by any means the *only* gift – enabling us to nurture one another in our life together. As we learn from God and God's people the disciplines, virtues and skills for expressing our sexuality appropriately, we build one another up in love. And as we build one another up, we bear witness to the fact that we belong to God and share together in the gracious play of God in creation, redemption and sanctification.

[38] For theological reflection on friendship see further the essays in Leroy S. Rouner, ed., *The Changing Face of Friendship* (Notre Dame: University of Notre Dame Press, 1994).

[39] See further Williams, *The Body's Grace*, 6, on sexual knowledge as 'political knowledge, a knowledge of what ordered human community might be'; and Linda Woodhead's discussion of 'Sex in the Church, Sex in Christ', in 'Sex in a Wider Context', 110–13.

Part Two

COMMUNITY

6

The Communal Dimension
of Earliest Christianity

In recent study of the New Testament, there has been an explosion of interest in the communal dimension of earliest Christianity. The very rapid growth of this field of study justifies a discussion which both attempts to put these scholarly developments in perspective and gives a survey of some of the more important contributions. In what follows, therefore, I seek first to trace the roots of this field of study, and then to select and summarize work done in this field over past decades, drawing a number of critical conclusions at the end.[1]

I. The roots of this field of study

The roots of the more recent interest in the ideas and practice of community in the period of Christian origins are complex and various. I would want to identify at least nine.

(i) Within biblical scholarship itself, the development of form criticism and subsequently redaction criticism has had a major impact. In the study of the Gospels, for example, form critics from Martin Dibelius and Rudolf Bultmann on have been very successful in showing that the Gospel traditions have a history, and that the various forms of the tradition relate to various settings (*Sitze im Leben*) in the life of Jesus or in the life of the post-Easter communities of

[1] The genesis of this essay is my much shorter piece on 'Community' in R. J. Coggins and J. L. Houlden, eds, *A Dictionary of Biblical Interpretation* (London: SCM Press, 1990), 135–8. The present expanded version was presented at the graduate seminar of the Department of Religious Studies in the University of Newcastle upon Tyne, in May 1990, and at the NT study group at Tyndale House, Cambridge in July 1990.

Life Together

believers.[2] Similarly, redactional investigations of the theologies of the evangelists have shown repeatedly the extent to which the Gospels in their final form represent responses of a pastoral kind to crises and controversies in communities of second-generation believers.[3]

(ii) In Roman Catholic scholarship, Vatican II has had a major impact on the study of ecclesiology and its foundation in the Bible and the Fathers. The crucial document, of course, is *Lumen Gentium* (or, the 'Dogmatic Constitution on the Church'),[4] and it is noteworthy how pervasive here is the influence of biblical ideas and images, as Avery Dulles acknowledges.[5] At least four of R. E. Brown's recent books[6] reflect this impact, as well as showing the complete convergence of methodologies for historical-critical study which has occurred between Catholic and Protestant exegetes.

(iii) In liberal Protestantism, Rudolf Bultmann's Lutheran theological hermeneutic, which tended to reduce New Testament theology to categories of individual human experience compatible with existentialist philosophy, has been subjected to extensive criticism at both the exegetical and theological levels. As Robert Morgan has pointed out in a recent essay,[7]

[2] See M. Dibelius, *From Tradition to Gospel* (ET London: Ivor Nicholson & Watson, 1934; German original 1919); R. Bultmann, *The History of the Synoptic Tradition* (ET Oxford: Blackwell, 1968, 2nd edn; German original 1931); and the survey of E. V. McKnight, *What is Form Criticism?* (Philadelphia: Fortress Press, 1969).

[3] See, for example, the essays on the Gospels in J. L. Mays, ed., *Interpreting the Gospels* (Philadelphia: Fortress Press, 1981); and the survey of N. Perrin, *What is Redaction Criticism?* (London: SCM Press, 1970).

[4] In A. Flannery, ed., *Vatican Council II* (Leominster, 1981), 350ff. Note, too, the statement in para. 19 of the 'Dogmatic Constitution on Divine Revelation' (= *Dei Verbum*) which recognizes explicitly the communal interest of the authors of the NT: 'The sacred authors, in writing the four Gospels, selected certain of the many elements which had been handed on, . . . others they synthesized or explained *with an eye to the situation of the churches*, the while sustaining the form of preaching, but always in such a fashion that they have told us the honest truth about Jesus' (Flannery, *Vatican Council II*, 761; my emphasis).

[5] See A. Dulles, *Models of the Church* (Dublin, 1976), 17ff.

[6] R. E. Brown, *The Community of the Beloved Disciple* (New York and London: Geoffrey Chapman, 1979); and *The Critical Meaning of the Bible* (London: Geoffrey Chapman, 1981); R. E. Brown and J. P. Meier, *Antioch and Rome* (New York: Paulist Press, 1983); and R. E. Brown, *The Churches the Apostles Left Behind* (New York: Paulist Press, 1984).

[7] R. Morgan, 'Rudolf Bultmann' in D. Ford, ed., *The Modern Theologians*, Vol. 1 (Oxford: Blackwell, 1989), 109–33 at 117–18.

Bultmann accepted Herrmann's contrast between the past history researched by historians, and a personal, inner, existential 'history' (*Geschichte*), which is said to be the locus of faith, genuine religion, and human meaning. This implied lack of religious interest in the social, historical world, and its concentration in ethics on the individual subject rather than on institutions and cultural values, is why many theologians today prefer Troeltsch to Herrmann, and are uneasy about Bultmann.

This kind of unease has generated a renewed focus on the social, communal and political dimensions of early Christian beliefs and practices. In Germany the writings of G. Theissen,[8] W. Schottroff and W. Stegemann[9] are instances of this development. Ironically, in view of Bultmann's predominant concern to contribute to the task of theology, it is his work in the history of traditions and the history of religions which has stood better the test of time.

(iv) The ethos of the 1960s, a period of rapid economic development, political protest, and social experimentation in the West, played a part also. At the academic level, the social sciences came into prominence in a new way and enormous attention was given to the seminal work of the 'founding fathers' of the discipline: Weber, Durkheim, Marx, Tönnies, and so on.[10] At the social level, there was a widespread quest of a countercultural kind for alternative lifestyles and patterns of community expressing the values of Romanticism.[11] And at the ecclesiastical level, there was a serious questioning of hierarchical and authoritarian church structures, along with various attempts to develop alternative churches on the 'small is beautiful' principle.[12] Much writing since then about

[8] G. Theissen, *The First Followers of Jesus* (ET London: SCM Press, 1978); and *The Social Setting of Pauline Christianity* (ET Edinburgh: T&T Clark, 1982).

[9] W. Schottroff and W. Stegemann, *God of the Lowly: Socio-Historical Interpretations of the Bible* (ET New York: Orbis, 1984).

[10] See, for example, T. Raison, ed., *The Founding Fathers of Social Science* (Harmondsworth: Penguin, 1969). The importance of the social sciences for helping to clarify how best 'community' might be studied is demonstrated in a book by A. P. Cohen, *The Symbolic Construction of Community* (London and New York: Tavistock Press, 1985).

[11] See the account of Bernice Martin, *A Sociology of Contemporary Cultural Change* (Oxford: Blackwell, 1981).

[12] See, for example, R. Banks, '"Small is Beautiful": The Relevance of Paul's Idea of Community for the Local Church Today', *Theological Renewal* 22 (1982), 4–18, and the literature cited there.

community in early Christianity is indebted, to some extent, to these kinds of developments.[13]

(v) Another factor is the impact of the charismatic movement, spread throughout a very wide range of Christian churches and denominations.[14] The custom of this movement to appeal to the charismatic element in Christian origins as a warrant for change in Christian understanding and practice today has influenced a number of accounts of community and the Spirit in the New Testament. A major case in point is the work of J. D. G. Dunn.[15] He has argued persuasively that charismatic experience was the bedrock of early Christian community, that authority in the early churches was primarily charismatic, and that the early Christian (and especially Pauline) ideal of the worshipping community was one which placed a premium on the exercise of a diversity of the 'gifts' of the Spirit by individual church members. In a noteworthy summary statement in *Jesus and the Spirit,* Dunn says:

> the early church's sense of community stemmed basically not from the first resurrection appearances but from Pentecost; not from an established hierarchy, not from an established tradition, not from an established liturgical or sacramental practice . . . but *from the common experience of the eschatological Spirit and the communal enthusiasm engendered thereby.*[16]

The influence of a particular theological and ecclesiological *Tendenz* is quite evident here. This same kind of *Tendenz* has made even very specific topics the object of extensive study: glossolalia being a good illustration.[17]

[13] See, R. Banks, *Paul's Idea of Community* (Exeter: Paternoster Press, 1979). For a general account of the social context of modern theology, see the works of Robin Gill, for example, *Theology and Social Structure* (London: Mowbrays, 1977), and *Theology and Sociology: A Reader* (London: Geoffrey Chapman, 1987).

[14] For an authoritative account see W. Hollenweger, *The Pentecostals* (London: SCM Press, 1976, 2nd edn).

[15] J. D. G. Dunn, *Baptism in the Holy Spirit: A Re-Examination of the New Testament Teaching on the Gift of the Spirit in Relation to Pentecostalism Today* (London: SCM Press, 1970); and *Jesus and the Spirit: A Study of the Religious and Charismatic Experience of Jesus and the First Christians as Reflected in the New Testament* (London: SCM Press, 1975); and 'Models of Christian Community in the New Testament', in D. Martin and P. Mullen, eds, *Strange Gifts?* (Oxford: Blackwell, 1984), 1–18.

[16] At p. 188 (author's emphasis).

[17] The 'guide to research' by W. E. Mills, *Speaking in Tongues* (Grand Rapids: Eerdmans, 1986), runs to 535 pages! See also K. Stendahl's essay, 'Glossolalia and the Charismatic Movement' in J. Jervell and W. A. Meeks, eds, *God's Christ and His People* (Oslo: Oslo University Press, 1977), 122–31.

(vi) Fashions in contemporary christology and ecclesiology have been influential also. A good example from the not-too-distant past is the curiously literal interpretation given to Paul's 'idea' of the church as 'the body of Christ' in the writings of scholars such as John Robinson and John Knox.[18] In an important although little-known critique of their work,[19] the ancient historian Edwin Judge points out that historical scepticism about Jesus and doubts about the viability of 'God' in the theology of the time were compensated for by an inflated theology of the church as, literally, the body of Christ.[20] Judge shows how this development was reflected, *inter alia*, in the frequent paraphrasing, in an 'incorporationist' direction, of the Pauline phrase 'in Christ' in the New English Bible (1961, 1970).[21] In general, he argues strongly that 'the body of Christ' is a metaphor whose plain sense is associational, and that it will not bear the literalist weight being imposed upon it. His discussion alerts us in a very clear way to the inevitable impact of doctrinal discussion on historical and exegetical studies of the early church.

(vii) Contemporary movements of liberation have been yet another force behind the study of community in the New Testament. Feminist scholars[22] have traced the roots of women's oppression in church and society today to the patriarchalization of authority in the early church. At the same time, they have discovered also prophetic, egalitarian strands and symbols of women's liberation in the New Testament texts. As Elisabeth Fiorenza puts it:

---

[18] J. A. T. Robinson, *The Body: A Study in Pauline Theology* (London: SCM Press, 1952); John Knox, *The Church and the Reality of Christ* (London: Collins, 1963).

[19] E. A. Judge, 'Demythologizing the Church: What is the Meaning of "The Body of Christ?"', *Interchange*, 11 (1972), 155–67.

[20] Judge, 'Demythologizing', 158: 'In spite of all the scepticism, our authors do in fact find themselves still believing in Christ. Because they cannot feel confident, however, of the traditional locus of the knowledge of Christ in the records of the past, they must find him in the only place they can take seriously, the community of those who follow him. It is intriguing that in Bishop Robinson's little book, *But That I Can't Believe!*, the church itself is a conspicuous absentee from the list of incredible things.'

[21] For example, 'incorporate in Christ' in Col 1.2; 'a member of Christ's body' in Col 1.28; 'incorporate in him' in Phil 3.9; and, in Eph 1.13, 'became incorporate in Christ'. The 'incorporationist' theology is still evident in the *Revised English Bible* (1989), though to a lesser extent. Compare 'as a mature member of Christ's body', in Col 1.28; and, 'in union with him', in Phil 3.9.

[22] See, for example, R. R. Ruether, *Sexism and God-Talk* (London: SCM Press, 1983); E. S. Fiorenza, *In Memory of Her* (London: SCM Press, 1983); and L. M. Russell, ed., *Feminist Interpretation of the Bible* (Oxford: Blackwell, 1985).

Feminist biblical interpretation must therefore challenge the scriptural authority of patriarchal texts and explore how the Bible is used as a weapon against women in our struggles for liberation. It must also explore whether and how the Bible can become a resource in this struggle.[23]

A similar critical ambivalence marks the response of those who come to the Bible from the viewpoint of political or liberation theology, and again, the focus on ideas of community and on the practice in early Christianity of solidarity with the oppressed and the marginalized is central.[24] For both feminist and liberationist interpreters it is a basic axiom that interpretation is a political act and that the hermeneutical key lies in the concrete, contemporary experience of the members of oppressed communities. So the interest in the study of community in the New Testament (and in the Bible as a whole) springs out of the strong communal concerns of the movements of liberation themselves.[25] In feminism, the hermeneutical centre is the 'women-church' or the '*ekklesia* of women'. In liberation theology, it is the Basic Christian Communities.

(viii) Developments in relations between Jews and Christians today, especially in the aftermath of the Holocaust, have provided particular stimulus for investigating relations between communities of Jews and Christians in the first century. A number of issues have been important in this regard. One issue has been how these groups defined their respective identities.[26] Historical study, such as that carried out by E. P. Sanders and Jacob Neusner,[27] has

[23] E. S. Fiorenza, 'The Will to Choose or to Reject: Continuing Our Critical Work', in L. M. Russell, ed., *Interpretation*, 125–36 at 129.

[24] See, for example, N. K. Gottwald, ed., *The Bible and Liberation: Political and Social Hermeneutics* (New York: Orbis, 1983); C. Rowland, *Radical Christianity* (Oxford: Polity, 1988); C. Rowland and M. Corner, *Liberating Exegesis: The Challenge of Liberation Theology to Biblical Studies* (London: SPCK, 1990).

[25] Cf. Rowland and Corner, *Liberating Exegesis*, 39: 'It is a reading which is emphatically communitarian, in which reflection on the story of a people can indeed lead to the appreciation of the *sensus ecclesiae* and a movement towards liberative action.'

[26] Note the collection of essays entitled '*To See Ourselves As Others See Us*': *Christians, Jews, 'Others' in Late Antiquity*, edited by J. Neusner and E. S. Frerichs (Chico: Scholars Press, 1985); and see the earlier essay by J. Z. Smith, 'Fences and Neighbours: Some Contours of Early Judaism' in W. S. Green ed., *Approaches to Ancient Judaism, II* (Chico: Scholars Press, 1980), 1–25.

[27] See E. P. Sanders, *Paul and Palestinian Judaism* (London: SCM Press, 1977); and *Jesus and Judaism* (London: SCM Press, 1985); J. Neusner, *Judaism in the Beginning of Christianity* (London: SCM Press, 1984).

made more clear than ever before that there was a wide diversity of ways of being a Jew in the first century and that the movement inaugurated by Jesus began as a messianic reform movement within Judaism.[28] A second and related issue has been the attempt to explain the 'parting of the ways' between Jews and Christians.[29] Here, attention has focused both on the controversies surrounding the important traditional boundary markers of Judaism (i.e. temple, law and circumcision), and on the cataclysmic effects of the fall of Jerusalem in 70 CE. A third issue has been the question of anti-Semitism in the New Testament, a question which has been raised by theologians as well as historians.[30] This has led, in the study of early Christianity, to attempts to distinguish different kinds of 'anti-Judaism' (rather than the more narrowly racial category, 'anti-Semitism') and to define more carefully the sociological factors and community dynamics which contributed to the phenomenon in its various forms. Even the rhetorical conventions of antiquity had their part to play, as Luke Johnson has shown.[31]

(ix) Three trends in recent New Testament historiography are worth mentioning as a final point. One is the development of a more genuine social-history approach, which tries to relate early Christian beliefs and practices to the material and social concerns of particular groups and strata in first-century society. I am thinking

---

[28] C. Rowland, *Christian Origins: An Account of the Setting and Character of the Most Important Messianic Sect of Judaism* (London: SPCK, 1985), 76, puts it quite bluntly: 'We cannot assume that the early Christians ever lost sight of their Jewish heritage, nor were they conscious of being anything other than Jews.'

[29] This has been a particular interest of G. N. Stanton, who has worked extensively on the evidence thrown up by Matthew: for example, 'The Gospel of Matthew and Judaism', *Bulletin of the John Rylands Library* 66 (1984), 264–84. Important also are A. F. Segal, *Rebecca's Children: Judaism and Christianity in the Roman World* (Cambridge: Harvard University Press, 1986) and J. D. G. Dunn, *The Partings of the Ways* (London: SCM Press, 1991).

[30] The literature is extensive. See, *inter alios* R. R. Ruether, *Faith and Fratricide. The Theological Roots of Anti-Semitism* (New York: Seabury, 1974); C. Thoma, *A Christian Theology of Judaism* (New York: Paulist Press, 1980); F. Mussner, *Tractate on the Jews: The Significance of Judaism for Christian Faith* (London: SPCK, 1984); J. G. Gager, *The Origins of Anti-Semitism: Attitudes Toward Judaism in Pagan and Christian Antiquity* (New York: Oxford University Press, 1985); P. Richardson, ed., *Anti-Judaism in Early Christianity, vol. 1 Paul and the Gospels* (Waterloo: Wilfrid Laurier University, 1986).

[31] L.T. Johnson, 'The New Testament's Anti-Jewish Slander and the Conventions of Ancient Polemic', *Journal of Biblical Literature* 108 (1989), 419–41.

here, for example, of the work of Edwin Judge and others[32] on schools, S. Scott Bartchy[33] on slaves, R. F. Hock[34] on artisans and tradespeople, F. W. Danker[35] on benefactors, D. L. Balch[36] on women and households, Bonnie B. Thurston[37] on widows, J. H Elliott[38] on 'resident aliens', P. Marshall[39] on relations of friendship and enmity, R. L. Wilken[40] on clubs and societies, F. Gerald Downing[41] on the Cynics, A. J. Malherbe[42] on the moral philosophers, and so on.

A second development is a specifically interdisciplinary one, involving the use of methods and models from the social sciences to describe more precisely the dynamics of community formation and boundary management in early Christianity. A powerful precedent existed already in the work of Max Weber on the sociology of charismatic authority, Ernst Troeltsch on sect–church typology, Karl Marx and Karl Kautsky on the economic and class basis of religious practice, Ludwig Feuerbach and Sigmund Freud on the psychological dimension of religion, Emile Durkheim on the social

---

[32] E. A. Judge, 'The Early Christians as a Scholastic Community', *Journal of Religious History* 1 (1960–1), 4–15, 125–37. On Matthew see K. Stendahl, *The School of St Matthew and its Use of the Old Testament* (Philadelphia: Fortress Press, 1968, 2nd edn); on the Fourth Gospel, see R. A. Culpepper, *The Johannine School* (Missoula: Scholars Press, 1975). Attention should also be drawn to the excellent essay by S. K. Stowers on the social location of Paul's preaching: 'Social Status, Public Speaking and Private Teaching: The Circumstances of Paul's Preaching Activity', *Novum Testamentum* 26 (1984), 59–82.

[33] *First-Century Slavery and the Interpretation of 1 Corinthians 7.21* (Missoula: Scholars Press, 1973).

[34] *The Social Context of Paul's Ministry: Tentmaking and Apostleship* (Philadelphia: Fortress Press, 1980).

[35] F. W. Danker, *Benefactor: Epigraphic Study of a Graeco-Roman and New Testament Semantic Field* (St Louis: Clayton, 1982).

[36] *Let Wives Be Submissive: The Domestic Code in 1 Peter* (Chico: Scholars Press, 1981); and 'Household Codes' in D. E. Aune, ed., *Greco-Roman Literature and the New Testament: Selected Forms and Genres* (Atlanta: Scholars Press, 1988), 25–50.

[37] *The Widows: A Women's Ministry in the Early Church* (Minneapolis: Fortress Press, 1989).

[38] *A Home for the Homeless: A Sociological Exegesis of I Peter, Its Situation and Strategy* (Philadelphia: Fortress Press, 1981).

[39] *Enmity in Corinth: Social Conventions in Paul's Relations with the Corinthians* (Tübingen: Mohr-Siebeck, 1987).

[40] *The Christians as the Romans Saw Them* (New Haven and London: Yale, 1984).

[41] *Jesus and the Threat of Freedom* (London: SCM Press, 1987).

[42] *Paul and the Thessalonians: The Philosophic Tradition of Pastoral Care* (Philadelphia: Fortress Press, 1987); and *Paul and the Popular Philosophers* (Minneapolis: Fortress Press, 1989).

function of religion, and Peter Berger and Thomas Luckmann on the sociology of knowledge, to name but a few of the major contributors.[43] It is probably true to say that some of the most innovative (if also most speculative) work on the communal dimension of early Christianity is indebted to interdisciplinary approaches which draw upon the social sciences. Some writers draw most heavily on sociology, others on the insights of social (or cultural) anthropology, others yet again on psychology.[44]

A third development which is still in its relative infancy, especially in so far as study of the New Testament is concerned, is that of canonical criticism.[45] It is important to mention this form of criticism here because at its very heart there lies a deep appreciation that the New Testament, and the Bible of which it is a part, is a product of community. As a natural development of form and redaction criticism, canonical criticism draws attention both to the canonical process and to canonical hermeneutics as witnesses to 'the function of the Bible as canon in the believing communities which formed and shaped it and passed it on to their heirs of today'.[46] As such, canonical criticism is an important counterweight against the rationalizing, individualizing and secularizing tendencies of post-Enlightenment exegesis, and serves to foster awareness of the integral relation of Bible, church and synagogue.

II. Overview of specific New Testament texts

Having surveyed the roots of contemporary study of community in the New Testament, it is necessary to give a selective overview of

---

[43] For important critical surveys see *inter alios* M. Hill, *A Sociology of Religion* (London: Heinemann, 1973); J. Bowker, *The Sense of God* (Oxford: Oxford University Press, 1973).

[44] See the excellent bibliography of D. J. Harrington, 'Second Testament Exegesis and the Social Sciences: A Bibliography', *BTB* 18 (1988), 77–85, which very usefully distinguishes works according to the broad category of social science method used. Even more comprehensive is G. Theissen, 'Auswahlbibliographie zur Sozialgeschichte des Urchristentums', in *Studien zur Soziologie des Urchristentums* (Tübingen: Mohr-Siebeck, 1989), 331–70.

[45] The two main, though diverging, contributors in this area are James A. Sanders and Brevard S. Childs, both primarily OT scholars. For Sanders see *Torah and Canon* (Philadelphia: Fortress Press, 1972) and *Canon and Community* (Philadelphia: Fortress Press, 1984). For Childs see *Introduction to the Old Testament as Scripture* (Philadelphia: Fortress Press 1979), and *The New Testament as Canon: An Introduction* (London: SCM Press, 1984).

[46] Sanders, *Canon and Community*, xv.

discussions relating to particular texts. This will show at least two things. First, at the historical level, that community formation and maintenance were all-pervasive concerns in early Christianity. Second, at the theological and phenomenological levels, that Martin Buber's characterization[47] of Christianity as a religion of the individual (over against Judaism as a religion of community) cannot be sustained.

1. *The Gospel of Matthew* shows much evidence of the editing of the traditions about Jesus to meet the needs of a community in transition in the period after the destruction of the temple in 70 CE. This has at least two aspects: community self-definition, and the maintenance of group boundaries and internal cohesion.

To distinguish his community from developments in Pharisaic Judaism, the evangelist identifies an alternative source of authority, Jesus the Son of God and Wisdom of God, and those appointed by him, notably Peter. Matthew's christology, in other words, has important social and communal ramifications – something which could be said for all of the christologies of the New Testament.[48] Further, to provide a normative basis for a common life under God (and apart from the synagogue communities), the evangelist presents an alternative and more rigorous interpretation of the law, and sets the tradition of the sayings and deeds of Jesus over against the traditions of the fathers as interpreted by the Pharisees (Matt 5–7). To provide the basis for reconstituting the people of God on terms which transcended the boundaries of the Jewish *ethnos*, he legitimates a strategy and practice of mission to Gentiles as well as Jews (Matt 10; 28.16–20).

To deal, on the other hand, with problems of community maintenance, the evangelist creates a kind of 'community rule' to deal with matters of internal discipline (Matt 18). He also gives prominence to what might best be called a 'scholarly' model of

---

[47] See M. Buber, *Two Types of Faith* (London, 1951), cited in H. C. Kee, 'Messiah and the People of God', in J. T. Butler, ed., *Understanding the Word* (Sheffield: JSOT, 1985), 341–58 at 341.

[48] See D. C. Duling, 'Insights from Sociology for New Testament Christology: A Test Case', in K. H. Richards, ed., *SBL 1985 Seminar Papers* (Atlanta: Scholars Press, 1985), 351–68; W. A. Meeks, *The Moral World of the First Christians* (London, 1987), esp. 136ff., on 'Messianic Biography as Community-Forming Literature'; and H. C. Kee, *Knowing the Truth: A Sociological Approach to New Testament Interpretation* (Minneapolis: Fortress Press, 1989), esp. ch. 4.

discipleship, where the stress is placed upon learning, obeying and handing on the tradition and, in so doing, preserving important elements of continuity with the past (cf. Matt 13.52). Potential sources of tension and conflict within the group are addressed by the attempt to encourage an ideal of the community as a non-hierarchical brotherhood (Matt 23.8–10), whose dominant ethos is one of forgiveness and pastoral care for the one who 'goes astray'. This ethos is reinforced both positively and negatively. In positive terms, there is the uniquely strong emphasis in Matthew upon the love commandment (Matt 5.43–48; 19.19b), upon the importance of 'bearing fruit' and doing works of 'righteousness', and upon attaining child-like humility (Matt 18.1–4) – all of which is modelled in the authoritative example of Jesus himself. Negative reinforcement comes in the form of apocalyptic threats of judgement: upon 'hypocrites', those whose love has grown cold, and those who show no regard for 'the little ones' (Matt 23–25).

The major contributions to the study of Matthew and his community are manifold. I would draw particular attention to the works of W. D. Davies,[49] W. G. Thompson,[50] E. Schweizer,[51] D. E. Garland,[52] B. Przybylski,[53] G. N. Stanton,[54] and J. A. Overman.[55]

2. Although redaction criticism of *the Gospel of Mark* went some way towards the identification of the Marcan community,[56] much greater precision was attained when this approach was combined with sociological analysis in studies such as the book by H. C. Kee, *Community of the New Age*.[57] Kee argues that Mark's audience is a missionary sect whose ethos is markedly at odds with dominant social mores and whose world view is apocalyptic. Membership is voluntaristic and inclusive, and the nurture of insiders has a strongly

[49] *The Setting of the Sermon on the Mount* (Cambridge: Cambridge University Press, 1964).

[50] *Matthew's Advice to a Divided Community* (Rome: Pontifical Biblical Press, 1970).

[51] 'Observance of the Law and Charismatic Activity in Matthew', *New Testament Studies* 16 (1970), 213–30; and *Matthäus und seine Gemeinde* (Stuttgart: KBW, 1974).

[52] *The Intention of Matthew 23* (Leiden: E. J. Brill, 1979).

[53] B. Przybylski, *Righteousness in Matthew and His World of Thought* (Cambridge: Cambridge University Press, 1980).

[54] *Inter alia* 'The Origin and Purpose of Matthew's Gospel: Matthean Scholarship from 1945–1980', *ANRW* II, 25, 3 (1983), 1889–1951.

[55] J. A. Overman, *Matthew's Gospel and Formative Judaism: The Social World of the Matthean Community* (Minneapolis: Fortress Press, 1990).

[56] For example, W. Marxsen, *Mark the Evangelist* (ET London: SPCK, 1970).

[57] London: SCM Press, 1977.

esoteric quality: '"To you has been given the secret of the kingdom of God, but for those outside everything is in parables . . ."' (Mk 4.11).

Kee's approach is strongly indebted to the sociology of knowledge. It has proved very fruitful and been taken further by others. A study by Joel Marcus,[58] for example, focuses upon the nature of Mark's epistemology and shows how strongly it reflects an apocalyptic viewpoint, similar in many respects to the world view of the Qumran sect, and arising out of the context of a community suffering persecution.[59] Another study by Francis Watson,[60] which appeared almost at the same time, comes to very similar conclusions. According to Watson, the theme of secrecy in Mark is understood adequately only if its social function is taken into account. He suggests that the secrecy motif expresses a doctrine of predestination which functioned, in a social context of persecution, both to reinforce the community's self-understanding as the elect, and to explain the incomprehension and hostility of outsiders.

Persecution and experiences of conflict do seem to have been of critical importance in shaping the outlook of Mark and his community.[61] But such persecution may have been itself a response to the novel, countercultural aspect of Mark's understanding of social relations. Feminist scholarship has emphasized, for example, the prominence given in Mark to women as followers of Jesus and models of bold faith and sacrificial service.[62] To this may be added

---

[58] 'Mark 4.10–12 and Marcan Epistemology', *JBL* 103 (1984), 557–74.

[59] See esp. Marcus, 'Epistemology', 572–3: 'This context of persecution helps us to see the cutting edge of Mark's epistemology for the community he is addressing. Confronted by a hostile world which for the most part seemed bent on denying the claims that they were making for Jesus, those within the Marcan community must have been asking themselves, "Why aren't people recognizing who Jesus is? If he has brought the kingdom of God, why isn't that kingdom being recognized by the world at large? Why is the world, in fact, opposing our message and persecuting us?" In a very direct way 4.10–12 is an answer to these questions. In it Jesus reassures the hard-pressed Marcan community that its sufferings . . . are only part of "the mystery of the kingdom of God," according to which those outside are blinded by the forces of darkness so that they oppose God's kingdom.'

[60] F. Watson, 'The Social Function of Mark's Secrecy Theme', *JSNT* 24 (1985), 49–69.

[61] The evidence is set out well by B. M. F. van Iersel, 'The Gospel According to St Mark – Written for a Persecuted Community?', *Nederlands Theologisch Tijdschrift* 34 (1980), 15–36.

[62] See esp. E. S. Malbon, 'Fallible Followers: Women and Men in the Gospel of Mark', *SEMEIA* 28 (1983), 29–48; and A. Gill, 'Women Ministers in the Gospel of Mark', *ABR* 25 (1987), 14–21.

the clear evidence of, *inter alia,* the rejection of the laws of purity (Mk 7.19b), hostility to material possessions (Mk 10.17–31), the radical subordination of family and occupational ties for the sake of mission (Mk 1.16–20; 10.28–30), and the potentially subversive understanding of power relations (Mk 10.13–16, 35–45; 12.13–17).

Yet another approach, which focuses on the mythological and parabolic dimensions of Mark, shows how the narrative functions both to establish a new world and to subvert the old. Using a form of structuralist exegesis, Elizabeth Malbon has shown in a number of quite innovative studies of the spatial dimensions (geopolitical, topographical and architectural) of the Marcan narrative[63] how the locus of the holy is related in a rather subversive way to being on the road or in the house or on the sea with Jesus rather than to Jerusalem and the temple.

3. Until recently, *Luke–Acts* has been read primarily, and quite properly, as a source for reconstructing the history of the early church and, in particular, of the primitive Christian community in Jerusalem. The focus of attention here has been the 'enthusiastic' ethos of the community and its various expressions of *koinonia,* such as the holding of goods in common and the regular gatherings for meals in members' houses.[64]

Philip Esler's book *Community and Gospel in Luke–Acts: The Social and Political Motivations of Lucan Theology* (Cambridge, 1987) breaks new ground by trying to give a sociological profile of the community of Luke's own day. He argues that Luke–Acts is best interpreted as written to provide legitimation for a Christian group whose relations with both the Jewish synagogue community and the wider Gentile society were fraught with the inevitable tensions and pressures arising from the Christian group's sectarian character. So, for example, the reason for Luke's interest in table fellowship is to legitimate Jew–Gentile commensality in his community and to maintain Jew–Gentile cohesion in the face of strong opposition from Jews and Jewish Christians who see the practice as a threat to the identity of the Jewish *ethnos.*

[63] See E. S. Malbon, 'TH OIKIA AYTOY: Mark 2.15 in Context', *New Testament Studies* 31 (1985), 282–92; and 'Mark: Myth and Parable', *BTB* 16 (1986), 8–17 and *Narrative Space and Mythic Meaning in Mark* (San Francisco: Harper & Row, 1986). Cf. also S. Freyne, *Galilee, Jesus and the Gospels* (Dublin: Gill & Macmillan, 1988), esp. ch. 2.

[64] See, for example, M. Hengel, *Property and Riches in the Early Church* (ET London: SCM Press, 1974); J. D. G. Dunn, *Jesus and the Spirit,* ch. 7.

Another study which focuses on table fellowship is Halvor Moxnes's essay, 'Meals and the new community in Luke'.[65] Moxnes sets his analysis firmly within a social anthropological framework, and quotes Marshall Sahlins's statement, 'Food dealings are a delicate barometer, a ritual statement as it were, of social relations, and food is thus employed instrumentally as a starting, a sustaining, or a destroying mechanism of sociability.'[66] Moxnes argues quite persuasively that meals in Luke (and especially the meal practice and table talk of Jesus) function as a challenge to the boundaries of the Jewish *ethnos*, as the starting mechanism of a new group, and as the basis for the internal ordering of the group, based now upon new criteria of acceptability and the reordering of the social hierarchy.

The recognition that the author of Luke–Acts was committed fervently to fostering a new pattern of community is now widespread. The delay of the parousia and concern about heretical developments of a gnostic kind[67] may well have been contributory factors. Luke's response is to present salvation not as a flight from history, but as the story of God's involvement in history as universal benefactor bringing a new people into being with Jesus as its head and exemplar.[68] The shorthand for describing this new people is 'the poor', those who acknowledge their utter dependence for salvation and sustenance upon God alone. For Luke, salvation works from the bottom up and from the margins in, and acceptance of this radical and novel reversal of conventional social-economic-political-religious norms is possible only on the basis of a thoroughgoing *metanoia*.

This helps to explain the symbolic significance and representative status of the many marginalized groups and individuals whom we encounter in the Lucan narrative: the 'tax collectors and sinners', the 'poor', women, a Samaritan leper, Gentiles, and so on. Among Lucan studies, Esler discusses Luke's theology of the poor against the backdrop of a highly stratified urban society and, on the basis

---

[65] *Svensk Exegetisk Arsbok* 51–2 (1986–7), 158–67; and see now his *The Economy of the Kingdom* (Philadelphia: Fortress Press, 1988), esp. ch. 8.

[66] M. Sahlins, *Stone Age Economics* (London: Tavistock, 1974), 215, quoted in H. Moxnes, 'Meals', 158.

[67] Cf. C. H. Talbert, *Luke and the Gnostics* (Nashville: Abingdon, 1966).

[68] F. W. Danker, *Luke* (Philadelphia: Fortress Press, 1976) elaborates the divine benefactor model to very good effect with respect to both the theology and christology of Luke–Acts.

of passages such as Luke 14.12–14, argues strongly that 'Luke intends Jesus' views on this subject to apply to the relationships between the rich and the poor *within* the Christian community'.[69]

The relative prominence given to women in Lucan salvation history has been noticed also. They too are among the 'poor' for whom the coming of Jesus is good news and, in numerous instances, they are presented as model disciples. Mary is a particular case in point, as excellent studies by Raymond Brown[70] and Joseph Fitzmyer[71] have shown. But lest we jump too readily to the conclusion that women exercised an unusual degree of authority in the church(es) of Luke, we do well to note Grassi's point[72] that the evangelist gives clear priority to the witness of Peter and the Twelve (since apostolicity is a more certain guard against heresy)[73] and Fiorenza's observation that Luke's history is biased androcentrically in such a way that the contribution of women as 'missionaries and leaders of churches in their own right' is neglected.[74]

4. It is recognized widely that *the Fourth Gospel and the Johannine Epistles* represent a distinctive trajectory in earliest Christianity. One explanation for this distinctiveness has to do with the character and history of the Johannine community. This has been the focus of a number of studies, including those of J. L. Martyn,[75]

---

[69] P. F. Esler, *Community and Gospel*, 194. Similarly, R. J. Karris, 'Poor and Rich: The Lukan *Sitz im Leben*', in C. H. Talbert, ed., *Perspectives on Luke–Acts* (Edinburgh: T&T Clark, 1978), 112–25, esp. 117: 'Luke's *Sitz im Leben* consists of propertied Christians who have been converted and cannot easily extricate themselves from their cultural mindsets. It also consists of Christians in need of alms. Luke takes great pains to show that Christians treat each other as friends and that almsgiving and care for one another is of the essence of the Way. If the converts do not learn this lesson . . . , there is danger that the Christian movement may splinter.'

[70] R. E. Brown *et al.*, *Mary in the New Testament* (Philadelphia: Fortress Press, 1978), 105–77.

[71] J. A. Fitzmyer, *Luke the Theologian: Aspects of His Teaching* (London: Chapman & Hall, 1989), 57–85.

[72] J. A. Grassi, *The Hidden Heroes of the Gospels: Female Counterparts of Jesus* (Collegeville: Order of St Benedict, 1979), esp. 83–91.

[73] For a bold attempt to demonstrate the presence of women at the Last Supper, in spite of Luke's silence (!) see Q. Quesnell, 'The Women at Luke's Supper', in R. J. Cassidy and P. J. Scharper, eds, *Political Issues in Luke–Acts* (New York: Orbis, 1983), 59–79.

[74] Fiorenza, *In Memory of Her*, 167; and '"You are not to be called Father": Early Christian History in a Feminist Perspective', *Cross Currents* 39 (1979), 301–23 at 308.

[75] *History and Theology in the Fourth Gospel* (Nashville: Abingdon, 1968, 1979[2]).

W. A. Meeks,[76] R. E. Brown,[77] F. F. Segovia,[78] and D. Rensberger.[79] By reading the Fourth Gospel as a kind of mirror of the community, the picture that has emerged is of a community radically estranged, not only from the wider society, but also from the society of the synagogue, and even from the society of other Christian groups. An introverted, 'us and them' ethos seems dominant. As D. Moody Smith puts it:

> ... it can probably be agreed that on any reading of the Gospel and Epistles there appears a sectarian consciousness, a sense of exclusiveness, a sharp delineation of the community from the world. ... Comparisons with community consciousness in Qumran, which is likewise related to a fundamental dualism, are entirely apposite and to the point.[80]

This sectarian ethos is reflected especially in the christology of the community. Just as the Jesus of the Gospel is a stranger to the world and even to his own people, so too is the Johannine community. This has been demonstrated brilliantly by Wayne Meeks and Marinus de Jonge[81] in studies which both take the encounter between Jesus and Nicodemus in John 3 as the epitome of the distance separating insiders from even sympathetic outsiders. Just as Jesus does not belong and is not understood, neither do those who believe in him find acceptance and understanding. The powerful use of path and residence metaphors (to use Margaret Pamment's phrase)[82] shows how strong is the sense of displacement. Now, Jesus exclusively is 'the way' to the Father, not Torah. Now, true worship takes place neither on Mount Gerizim nor on Mount Zion, but 'in spirit and in truth' (4.19ff.). Now, the only temple where God is to be encountered is the temple of Jesus' own body. In fact, almost every major symbol of belonging as a Jew to the people of God – Torah, temple, festival calendar, sabbath observance,

---

[76] 'The Man from Heaven in Johannine Sectarianism', *JBL* 91 (1972), 44–72.

[77] *The Community of the Beloved Disciple* (New York: Paulist Press, 1979).

[78] *Love Relationships in the Johannine Tradition* (Chico: Scholars Press, 1982).

[79] D. Rensberger, *Johannine Faith and Liberating Community* (Philadelphia: Fortress Press, 1988).

[80] D. M. Smith, 'Johannine Christianity: Some Reflections on its Character and Delineation', *NTS* 21 (1975), 224–48 at 223–4.

[81] See W. A. Meeks, 'The Man from Heaven'; and M. de Jonge, *Jesus Stranger from Heaven and Son of God* (Missoula: Scholars Press, 1977), esp. ch. 2.

[82] 'Path and Residence Metaphors in the Fourth Gospel', *Theology* 88 (1985), 118–25.

the land, the scriptures and the patriarchs – is displaced in a quite countercultural way by the Jesus of John.[83]

The highly polemical portrayal of 'the Jews' is best seen as a negative interpretation of the time of Jesus in the light of subsequent experiences of expulsion from the synagogue and conflict between Jews and Christians, especially in the period of Jamnia, 'when the Pharisees were making strenuous efforts to preserve the purity of the people and the integrity of the Law'.[84] The escalating severity of this conflict is reflected in the warning attributed to Jesus in 16.1–2: 'I have said all this to you to keep you from falling away. They will put you out of the synagogues; indeed, the hour is coming when whoever kills you will think he is offering service to God.' On this kind of reading, the Farewell Discourses represent an authoritative attempt to prepare the community for conflict, to warn against the twin dangers of disunity and apostasy, and to overcome anxiety through the promise of the presence of 'another Paraclete'. They deal both with problems internal to the life of the community – problems about authority, rank and succession after the departure of the original charismatic leader;[85] and they deal also with problems arising in relations with outsiders.[86]

The reinterpretation of the sacraments in the direction of a far more fundamental concern with the symbolism of belief and unbelief,[87] the shift of attention away from the twelve apostles and towards the life of the individual believer, the charismatic theological emphasis on the availability of the Spirit-Paraclete to each and every believer, the striking prominence accorded women as outspoken witnesses to the truth[88] – such phenomena are interpreted now as

---

[83] David Rensberger, in *Johannine Faith*, has shown that this countercultural aspect of the Fourth Gospel also has a political dimension that bears directly upon attitudes toward Roman authority. This comes out in his analysis of the narrative of the trial of Jesus in ch. 5.

[84] B. Lindars, 'The Persecution of Christians in John 15.18 – 16.4a', in W. Horbury and B. McNeil, eds, *Suffering and Martyrdom in the New Testament* (Cambridge: Cambridge University Press, 1981), 49.

[85] See D. B. Woll, *Johannine Christianity in Conflict* (Chico: Scholars Press, 1981). Another study which emphasizes the intra-mural dimension of the problems in the Johannine community is F. F. Segovia, 'The Theology and Provenance of John 15.1–17', *JBL* 101 (1982), 115–28.

[86] So, B. Lindars, 'The Persecution of Christians', who follows J. L. Martyn's position.

[87] See the excellent essay by John Painter, 'Johannine Symbols: A Case Study in Epistemology', *Journal of Theology for Southern Africa* 27 (1979), 26–41.

[88] On each of these points, see *inter alios* Brown, *The Churches the Apostles Left Behind*, chs 6–7, and the literature cited there.

further hints that the Johannine community was an isolated and idiosyncratic community at odds with developments reflected in the post-Pauline tradition of the Pastoral Epistles and Luke–Acts. Striking, instead, is the concern of an egalitarian kind[89] with the intensification of individual members' faith and knowledge and the emphasis on the need for love within (rather than without) the brotherhood. The Johannine Epistles give evidence of the fissile, unstable character of the Johannine community.

5. The study of community in the New Testament has reached its greatest precision in relation to *the letters of Paul.* This is because, to a degree more obvious than in the case of the Gospels, Paul's writings are occasional pieces directed to particular groups in particular places. Close study of the letters has made it possible to reconstruct the character of the groups founded by the apostle, the social level of their members, relations within the groups and between them, their beliefs and practices, their disciplinary procedures and attitudes to outsiders, and their struggle to establish boundaries and a sense of identity over against various alternative groups and patterns of association. In my view, two of the most important contributions in this area are the essays of Gerd Theissen on Corinth, collected in translation as *The Social Setting of Pauline Christianity* (Philadelphia and Edinburgh, 1982), and Wayne A. Meeks's magisterial study *The First Urban Christians: The Social World of the Apostle Paul* (New Haven and London, 1983). But there has been a plethora of other important work.

(*a*) Some scholars have proceeded by focusing on Paul's relations with his churches.[90] Important here is the question of power and its interpretation by Paul in his dealings with both the Jerusalem church and his own communities. Bengt Holmberg's analysis of the 'organic' authority structure of the early church as a whole and, within that, of Paul's authority in the churches he founded himself, is particularly insightful. Of the latter, he says, for example:

[89] See esp. Brown, *The Churches the Apostles Left Behind*, 109: 'there are no second-class Christians *in terms of status* . . . there are no second-class Christians *geographically* . . . there are no second-class Christians *chronologically*' (Brown's emphasis.)

[90] For example, J. H. Schütz, *Paul and the Anatomy of Apostolic Authority* (Cambridge: Cambridge University Press, 1975); and B. Holmberg, *Paul and Power. The Structure of Authority in the Primitive Church as Reflected in the Pauline Epistles* (Lund: Gleerup, 1978).

Paul's actual power is not strictly formalized, and we cannot make out a catalogue of well-specified apostolic rights with a corresponding list of obligations on the part of the church even if rights and obligations obviously existed. Instead we find in all letters, except Rom, the conception of apostolic fatherhood and imitation (*mimesis*), which, as a description of the relation between apostle and local church is milder and at the same time more demanding than a list of rights and obligations. It is milder because it signifies an affectionate relation, but it is also more demanding – when are you free from the obligation of respecting and obeying 'father', and when have you repaid the debt of gratitude to the person who has given you life (eternal)?[91]

(*b*) Others have attempted to delineate the most important aspects of Paul's understanding of community.[92] Here, the emphasis has fallen upon Paul's doctrine of freedom and new creation 'in Christ' and upon the local believing community as the locus for shared experience of the eschatological Spirit. Hence, Paul's conception of authority and ministry in the community is seen as essentially charismatic, with a strong recognition of the mutual interdependence of members and an ideal of unity as the outworking of the diversity of members' contributions.

(*c*) Yet another focus for scholars has been the social setting of Paul's groups. E. A. Judge[93] broke new ground in showing that early Christian ideas of social obligation need to be interpreted in relation to the particular social institutions which they presuppose: the city state, the household, and the unofficial association. More recent work has taken the study of these three kinds of institution considerably further:[94] (i) The urban ethos of Paul's groups has been explored by Gerd Theissen and Wayne Meeks in the works mentioned already. (ii) The significance of the household as providing the churches' setting and constituency, their role relations and dominant authority patterns, as well as potential sources of conflict, was mooted early on by Floyd Filson,[95] and has

---

[91] *Paul and Power*, 81.

[92] For example, E. Schweizer, *The Church as the Body of Christ* (Atlanta: John Knox, 1964); Dunn, *Jesus and the Spirit*, chs 8–10; Banks, *Paul's Idea of Community*; Meeks, *Urban Christians*, ch. 6.

[93] *The Social Pattern of Christian Groups in the First Century* (London: Tyndale, 1960).

[94] See, in general, J. Stambaugh and D. Balch, *The Social World of the First Christians* (London: SPCK, 1986).

[95] 'The Significance of the Early House Churches', *JBL* 58 (1939), 105–12.

been studied further by, *inter alios*, Robert Banks,[96] Abraham Malherbe,[97] Norman Petersen,[98] John Koenig,[99] and Larry Yarbrough.[100] A study of my own, drawing especially upon the anthropology of social boundaries, attempts to assess the extent to which conflict in the Corinthian churches was indebted to the ambiguity of the boundary between church (*ekklēsia*) and household (*oikos*).[101] (iii) Comparison with Graeco-Roman voluntary associations is still at a fairly preliminary stage in so far as detailed analysis is concerned, but advances have been made. A useful essay on 'Patrons and Offices in Club and Church' was presented by William Countryman at the SBL meeting in 1977;[102] Greg Horsley and myself published a detailed analysis of one piece of epigraphic evidence from Philadelphia in Asia Minor, in 1981;[103] and R. L. Wilken discusses 'Christianity as a Burial Society' in his book of 1984.[104]

(*d*) Influenced in part by the feminist movement, many attempts have been made to interpret and explain the rather confusing evidence about the role of women in the churches of Paul. It is accepted widely that, whereas Paul was a social radical in his insistence on the removal of boundaries separating Jew and Gentile in the people of God, his position on the roles and status of women (and slaves) in the Christian gatherings was more conservative and pragmatic, in spite of his wholehearted endorsement

[96] *Paul's Idea of Community.*

[97] A. J. Malherbe, *Social Aspects of Early Christianity* (Philadelphia: Fortress Press 1983[2]), esp. chs 3, 4.

[98] N. R. Petersen, *Rediscovering Paul: Philemon and the Sociology of Paul's Narrative World* (Philadelphia: Fortress Press 1985). Cf. also on Philemon, J. H. Elliott, 'Philemon and House Churches', *The Bible Today* 22/3 (1984), 145–50.

[99] *New Testament Hospitality* (Philadelphia: Fortress Press 1985), esp. ch. 3.

[100] O. L. Yarbrough, *Not Like the Gentiles: Marriage Rules in the Letters of Paul* (Atlanta: Scholars Press, 1985).

[101] S. C. Barton, 'Paul's Sense of Place: An Anthropological Approach to Community Formation in Corinth', *NTS* 32 (1986), 225–46.

[102] *SBL 1977 Seminar Papers*, ed. P. J. Achtemeier (Missoula, 1977), 135–41.

[103] S. C. Barton and G. H. R. Horsley, 'A Hellenistic Cult Group and the New Testament', *Jahrbuch für Antike und Christentum* 24 (1981), 7–41.

[104] R. L. Wilken, *The Christians as the Romans Saw Them* (New Haven and London: Yale, 1984); cf. 'Collegia, Philosophical Schools, and Theology', in S. Benko and J. J. O'Rourke, eds, *Early Church History: The Roman Empire as the Setting of Primitive Christianity* (London: Oliphants, 1972), 268–91.

of the eschatologically oriented baptismal formula which he cites in Galatians 3.27–28.[105]

(*e*) The novel, experimental and charismatic ethos of Paul's groups made them prone to conflict. Such conflict has been a further area of investigation. Some, like Walter Schmithals,[106] have emphasized the doctrinal elements in the conflicts. Others, have drawn attention to sociological factors and have tried to correlate the sociological and the doctrinal.[107] Here, one thinks of Gerd Theissen on the 'strong' and the 'weak' in Corinth,[108] and Robert Jewett's work on millenarian radicalism in Thessalonica.[109] One thinks also of the 'new look' on the law and justification in the teaching of Paul, associated especially with the names of Krister Stendahl and E. P. Sanders, where much greater weight is given to placing Paul's polemical doctrines within the social context of his mission to the Gentiles.[110] Increasing recognition is being given as

---

[105] Important contributions to this question have come, *inter alios*, from K. Stendahl, *The Bible and the Role of Women* (Philadelphia: Fortress Press 1966); W. A. Meeks, 'The Image of the Androgyne: Some Uses of a Symbol in Earliest Christianity', *HR* 13 (1974), 165–208; Fiorenza, *In Memory of Her*; W. O. Walker, Jr, 'The "Theology of Woman's Place" and the "Paulinist" Tradition', *SEMEIA* 28 (1983), 101–12; M. Hayter, *The New Eve in Christ* (London: SPCK, 1987); and B. Witherington III, *Women in the Earliest Churches* (Cambridge: Cambridge University Press, 1988).

[106] *Paul and the Gnostics* (ET Nashville: Abingdon, 1972).

[107] See, for example, S. C. Barton, 'Paul and the Cross: A Sociological Approach', *Theology* 85 (1982), 13–19; and 'Paul and the Resurrection: A Sociological Approach', *Religion* 14 (1984), 67–75. An important methodological essay is Bengt Holmberg, 'Sociological versus Theological Analysis of the Question Concerning a Pauline Church Order', in S. Pedersen, ed., *Die Paulinische Literatur und Theologie* (Arhus: Aros, 1980), 187–200.

[108] *Pauline Christianity*, ch. 3.

[109] *The Thessalonian Correspondence: Pauline Rhetoric and Millenarian Piety* (Philadelphia: Fortress Press 1986).

[110] See K. Stendahl, *Paul Among Jews and Gentiles* (London: SCM Press, 1977); Sanders, *Paul and Palestinian Judaism*; also, F. Watson, *Paul, Judaism and the Gentiles* (Cambridge: Cambridge University Press, 1986). The debate has been taken an important stage further by J. D. G. Dunn, in his essay, 'The New Perspective on Paul', in his *Jesus, Paul and the Law* (London: SPCK, 1990), 183–214. He concludes: 'All this confirms the earlier important thesis of Stendahl, that Paul's doctrine of justification by faith should not be understood primarily as an exposition of the individual's relation to God, but primarily in the context of Paul the Jew wrestling with the question of how Jews and Gentiles stand in relation to each other within the covenant purpose of God now that it has reached its climax in Jesus Christ. . . . Paul's solution does not require him to deny the covenant, or indeed the law as God's law, but only the covenant and the law as "taken over" by Israel' (p. 202).

well to the pastoral aspects of Paul's self-understanding and practice as an apostle and to his theology as pastoral theology.[111]

6. Until recently, the study of *1 Peter* has focused on the extent of the epistle's indebtedness to a (hypothetical) early Christian baptismal liturgy.[112] Two studies, however, have brought communal concerns to the fore. Coincidentally, these two studies were published in the same year, 1981. D. L. Balch's book, *Let Wives Be Submissive: The Domestic Code in I Peter*[113] argues that the rules in 1 Peter about social obligations generally, and the ordering of house hold relations in particular, have an apologetic function and are intended to counter slanderous accusations of outsiders that the Christian groups, like other cults from the Greek east, were a threat to the Roman 'constitution'. On this view, the domestic code represents an assimilation of group norms to the norms of the wider society.

In some tension with this interpretation, although once again concentrating upon the household as the locus of early Christian community, is J. H. Elliott's *A Home for the Homeless: A Sociological Exegesis of I Peter* (Philadelphia, 1981). Elliott argues that the addressees of the epistle are marginalized 'resident aliens' (*paroikoi*) of Asia Minor whose conversion has increased the antagonism of the native residents towards them. They constitute, therefore, a 'conversionist sect' in tension with the society at large. The strategy of the letter is to confirm the believers in their social and religious separation from outsiders and to emphasize their incorporation into an alternative family, the 'household of God' (cf. 1 Pet 2.5; 4.17).

So, whereas Balch interprets the household code as intended to promote greater integration into Graeco-Roman society, Elliott sees the code functioning to encourage sectarian isolation. A more recent essay on the teaching about citizenship in Romans 13.3–4 and 1 Peter 2.14–15, by B. W. Winter[114] tips the balance of the

[111] For example, A. J. Malherbe, *Paul and the Thessalonians*; and E. Best, *Paul and His Converts* (Edinburgh: T&T Clark, 1988).
[112] For example, F. L. Cross, *I Peter: A Paschal Liturgy* (London: SPCK, 1954); T. C. G. Thornton, 'I Peter: A Paschal Liturgy?', *JTS*, n.s. 12 (1961), 14–26.
[113] Chico: Scholars Press, 1981. See also the recent summary of scholarly interpretation in 'Household Codes', in D. E. Aune, ed., *Greco-Roman Literature and the New Testament* (Atlanta: Scholars Press, 1988), 25–50.
[114] 'The Public Honouring of Christian Benefactors: Romans 13.3–4 and 1 Peter 2.14–15', *JSNT* 34 (1988), 87–103.

argument against Elliott.[115] By adducing numerous parallels from benefaction inscriptions of the time, Winter shows that the teaching of Paul and 1 Peter is intended to encourage 'rich Christians to contribute to the well-being of the community at large' in the clear expectation of recognition and gratitude by the public authorities. Not withdrawal, therefore, but 'high-profile good works'.[116]

7. The interpretation of the ideas about community in *the Pastoral Epistles* has been dominated by the debate over 'Early Catholicism' (*Frühkatholizismus*) in the New Testament, a debate which goes back at least to F. C. Baur and the Tübingen school in the mid-nineteenth century and whose most vigorous prosecutor this century has been Ernst Käsemann.[117] The Pastorals, along with Luke–Acts and other late New Testament texts, have been seen as literary expressions of certain developments in second-generation Christianity: the fading of the parousia hope, the deaths of the apostles, the tendency toward increasing institutionalization as a response to growth, the normalizing of relations with the society at large, and the crystallization of Christian beliefs into set forms in order to guard against 'enthusiasm' and heresy.[118]

Certainly, it is commonly accepted that the ideas about authority and community in the Pastorals constitute a substantial modification of the more Pauline ideal of participatory, charismatic community in the direction of hierarchy and patriarchy in matters of governance, and orthodoxy and tradition in matters of belief.[119] Advances

---

[115] Antoinette Wire's important review article (in *RSR* 10/3 (1984), 209–16) shows that the respective hypotheses of Balch and Elliott about the strategy of 1 Peter are not incompatible, however.

[116] 'Christian Benefactors', 95.

[117] See E. Käsemann, 'Paul and Early Catholicism' (ET of 'Paulus und der Frühkotholizismus'), in his *New Testament Questions of Today* (London: SCM Press, 1969), 236–51. Cf. also H. von Campenhausen, *Ecclesiastical Authority and Spiritual Power in the Church of the First Three Centuries* (ET London: A&C Black, 1969).

[118] See, for example, Dunn, *Unity and Diversity in the New Testament* (London: SCM Press, 1977), ch. 14; and D. Harrington, *Light of All Nations: Essays on the Church in New Testament Research* (Wilmington and Dublin, 1982), esp. ch. 3.

[119] See, for example, Brown, *The Churches the Apostles Left Behind*, ch. 2. His comment on Paul is apt: 'Indeed, Paul might not have been able to meet several requirements the Pastorals would impose on the presbyter-bishops. "Not quick-tempered" (Titus 1.7) would scarcely describe the Paul who called the Galatians "fools" (Gal 3.1). "Dignified" (1 Tim 3.2) would not fit the Paul who wished that his circumcising adversaries would slip with the knife and castrate themselves (Gal 5.12) ... Rough vitality and a willingness to fight bare-knuckled for the gospel were part of what made Paul a great missionary, but such characteristics might have made him a poor residential community supervisor' (p. 35).

in the study of these developments have been considerable and
have involved, in part, a reaction against the too simple (and often
polemical) dichotomy between charisma and office.

Three studies may be mentioned here. First, John G. Gager's
Kingdom and Community makes effective use of insights from
Weberian sociology to argue for the inevitability and necessity of
the processes of routinization in earliest Christianity if the movement
was to survive and grow. According to Gager,

> if we accept as a fundamental law the transformation from no rules
> to new rules, we may not at the same time lament the routinization of
> the primitive enthusiasm that characterizes all charismatic or millen-
> narian movements in their second generation and sometimes even
> earlier.[120]

And, in criticism of Bultmann, he adds: 'By failing to pursue the
full consequences of his own observation about the inevitability of
regulations, he and numerous others have given up consistent
historical analysis. Consequently, a good deal of nonsense has
been written about the decline of primitive Christianity into "early
Catholicism".'[121]

In agreement with Gager on this and drawing likewise on
Weberian and other sociological models, is Margaret MacDonald's
book *The Pauline Churches*.[122] This comprehensive study seeks to trace
the process of institution-building in the churches of the Pauline
tradition after the apostle's death. Rather than contrast ideas of
community in Paul and the Pastorals in a simplistic way, MacDonald
attempts to discover 'relations between the stages in terms of the
institution building process'.[123] Focusing on developments in the
Pauline and post-Pauline literature in four aspects of community
life – ethics, ministry, ritual, and belief – she suggests that three
stages of institutionalization become evident: Paul's letters are to
do with community *building*, Colossians and Ephesians are to do
with community *stabilizing*, and the Pastorals are to do with
community *protecting*.

For feminist biblical scholarship, with its commitment to making
early Christian women visible by a reconstruction of Christian origins

[120] *Kingdom and Community* (Englewood Cliffs: Prentice-Hall, 1975), 67.
[121] Ibid.
[122] M. Y. MacDonald, *The Pauline Churches: A Socio-Historical Study of Institutionalization in the Pauline and Deutero-Pauline Writings* (Cambridge: Cambridge
University Press, 1988).
[123] Ibid. 8.

on the basis of a feminist hermeneutic of suspicion, the Pastorals are evidence, not just of the institutionalization of the early church, but of its patriarchalization as well. This has been argued most forcefully by Elisabeth Fiorenza in *In Memory of Her*.[124] She traces the gradual adaptation of early Christian authority structures to that of the patriarchal household,[125] and the 'genderization of ecclesial office' represented, for example, by the prohibition against the teaching of men by women (1 Tim 2.12) and the instructions concerning the order of widows in 1 Timothy 5.3–16.[126] According to Fiorenza, the teaching about virgins and widows is to be seen as a mechanism of control. Their protection is an obligation in a patriarchal society: it is also a means of prescribing limits to their roles and status. In sum, the countercultural 'discipleship of equals' which she discerns in the practice of Jesus and in the Christianity of the first generation is marginalized thoroughly in the post-Pauline and post-Petrine trajectories.

8. A convergence of a number of trends in biblical interpretation and theology has brought a renewed interest in *the Book of Revelation* and the situation of its addressees.

(*a*) Following in the tradition of historical geography and social history, as exemplified at the turn of the last century by the work of Sir William Ramsay, is C. J. Hemer's book *The Letters to the Seven Churches of Asia in Their Local Setting* (Sheffield, 1986). This study draws upon a mass of literary, archaeological and epigraphic data in order to throw light upon local conditions likely to have affected the Christian groups in Asia Minor. In the same tradition are the volumes entitled *New Documents Illustrating Early Christianity*, edited by G. H. R. Horsley.[127]

(*b*) The sociological trend has been important also. With respect to the interpretation of biblical, Jewish and Christian apocalyptic generally, the social sciences have been employed to help clarify

---

[124] See my review in *Theology* 88 (1985), 134–7. Cf. also Fiorenza's essay, 'Feminist Theology and New Testament Interpretation', *JSOT* 22 (1982), 32–46.

[125] For further discussion, from a social history perspective, on the approximation of the church to the household in the Pastorals, see D. C. Verner, *The Household of God: The Social World of the Pastoral Epistles* (Chico: Scholars Press, 1983), esp. ch. 4.

[126] See also, most recently, Thurston, *The Widows*, for fuller discussion.

[127] *New Documents* is published by the Ancient History Documentary Research Centre, Macquarie University, New South Wales, Australia.

what kinds of groups develop an apocalyptic world view and millennialist hopes and under what kinds of conditions.[128] Typically, apocalyptic literature represents the response of an alienated, marginalized and persecuted group in a society undergoing rapid cultural change. The apocalyptic vision offers a new conception of reality and an alternative (i.e. countercultural) symbolic universe in terms of which the alienated group can sustain its life. Among studies of the Johannine Apocalypse from this point of view, the following may be noted.[129]

J. G. Gager discusses the 'therapeutic' function of the myth of the millennium for the persecuted community. He suggests that the mythological dimension of the Apocalypse is indispensable to the seer's message of consolation. Within the community of oppressed believers gathered for worship, the myth functions to suppress or transcend the time between present woe and future bliss, the effect of which is 'to make possible an experience of millennnial bliss as living reality'.[130]

In an essay of relevance to the study of early Christian anti-Judaism, Adela Yarbro Collins shows how the language of vilification of enemies in the Apocalypse plays an important role in the self-definition of the community.[131] The vilification of 'those who call themselves Jews and are not, but are rather a synagogue of Satan' (Rev 2.9; 3.9) has a social function. It defines the Christians as 'the genuine Jews, the heirs of the promises to Israel' over against their rivals. Similarly, the vilification of Rome and her allies in Revelation 13, expresses these Christians' rejection of imperial authority and values in favour of an alternative symbolic universe focused on the risen and glorified Jesus. Yet again, the vilification of Christian rivals in the seven letters (cf. 2.14–15, 20–23) reflects an attempt by the prophet John to consolidate his own authority by encouraging the

---

[128] See, for example, N. Cohn, *The Pursuit of the Millennium* (London: Granada, 1957); K. Burridge, *New Heaven New Earth* (Oxford: Blackwell, 1969); J. G. Gager, *Kingdom and Community*, ch. 2.

[129] This is a burgeoning area of study. See, *inter alios*, C. Rowland, *The Open Heaven: A Study of Apocalyptic in Early Judaism and Christianity* (London: SPCK, 1982); P. D. Hanson, ed., *Visionaries and Their Apocalypses* (Philadelphia and London: Fortress/SPCK, 1983); and D. Hellholm, ed., *Apocalypticism in the Mediterranean World and the Near East* (Tübingen: Mohr/Siebeck, 1983).

[130] J. G. Gager, *Kingdom and Community*, 49ff. at 55.

[131] 'Vilification and Self-Definition in the Book of Revelation', *HTR* 79 (1986), 308–20 at 314.

churches in the direction of his own policy of strict social non-conformity.[132]

(c) Emphasis on apocalyptic as the protest literature of the socially and politically marginalized has corresponded with the concerns and interests of liberation theology.[133] From the liberationist perspective, the ideas about reality, community and society in Revelation are still relevant today: the unmasking of, and resistance to, the ideology of the oppressor; the hostility towards idolatry in all its manifestations; the vision of heavenly realities which serves as a powerful critique of earthly powers and dominions; and the call to prophetic protest and to a common life which does not accommodate to the perverse values of the society at large. In contemporary British scholarship, the writings of Christopher Rowland have done much, both to bring the study of apocalyptic to the centre of academic debate and to relate such study to the concerns of the liberation theology movement.[134]

III. Conclusion

It remains to suggest, however partially, where further investigation could profitably be made and where current debate needs to be extended. First, and perhaps surprisingly, renewed attention needs to be given to the communal dimension of the activity of Jesus. As I engaged in the present study, the relative absence of scholarly endeavour in this area struck me as noteworthy.[135]

---

[132] On this last point, cf. also the excellent essay by D. E. Aune, 'The Social Matrix of the Apocalypse of John', *Biblical Research* 26 (1981), 16–32. Aune focuses attention on antagonism between rival, translocal, prophetic circles in the seven churches, and suggests that the antagonism arose in relation to the problem of social conformity. John himself advocates strict nonconformity to the values and practices of the dominant culture, 'Jezebel': the Nicolaitans have adopted a liberal policy of cultural accommodation, and a majority of church members are 'lukewarm' and stand somewhere in between. According to Aune, 'John's intense opposition to "Jezebel" and the Nicolaitans appears to have been grounded, not only in the pagan practices they encouraged, but also in the prophetic role they played in legitimating their behavior. John's battle with the Nicolaitans and "Jezebel" was, in a word, a conflict between prophets' (p. 28).

[133] For example, Allan Boesak, *Comfort and Protest* (Edinburgh: Saint Andrew Press, 1987).

[134] See Rowland, *The Open Heaven* and *Radical Christianity* (esp. ch. 3); and Rowland and Corner, *Liberating Exegesis*, esp. ch. 4.

[135] But see G. Lohfink, *Jesus and Community: The Social Dimension of Christian Faith* (ET London: SPCK, 1985).

112 *Life Together*

It is due, no doubt, to the now widespread recognition that the question, Did Jesus found the church? is anachronistic from a historical point of view. It is due also to the passing of interest in questions from a previous agenda to do with the nature of apostleship, its relation to 'the twelve' and to the doctrine of apostolic succession.[136] And, of course, the disciplines of form and redaction criticism have focused our attention away from the pre-Easter community to the shaping of the tradition in the *Sitze im Leben der Kirche*. Now, however, the time is right for a more historically and sociologically sensitive return to the historical-Jesus quest, with a specific view to the societal and communal dimensions of his activity. This is possible, partly because of recent advances in our knowledge of Palestinian Judaism at the time of Jesus,[137] partly because the study of (what Peter Berger calls) the social construction of reality has gained wide acceptance in the study of the New Testament, and also because there has been a revival of interest in Christian social teaching and, in particular, in the ethics of Jesus.[138] Among scholars who have begun to give this matter serious attention, the work of Richard Horsley is especially important. Representative of his position is the following:

> In the 'kingdom of God' sayings and the related preaching and actions of Jesus, the focus is almost always on the people, and the concern is not abstract or even primarily religious, but is with the people's concrete circumstances, both somatic and psychic, both material and spiritual. The *rule* of God entails a *society* of God, a society in which social relations are transformed . . .[139]

---

[136] Cf. E. Schweizer, *Church Order*, 20ff., 211ff.; and C. K. Barrett, *Signs of an Apostle* (London: SPCK, 1970).

[137] For example, S. Freyne, *Galilee from Alexander the Great to Hadrian 323 BCE to 135 CE* (Notre Dame: University of Notre Dame Press, 1980); M. Hengel, *Judaism and Hellenism*, 2 vols (ET London: SCM Press, 1974); A. Saldarini, *Pharisees, Scribes and Sadducees in Palestinian Society: A Sociological Approach* (Edinburgh: T&T Clark, 1989); E. P. Sanders, *Jesus and Judaism.*

[138] For example, L. W. Countryman, *Dirt, Greed and Sex* (London: SCM Press, 1989); Downing, *Jesus*; A. E. Harvey, *Strenuous Commands: The Ethic of Jesus* (London: SCM Press, 1990); K. Wengst, *Pax Romana and the Peace of Jesus Christ* (ET London: SCM Press, 1987).

[139] R. A. Horsley, *Jesus and the Spiral of Violence: Popular Resistance in Roman Palestine* (San Francisco: Harper & Row, 1987). The quotation comes from Horsley's own summary article, 'Jesus and the Spiral of Violence', *Forum* 5/4 (1989), 3–17 at 10. Mention should also be made of Gerd Theissen's two books on Jesus: *First Followers*, and *The Shadow of the Galilean* (ET London: SCM Press, 1987).

A second area for further development concerns the 'turn to the reader' in some current biblical interpretation: the shift from the historical paradigm to the literary-critical paradigm for the interpretation of texts.[140] Meaning, here, is understood more in terms of the aesthetic and intuitive appreciation of the world of the story than in terms of the ability to demonstrate a correspondence between the text and something extrinsic to it. Thus, the community spoken of is not the (hypothetical) community *behind* the text: the Marcan community 'lying behind' the Gospel of Mark, for example. Instead, it is the community which the reader discovers when he or she enters the 'story world' of the text itself.[141] This kind of 'text-immanent' approach is not necessarily antagonistic to historical concerns, since historical information can enable the reader to enter the story world of the text in a more sensitive and better-informed way. However, it is an approach which eschews history-of-traditions concerns in favour of the final form of the text, and it is therefore an approach which challenges attempts of an 'archaeological' kind to reconstruct the history of the post-Easter communities from the tracing of the evolution of the tradition.[142] It is still relatively early days in the application of literary-critical insights to the study of community in the New Testament.[143] It is important to recognize, however, that serious questions have been raised about the more traditional literary-historical methods, and that, at the very least, the hegemony of those methods has been broken.

A third area for continuing debate, once more methodological, must be the application of insights from the sociology of literature to the study of the Gospels in particular. For the way in which the Gospels are read often as virtual allegories of communities or groups, whose needs, interests and history they are supposed to reflect in a quite transparent way, is open to serious doubt. So, for example, it is not necessarily the case that documents reflecting a hostility to

[140] An excellent guide to the burgeoning literature in this field is Stephen D. Moore, *Literary Criticism and the Gospels* (New Haven: Yale University Press, 1989).

[141] See, for example, D. Rhoads and D Michie, *Mark as Story* (Philadelphia: Fortress Press 1982), 1–4.

[142] See on this N. R. Petersen, *Literary Criticism for New Testament Critics* (Philadelphia: Fortress Press 1978), esp. 11ff.

[143] On the Gospels, there is Sean Freyne's innovative work *Galilee, Jesus and the Gospels*, which combines literary and historical approaches; and on the Epistles there is N. R. Petersen's *Rediscovering Paul: Philemon and the Sociology of Paul's Narrative World* (Philadelphia: Fortress Press 1985), which combines literary and sociological approaches.

114 *Life Together*

wealth come from a community of the poor;[144] nor that documents which contain sayings apparently inimical to family ties come from groups of 'wandering charismatics'.[145] Such assumptions are liable to the accusation that a crude functionalism underpins the interpretation. To avoid such accusations, a much greater methodological accountability is called for, of the kind outlined recently by one of the leading practitioners of sociological interpretation, Bengt Holmberg.[146] As Holmberg says:

> The postulate of complete and positive correlation between a text and the social group that carries and receives it is implausible. . . . A text can just as well be standing in a negative correlation to the situation of the receivers. . . . And the uncertainty concerning what type of correlation we encounter applies especially where the texts use symbolic language, which often is a kind of double talk that has metaphorical or distant references, or may be charged with irony.[147]

One final area for further investigation suggests itself, and is of particular relevance to hermeneutics, the history of ideas, and contemporary ecclesiology. I refer to the way in which biblical and specifically New Testament ideas of community have been used at various times and in various places since the period of Christian origins.[148] This involves a study in community as an ideological concept, as part of a wider system of meaning and values, as something people *believe in* and which enhances (or diminishes) their sense of identity and belonging. What is important in study of this kind is how biblical ideas of community become normative and take on a prescriptive role, often coming into conflict with alternative definitions and functioning as a lever for social and institutional change. The roots in the social changes of the 1960s of much contemporary interest in the communal dimension of earliest Christianity, mentioned earlier, is hardly coincidental, and is a prime example of what I have in mind.

[144] Cf. T. E. Schmidt, *Hostility to Wealth in the Synoptic Gospels* (Sheffield: JSOT, 1987), who argues that hostility to wealth is a religious-ethical tenet and is not related to the socio-economic circumstances of the time; and contrast D. L. Mealand, *Poverty and Expectation in the Gospels* (London: SPCK, 1980).

[145] The position of Theissen in *First Followers*.

[146] B. Holmberg, *Sociology and the New Testament: An Appraisal* (Minneapolis: Fortress Press 1990).

[147] Ibid. 124–5; and see further 134ff.

[148] For one attempt see H. von Campenhausen, *Ecclesiastical Authority and Spiritual Power*.

There is no sign that study of the communal dimension of earliest Christianity is abating. The preceding survey shows that all the signs are to the contrary. In my view, this is all to the good, for at least the following reasons:

1. Such investigation is an important corrective to interpretations of either a phenomenological or theological kind which put too much emphasis on Christianity as a religion of the individual. It shows how, from the very beginning, following Jesus was a thoroughly social commitment,[149] which involved the shaping of a corporate life engaged in an all-pervasive (if sometimes implicit) way with questions of morality, politics, economics, law and culture. From the perspective of Christian origins, therefore, it is impossible to justify a separation of personal salvation and spirituality, on the one hand, and corporate identity and responsibility, on the other.

2. Such investigation also encourages the recognition that early Christian beliefs and practices (*including* beliefs about community) were conditioned, not only historically,[150] but sociologically as well. This means that due attention has to be given, in the interpretation of the early Christian writings, to the effects of social stratification, role expectations, conflict and competition, power relations, types of authority, the construction of gender, dominant social symbols, ideologies of legitimation, and the like. Discussion of 'church order' in New Testament times is likely to be abstract, doctrinaire and 'docetic' if it fails to take sociological factors such as these fully into account.[151] On the other hand, awareness of the sociological dimension in interpretation offers the possibility of a much more richly textured, and also critical, appreciation of the nature of early Christian attempts to build and sustain a common life.

3. Finally, such investigation is important for the attention it draws to the hermeneutics of the study of community in earliest

---

[149] Important here is Gerhard Lohfink's *Jesus and Community*.
[150] As Wayne Meeks puts it, in *The Moral World of the First Christians*, 97. 'If therefore we are looking for some "pure" Christian values and beliefs unmixed with the surrounding culture, we are on a fool's errand. What was Christian about the ethos and ethics of those early Christian communities we will discover not by abstraction but by confronting their involvement in the culture of their time and place and seeking to trace the new patterns they made of old forms, to hear the new songs they composed from old melodies.'
[151] So, too, Holmberg, 'Sociological versus Theological Analysis'.

Christianity. Again and again one observes the extent to which various scholarly reconstructions are indebted strongly to the hermeneutical presuppositions of the interpreter, be they liberal-objectivist, materialist, charismatic, feminist, liberationist, high or low church, or whatever. There is no harm in this: it is what the sociology of knowledge would lead us to expect.[152] The reality of communal life in earliest Christianity will have been complex and many-sided. To approach it from a wide variety of perspectives helps both to bring that reality more clearly into view, and to evaluate and (where possible) appropriate it more responsibly.

---

[152] See Kee, *Knowing the Truth*, esp. chs 1, 2.

7

Early Christianity and the
Sociology of the Sect

I. Introduction

This essay is an attempt to address and evaluate the wave of studies which, over the past two decades, have used models and methods from the social sciences to interpret the biblical literature.[1] The field is very large already, so we need to narrow our focus. Even if we confine ourselves to the New Testament alone, the mass of secondary literature is very considerable, as several bibliographical essays show;[2] and there exist already a number of competent book-length introductions to the field, such as those by Bruce Malina (1981), Derek Tidball (1983), Howard Clark Kee (1989) and Bengt Holmberg (1990).[3]

As a way through, therefore, I have chosen to focus on one particular issue in the social-scientific interpretation of the New Testament – namely, the appropriateness or otherwise of describing

[1] I am grateful to Joel B. Green of New College, Berkeley, for his helpful comments on this paper; and to Leslie Houlden and Francis Watson for the original invitation to write and present it.

[2] For example, D. J. Harrington, 'Second Testament Exegesis and the Social Sciences: A Bibliography', *Biblical Theology Bulletin* 18 (1988), 77–85; G. Theissen, 'Auswahl-bibliographie zur Sozialgeschichte des Urchristentums', in his *Studien zur Soziologie des Urchristentums* (Tübingen: Mohr/Siebeck, 1989), 331–70; and S. C. Barton, 'The Communal Dimension of Earliest Christianity: A Critical Survey of the Field', *Journal of Theological Studies* 43/2 (1992), 399–427 (reprinted in the previous chapter).

[3] See B. J. Malina, *The New Testament World: Insights from Cultural Anthropology* (Atlanta: John Knox, 1981); D. Tidball, *An Introduction to the Sociology of the New Testament* (Exeter: Paternoster Press, 1983); H. C. Kee, *Knowing the Truth: A Sociological Approach to New Testament Interpretation* (Minneapolis: Fortress Press, 1989); and B. Holmberg, *Sociology and the New Testament: An Appraisal* (Minneapolis: Fortress Press, 1990).

early Christianity as a 'sect'. Several factors explain my choice. First, as will become clear, the application of the sociological model of the sect to various aspects of early Christianity is a commonplace now. Whether the text under examination is a gospel or an epistle or an apocalypse, its social setting invariably attracts the label 'sectarian'. Perhaps this is an opportune time to test this remarkably widely held consensus to see whether or not its foundations are secure.[4]

Second, the sect model has a distinguished pedigree, both in the social sciences and in the historiography of early Christianity. So this is no hermeneutical 'fly-by-night' to which we are giving our attention. On the contrary, the sociology of sects is a century old at least, and boasts names like Max Weber, Ernst Troeltsch, Georg Simmel, H. Richard Niebuhr, and more recently, Werner Stark and Bryan Wilson.[5] The discussion has a history, therefore; and it will be important to see whether or not an awareness of that history informs accounts given by New Testament scholars of early Christianity as sectarian.

Third, to label early Christianity as a sect is to employ a category which is not native to the first Christians themselves. A twentieth-century Western social-science category is being applied to a phenomenon of the first-century Mediterranean world. This is not objectionable in itself. On the contrary, we do this all the time as a way of making greater sense of the past or of cultures other than our own in terms which are intelligible to us. Nevertheless, it is important to recognize that such categories – etic (outsider) rather than emic (insider), to use the anthropological jargon – are likely to be distorting of what they describe, as well as illuminating, depending on where resides the final court of appeal.[6] In a nutshell, interpretations of early Christianity as a sect are likely to tell us as much about ourselves as interpreters as about the first Christians and their literary deposit. So the present paper is a case study in interpretation which may be of interest not

---

[4] See also the helpful essay by L. Michael White, 'Shifting Sectarian Boundaries in Early Christianity', *Bulletin of the John Rylands Library* 70 (1988), 7–24.

[5] For a useful survey of the sociological debate, see M. Hill, *A Sociology of Religion* (London: Heinemann, 1973), 47–70. On the work of Wilson in particular, see D. E. Miller, 'Sectarianism and Secularization: The Work of Bryan Wilson', *Religious Studies Review* 5/3 (1979), 161–74.

[6] This point is made well in Mark Brett's recent book, *Biblical Criticism in Crisis?* (Cambridge: Cambridge University Press, 1991), 18.

only to students of early Christianity and its social forms, but also to students of the art of interpretation itself. To put the matter pointedly: Do interpreters of early Christianity as a sect find what they are looking for already?

II. Early Christianity as a sect?

Perhaps the best way to proceed is to look critically at specific accounts of early Christianity as sectarian. This will give some indication of how strong is the present consensus that the first Christians did constitute a sectarian movement. It will provide also a basis for judging some of the promise and pitfalls of this kind of sociological analysis.[7]

1. Robin Scroggs on the Jesus movement

A good place to begin is Robin Scroggs's wide-ranging essay of 1975, 'The Earliest Christian Communities as Sectarian Movement'.[8] Here Scroggs claims that the sect model has never previously been applied in detail to the emergence of Christianity, and states his thesis thus:

> It is my conviction that the community called into existence by Jesus fulfills the essential characteristics of the religious sect, as defined by recent sociological analyses. Should this prove so, then the sect model provides us with a new perspective from which to view our material, one which will help gestalt the fragmentary data, and which will illumine the cares and concerns of the people who were attracted to Jesus and who formed the nucleus of the Christian communities. It will help us understand the quality of the experience in these communities.[9]

Scroggs then identifies seven characteristics of the sect as an ideal type before going on to show how the early Christian communities in fact exhibited these traits. The traits are that the sect (i) originates in protest against economic and societal repression, (ii) rejects the

---

[7] On the wider front see T. F. Best, 'The Sociological Study of the New Testament: Promise and Peril of a New Discipline', *Scottish Journal of Theology* 36 (1983), 181–94; also S. K. Stowers, 'The Social Sciences and the Study of Early Christianity', in W. S. Green, ed., *Approaches to Ancient Judaism*, vol. 5 (Chico: Scholars Press, 1985), 149–81.

[8] In J. Neusner, ed., *Christianity, Judaism and Other Greco-Roman Cults*, pt 2 (Leiden: E. J. Brill, 1975), 1–23.

[9] Ibid. 2–3.

values and ideology of the establishment, (iii) adopts a counter-cultural, egalitarian ethos according to which status distinctions in 'the world' are left behind, (iv) offers adherents love and acceptance not found outside, (v) exists as a voluntary association to which members belong by conviction and conversion rather than by birth, (vi) demands total commitment maintained by group discipline, and (vii) is often adventist or apocalyptic in its orientation on history.[10]

Setting aside the Acts of the Apostles as 'late, tendentious, and offer[ing] few traditions that can be sociologically evaluated',[11] and disregarding Paul's letters as well, Scroggs focuses on the Gospel traditions, and finds in them evidence of the seven characteristics of the sect he has just elaborated. Jesus was the leader of a protest movement of the predominantly socially and economically dis-possessed; the movement he inaugurated rejected and was in turn rejected by society at large and by the official establishment; within the movement, communal life was organized on strongly egalitarian, anti-hierarchical lines, and members found love and mutual acceptance; membership was voluntary and totally demanding; and so on.[12] So Scroggs concludes:

> [T]he earliest church meets all the essential characteristics of the religious sect. . . . The use I have made of Synoptic pericopae in this paper illustrates how the gestalt changes the way the material is viewed. The church becomes from this perspective not a theological seminary but a group of people who have experienced the hurt of the world and the healing of communal acceptance. The perspective . . . helps us to see that the church in its own way dealt with the problems individuals faced in repressive social circumstances.[13]

What are we to make of this early stab at a sociological analysis of early Christianity in terms of the sect model? Its strength lies in its bold attempt to wrest the New Testament documents from what Scroggs sees as the narrow concerns of dogmatic theology or the romanticizing tendencies of Christian piety, and to show that these documents bear testimony to the often harrowing real-life situations of communities of believers trying to protest against or come to terms with the harsh political, economic and religious

[10] Ibid. 3–7.
[11] Ibid. 8, n. 26.
[12] Ibid. 19–21.
[13] Ibid. 21.

realities of life in the world of their time. Interpreting the early church in sectarian terms allows us to recapture the innovative, countercultural, protest dimension at the very core of the Christian heritage: and this may function as a corrective or rebuke to conservative religious establishments today. Says Scroggs: 'Traditional Christianity, full of support for law and order . . has lost all feeling for the sectarian protest of the earliest church. From the standpoint of sectarian reality, however, the death of Jesus offers a powerful symbolism for the outcast and alienated.'[14]

But there are weaknesses to this kind of approach as well. Above all, it is quite clear from the article that Scroggs's sociological analysis is wedded to his own theological and ideological agenda. There is no sense in which Scroggs hides his light under a bushel on this score. In the second sentence of his essay, for example, he refers to 'the poison of over-theologizing which has been characteristic of so much New Testament scholarship during the neo-orthodox era'.[15] It is by no means coincidental that he finds the sect model so apposite for interpreting early Christianity, for his own ecclesiology is one of the church as a protest movement from below standing over against the conservative values of the establishment. Is it the case, then, that Scroggs has chosen a model to produce a result which he has arrived at already on other grounds? Do we not have here a classic example of the problem of the hermeneutical circle, and, if we are predisposed not to accept Scroggs's own theological and ecclesiological presuppositions, shall we not want to say that the hermeneutical circle is a vicious one? Will not those who suspect that sociological analysis generally is little more than an ideological tool of the political Left or Right have their suspicions confirmed? What claims to be explanatory turns out in practice to be not-so-subtle ideological rhetoric.

Even if we accept that the sect model may throw new light on Christian origins, there are other weaknesses in Scroggs's analysis. Briefly, they are as follows. First, there is the problem of gross oversimplification. On the one hand, the idea of the sect itself is described in a very general and monolithic way, so that it is hardly surprising that the early church can be described as sectarian, especially when one begins to suspect that the characteristics of the ideal type have been taken from early Christianity in the first place!

[14] Ibid. 22.
[15] Ibid. 1.

On the other hand, early Christianity is described also in a general and monolithic way as a peasant protest movement reacting against oppression and marginalization from an equally undifferentiated body called 'the establishment'. There is little sense in what Scroggs says of either the diversity of identity in early Christianity, or of the diversity – often of a quite sectarian kind, perhaps – within Judaism. So, as a tool of analysis, the sect model as used by Scroggs seems to be a very blunt one indeed.

Second, if the sect as an ideal type is used to 'help gestalt the fragmentary data',[16] it functions also to block other data out. So general are the characteristics of the sect, so loaded are they with evaluative terms – like 'protest', 'counterculture', 'egalitarian', 'love and acceptance', 'voluntary' and 'commitment' – that a powerful rhetoric may blind us to other data and other possibilities of interpretation. So, for example, Scroggs can do little with evidence that the socio-economic status and socio-ecological location of the early Christians was variable,[17] since his model assumes agrarian impoverishment and protest from below. His omission of the evidence of Acts is significant in this regard. Likewise, evidence that the early Christians shared the values, practices and prejudices of the society at large passes unmentioned. The admonition in Matthew 17.24–27 to continue to pay the temple tax does not sit easily with the anti-establishment sect model. Nor, in the same Gospel, does the role diversity and status differentiation implied in what is said about Peter (cf. Matt 16.17–19) or in what is said about the 'prophet' and 'scribe' (cf. Matt 10.41; 13.52) fit well with the idea of the sect as egalitarian.

Third, early Christian beliefs and doctrines assume an epiphenomenal status in Scroggs's analysis. What 'really' matters are social and economic relations and the formation of communities of protest. In short, in reacting against what he sees as a kind of theological reductionism, Scroggs leaves little place for an early Christian theological consciousness at all. No one is likely to dispute Scroggs's claim that the early church was not a theological seminary, but it is highly questionable to imply that matters of doctrine, scriptural interpretation, spiritual discernment and (what we would call) ethics were not a constant focus of attention. Well before

[16] Ibid. 3.

[17] On which see, for example, A. J. Malherbe, *Social Aspects of Early Christianity* (Philadelphia: Fortress Press 1983[2]), 29–59.

Scroggs's article, at least one ancient historian saw fit to write a major essay depicting the early Christians as a 'scholastic community'.[18] It is arguable that the designation 'scholastic community' does more justice to certain aspects, at least, of the evidence about early Christianity than does the designation 'sect'.

2. Wayne Meeks on the Fourth Gospel

We turn, next, from social-scientific criticism of the Synoptic traditions to work done on the Fourth Gospel. Roughly contemporary with Robin Scroggs's work is an important and influential essay by Wayne Meeks, entitled 'The Man from Heaven in Johannine Sectarianism', published in 1972.[19] Here Meeks argues that a major clue to the distinctiveness of this Gospel – and of its discourses in particular – lies not so much in *religionsgeschichtlich* factors to do with John's indebtedness or otherwise to gnosticism or heterodox Judaism, but in sociological factors to do with the kind of community to which the Gospel is addressed. The distinctiveness of the discourses is to be sought, not so much in the history of ideas, as in the social function of the Gospel's persistently riddling, repetitive, opaque, symbolic and mythological language. To outsiders – even sympathetic ones like Nicodemus – what Jesus says is a cause of misunderstanding and offence: to insiders it is divine revelation. Just as the Jesus of John is a stranger to the world and even to his own people, so too is the Johannine community. Meeks sums up his thesis thus:

> *The book functions for its readers in precisely the same way that the epiphany of its hero functions within its narratives and dialogues.* . . . In telling the story of the Son of Man who came down from heaven and then re-ascended after choosing a few of his own out of the world, the book defines and vindicates the existence of the community that evidently sees itself as unique, alien from its world, under attack, misunderstood, but living in unity with Christ and through him with God. It could hardly be regarded as a missionary tract, for we may imagine that only a very rare outsider would get past the barrier of its closed metaphorical system. It is a book for insiders.[20]

[18] See E. A. Judge, 'The Early Christians as a Scholastic Community', *Journal of Religious History* 1 (1960–1), 4–15, 125–37.

[19] In *Journal of Biblical Literature* 91 (1972), 44–72. My references are to the reprinted version in J. Ashton, ed., *The Interpretation of John* (London/Philadelphia: SPCK/Fortress Press 1986), 141–73.

[20] Meeks, 'Sectarianism', 162–3 (author's emphasis).

Meeks is not alone in his view that the Fourth Gospel betrays a
sectarian, in-group consciousness. Among others who take this view
we may cite J. Louis Martyn, Raymond Brown, Fernando Segovia
and David Rensberger.[21] D. Moody Smith reflects a widely held
consensus when he says:

> ... it can probably be agreed that on any reading of the Gospel and
> Epistles there appears a sectarian consciousness, a sense of exclusiveness,
> a sharp delineation of the community from the world. . . . Comparisons
> with community consciousness in Qumran, which is likewise related to
> a fundamental dualism, are entirely apposite and to the point.[22]

Interpreting the Johannine literature in sectarian terms has much
to commend it. It helps to explain the vilification of 'the Jews' and
the strong sense of mutual hostility between them and believers in
Jesus. The hostility is so sharp and the possibility of accommodation
so meagre because, like an argument in the family, each side knows
the other only too well and the psycho-social stakes are too high. It
helps also to make sense of the uncompromising exclusiveness
of Johannine christology and soteriology, whereby now, Jesus exclusively is the way to the Father, not Torah.

At the same time, the sect model makes intelligible the hints
we are given of the ethos of the Johannine community, in spite
of the absence of any explicit ecclesiology. I have in mind, for
example, the strongly centripetal character of the love commandment; the emphasis on humility and equality in interpersonal
relations dramatized in the episode of the footwashing (Jn 13.1–
20); the predominant orientation of the Johannine symbols on
nurture, sustenance, abiding and unity; the charismatic emphasis
on the availability of the Spirit-Paraclete to the members of the
group; and the overwhelmingly pessimistic outlook on relations with
'the world' and its institutional manifestations, whether Jewish or
Roman.

What distinguishes Meeks's use of social science categories
from that of Scroggs? Primarily the fact that in Meeks's hands the

---

[21] J. Louis Martyn, *History and Theology in the Fourth Gospel* (Nashville: Abingdon,
1968, 1979²); R. E. Brown, *The Community of the Beloved Disciple* (New York: Paulist
Press, 1979); F. F. Segovia, *Love Relationships in the Johannine Tradition* (Chico:
Scholars Press, 1982); D. Rensberger, *Johannine Faith and Liberating Community*
(Philadelphia: Fortress Press 1988).

[22] D. M. Smith, 'Johannine Christianity: Some Reflections on its Character and
Delineation', *New Testament Studies* 21 (1975), 224–48 at 223–4.

social-science tools are used in a much more refined way, such that explanation of the data is not confused with political and religious advocacy. Instead of imposing a rather undifferentiated sect model on a similarly undifferentiated range of Gospel textual data, Meeks begins with a widely recognized literary and hermeneutical puzzle in Johannine studies (i.e. how to explain the 'special patterns of language' of the Johannine Christ, including the motif of the ascending and descending redeemer), demonstrates the inadequacy of previous *religionsgeschichtlich* attempts to solve the puzzle, and then draws in perspectives from the structuralist anthropology of Edmund Leach in order to suggest that a solution to the puzzle can be found if the model of interpretation shifts from the theological and historical to the sociological, to how mythological language functions in the communities who use it. Meeks says:

> It is only, therefore, by paying attention to the underlying structure of the components in a system of myths that an interpreter can 'hear' what the myths are 'saying' or, to put it another way, can discover the function which the myths have within the group in which they are at home. It is astonishing that attempts to solve the Johannine puzzle have almost totally ignored the question of what *social* function the myth may have had.[23]

So Meeks uses a very specific social scientific tool of analysis to help resolve a very specific problem of interpretation. And he chooses a tool of analysis which has, arguably, a natural congruence or compatibility with the literary puzzle he is working to solve. Unlike Scroggs, he resists the temptation to claim too much for his model or to try to do too much with it. The sociological dimension helpfully supplements the theological and historical dimensions without being in such danger of reducing them to the epiphenomenal.[24]

Nevertheless, having seen how strong is the sect model in relation to John, how suggestive it is for the attempt of the historical and sociological imagination to relate Johannine christology to Johannine community, it is important also to highlight some of the weaknesses, problems or unanswered questions. There is, for

---

[23] Meeks, 'Sectarianism', 144–5 (author's emphasis).

[24] I notice that Mark Stibbe also finds Meeks's approach a persuasive and important advance in Johannine interpretation, in *John as Storyteller: Narrative Criticism and the Fourth Gospel* (Cambridge: Cambridge University Press, 1992), esp. 61–3.

example, the persistent problem, not at all unique to the interpretation of John, of drawing sociological inferences from a very small literary deposit, even if we include the Johannine Epistles as well. Meeks's claim, extended to an extreme degree by Raymond Brown in *The Community of the Beloved Disciple*, that the story of the Johannine Jesus is, in effect, a cypher for the history and sociology of the Johannine community is creative and imaginative, certainly. But it must be questioned whether or not interpreting the Gospel narrative as a kind of allegory of the Johannine community runs too great a risk of finding what is not there or what, by the nature of the evidence, cannot be found.

Certainly, the evidence is ambiguous, and that alone should give us reason for caution. Meeks makes a lot, for example, of the sectarian, 'us-versus-them', consciousness which can be read off the encounter between Jesus and Nicodemus, in John 3.[25] But it may be questioned whether Nicodemus is cast in the outsider role which Meeks attributes to him; whether also he plays the role of an uncomprehending fool – any more, say, than a Samaritan woman or a Thomas or a Peter; and whether what is being conveyed in the dialogue is only that Jesus is incomprehensible, as Meeks claims. A more sympathetic reading is certainly possible, and if it is, then a crack begins to appear in Meeks's sectarian edifice. Notably, Raymond Brown, who is at most points sympathetic to Meeks's approach, says of Nicodemus that '[his] role is not to illustrate or personify the attitudes of a contemporary group in the Johannine experience, but to show how some who were attracted to Jesus did not immediately understand him'.[26]

Doubt may also be cast on Meeks's claim that the Fourth Gospel shows all the signs of being a 'book for insiders', since 'only a very rare outsider would get past the barrier of its closed metaphorical system'.[27] This strikes me as a *tour de force*. On this view, it is a wonder that anyone made it into the Johannine community at all! Are metaphors like *logos*, light, bread, living water, good shepherd, true vine, Son of God, and so on – each of them with deep roots in the biblical and Jewish traditions and not without a certain currency in the wider Hellenistic milieu, either – as opaque as Meeks makes them out to be? If they are not, and if we recall in addition the

[25] Meeks, 'Sectarianism', 147–52.
[26] Brown, *Community*, 72 n. 128.
[27] Meeks, 'Sectarianism', 163.

strong, universalizing missionary thrust of John, then a further crack appears in Meeks's sociological interpretation.

An important caution is constituted also by Martin Hengel's book *The Johannine Question*.[28] Whereas Meeks insists in his essay that 'the Johannine literature is the product not of a lone genius but of a community or group of communities that evidently persisted with some consistent identity over a considerable span of time',[29] Hengel argues that a single theological genius does indeed lie behind the Johannine corpus and that claims that the Fourth Gospel is somehow a community product are spurious. Hengel does not deny that the Gospel and Epistles took shape in a communal context. For Hengel, however, this context is best understood as a school of disciples over which John the elder presided for many years. It is not some anonymous sectarian consciousness that explains the distinctiveness of the Johannine material, therefore, but the creative theological activity of John. Says Hengel:

> Here, then, was a towering creative teacher who ventured with reference to the activity of the Spirit Paraclete to paint a quite different picture of the activity and proclamation of Jesus from that which we can see in the Synoptic tradition, and who introduced the post-Easter pre-existence and exaltation christology quite massively into his description of the Galilean master. We must assume that such a 'theologian', who was the opposite of a mere tradent did not fix the dialectical positions that he expressed at one stage once and for all as inviolable principles. In a specific situation of crisis he ventured to take up new focal points and even in some circumstances to correct himself – dialectically. . . . That such a teacher possessing the highest authority and with rich experience going back over two generations could react sharply and clearly to a controversy with a group of pupils who were adapting themselves to 'the spirit of the time' is not surprising. In his view these former pupils of his (and their seducers coming from outside) threatened the existence of his school and all the Christian communities in Asia.[30]

Significantly, Hengel makes no mention of Meeks's prior essay; and, as with our evaluation of Robin Scroggs's position, we are left wondering whether an alternative social model, more firmly grounded historically – that of the school – is not more convincing

[28] M. Hengel, *The Johannine Question* (London: SCM Press, 1989).
[29] Meeks, 'Sectarianism', 145.
[30] Hengel, *Question*, 104–5.

than that of the religious sect. Be that as it may, Hengel's study is a powerful reminder that Meeks's basically functionalist sociological interpretation shows a tendency towards determinism in its account of the relation between text and community and that it may be in danger of leaving insufficient room for the role of the creative individual, the evangelist himself.[31]

Interestingly, C. K. Barrett, in the second edition of his massive commentary on John (published in 1978), does not refer to Meeks's essay either (even though he does make wide use of Meeks's 1967 monograph *The Prophet-King*)! I do not know why this is so. Perhaps it has something to do with a reticence in British biblical scholarship – at least in the 1970s – to consider seriously the possibilities for interpretation opened up by the social sciences. Perhaps it is explained by the likelihood that Barrett holds to a different view of the purpose of John, where the emphasis lies not on the influence of sociological factors so much as on the primacy of theological considerations, especially the evangelist's concern to present a universalizing articulation of the Christian message. As Barrett says in an article on 'St John: Social Historian': 'Undoubtedly it is true that we must look to John for theology rather than sociology' – even though he immediately qualifies this by adding, 'But this is not quite all. Few works of theology are generated within an exclusively theological environment, and the great works of theology have owed a good deal to their social environment.'[32] That Barrett's position seems to be shifting is reflected in his essay of 1989 for the Eduard Lohse *Festschrift*, where he argues that we are likely to misunderstand the nature of Christian community (both then and now) unless we take seriously the fact that in its origins it had characteristics both of the school and of the conventicle or sect.[33] But this is still a long way – and with good reason, perhaps? – from a systematic attempt to interpret the Johannine corpus in terms of the sociology of sectarianism. Barrett appears to share with Hengel an overriding commitment to historical-contextual and traditio-historical method in a form which is exclusive of sociological analysis,

---

[31] For an important critique of Meeks's functionalist sociology see Stowers, 'Social Sciences', *passim*.

[32] C. K. Barrett, 'St. John: Social Historian', *Proceedings of the Irish Biblical Association* 10 (1986), 26–39 at 26.

[33] C. K. Barrett, 'School, Conventicle, and Church in the New Testament', in K. Aland and S. Meurer, eds, *Wissenschaft und Kirche: Festschrift für E. Lohse* (Bielefeld: Luther-Verlag, 1989), 96–110.

even though, confusingly, both writers are prepared at times to use sociological terminology.[34]

A quite different kind of problem, not just with Meeks's interpretation but with sociological and social science interpretations generally, is whether or not interpreting John in the light of the sociology of the sect is a *distraction* in the reading of the text. This can be put in a number of ways. But in general terms, the point is that whether or not a method or model of interpretation is valid depends upon who is doing the reading and for what purpose.

Thus, from the viewpoint of certain forms of literary criticism, meaning lies within the narrative world of the text and is generated by the interaction of the reader and the autonomous text.[35] It is what happens on *this* side of the text which is important, not the prehistory of the text or claims about communities or whatever lying *behind* the text, claims which in any case have no way of being substantiated. On this view, Meeks's attempt to establish a correlation between distinctive and disturbing features of the gospel and a distinctive, sectarian community lying behind the gospel are futile and ill-conceived. Rather, the meaning of the text is literary and aesthetic. It does not depend on referentiality outside the text. The *aporiae* of the text are not an invitation to hypothesize about the social function of the language: they are a provocation to the imagination and aesthetic sensibilities of the reader.

Another way this objection can be put comes from the perspective of canonical criticism. According to this approach, what is of central validity for interpretation is the meaning of John's Gospel as part of the canon of Scripture and as the fourth of the four Gospels. Here, what is important is to hear the written words in the way in which they have been heard traditionally in the life and worship of the church – as Scripture and as gospel, the Word of God. Historical-exegetical methodology may contribute to the reader's appreciation of what the text meant to its original readers and listeners, and sociological analysis may help to explain the social and communal dialectic of which the text is somehow a product, but valid interpretation in terms of canonical criticism will accord these approaches subordinate status only and will acknowledge only

[34] One thinks, for example, of Hengel's monograph *Nachfolge und Charisma* (Berlin: de Gruyter, 1968), translated into English by J. C. G. Greig as *The Charismatic Leader and His Followers* (Edinburgh: T&T Clark, 1981).
[35] For an authoritative account see Stephen Moore, *Literary Criticism and the Gospels: The Theoretical Challenge* (New Haven: Yale University Press, 1989).

an indirect relationship between canonical interpretation and historical or sociological interpretations. For what is important above all is hearing the text itself as Scripture, addressed to every successive generation. Thus, Brevard Childs, in discussing John 9, a text which J. L. Martyn had made the centre of his very valuable attempt to reconstruct the history of the Johannine community 'behind' the text, says:

> There is a wide consensus that Martyn has greatly illuminated the text by seeing it in relation to the expulsion from the synagogue. . . . Yet the crucial hermeneutical issue remains whether Martyn has correctly assessed the canonical function of this material within the final shape of the text. . . . I would argue that to take the canonical shape of the Gospel seriously is to recognize that the text's authoritative, kerygmatic witness is not identical with its historical development, but must be discerned from the literary form of the text itself.[36]

Now, it is unfair of course to judge Meeks's work and the work of others in the same line according to the criteria of models of interpretation which they do not employ. However, the more modest point is worth making: that what you see depends upon where you stand. As we have seen, from at least one literary-critical point of view, the social function of a text in its original historical context is not relevant to the art of interpretation. And from the point of view of canonical criticism, the claim that the Gospel of John betrays a sectarian consciousness is a distraction.

3. *Philip Esler on Luke–Acts*

Up until recently, Luke–Acts has been read either as a source for reconstructing the history of the early church or as a theological narrative designed to convey the evangelist's response to the doctrinal and existential dilemmas of his readers in the last decades of the first century. Attempts to give a sociological interpretation of Luke's two volumes have been almost entirely lacking. Philip Esler's book, *Community and Gospel in Luke–Acts: The Social and Political Motivations of Lucan Theology*, published in 1987,[37] is an important attempt to fill this gap, and heavy use is made of the sociology of sectarianism.

---

[36] Brevard S. Childs, *The New Testament as Canon: An Introduction* (London: SCM Press, 1984), 133.

[37] Cambridge: Cambridge University Press, 1987.

In company with redaction critics, Esler does not see Luke as a disinterested recorder of the story of Jesus and the early church. Nor, however, is Luke to be seen as some kind of armchair theologian 'who ponders over purely religious questions before issuing forth from his scriptorium to enlighten his fellow-Christians as to the correct attitude which they and their community should adopt to their social and political environment'.[38] Rather, as the book's subtitle suggests, Luke's is applied theology from the start, motivated by strong social and political interests, and written for a specific historical community whose needs are as much material as spiritual.

Using a method he calls 'socio-redaction criticism', Esler argues that Luke–Acts is best interpreted as written to provide legitimation for a Christian community whose relations with both the synagogue community and the wider Gentile society are fraught with the inevitable tensions and pressures arising from the Christian group's sectarian status.[39] Luke's theological narrative is given a strongly functionalist orientation: it legitimates and justifies the beliefs and practices of his group over against those of alternative social worlds which have been left behind at conversion. To quote Esler:

> One obvious way to provide the necessary reassurance, to legitimate the sectarian status of his *ekklesia*, was for Luke to write a history of the beginnings of Christianity which pinned the blame for the subsequent split firmly on the Jews, especially their leaders, and which explained and justified early developments, such as Jewish-Gentile table-fellowship, which were still of significance to his Christian contemporaries. From this viewpoint, history is important for Luke not, as Conzelmann suggests, as a replacement for the imminent expectation of the early church, but as a way of accounting for the present situation of his community. In other words, the key to Lucan historiography is not eschatology but etiology.[40]

The picture of Luke's community which emerges is a fascinating one. Contrary to the widely held view that Luke's audience is Gentile, Esler argues that many in Luke's group are converts from Judaism or Gentile God-fearers. The reason for Luke's interest in table fellowship is to legitimate Jew–Gentile commensality in his community and to maintain Jew–Gentile cohesion in the face of strong opposition from synagogue Jews and Jewish Christians who see the

[38] Esler, *Community*, 1.
[39] See esp. Esler, *Community*, ch. 3.
[40] Ibid. 67.

practice as a threat to the identity of the Jewish *ethnos*. An essential
'sectarian strategy' adopted by Luke is to defend the practice by
appealing to, and rewriting, history. The great apostles Peter and
James, together with the Jerusalem church, are portrayed now by
Luke as giving their backing to Jew–Gentile table fellowship.

A similar interpretation is placed upon other major themes of
Luke–Acts – the status of the Jewish law, the place of the temple,
attitudes to poverty and wealth, and attitudes to Roman authority.
In each case, Esler argues that Luke's writing betrays strong political
and social concerns which reflect both the socially and religiously
mixed character of his community and its vulnerability as a sect to
pressures from outside, above all from Judaism. In the chapter
entitled 'The Poor and the Rich', for instance, Esler argues that
Luke developed a specific theology of poverty in order to address
the problems of social stratification and economic disparity which
threatened the fellowship; and Esler is sharp in his criticism of
'spiritualizing' and 'individualizing' interpretations. He says:

> That the Lucan Gospel imposes on the rich an indispensable require-
> ment, quite at odds with the social values of their own society, to provide
> the destitute with food and other necessities of life in this world sounds
> the death-knell over all such interpretations of his theology as, affected
> by middle-class bias, present salvation as a reality reserved for the
> individual in the after-life.[41]

Esler certainly gives the lie to Scroggs's curious claim, noted
earlier, that Luke's writings, especially the Acts, offer few traditions
that can be sociologically evaluated. The sect typology of Bryan
Wilson and the model of sect development opened up by H. Richard
Niebuhr are used to powerful explanatory effect in Esler's study to
bring to our attention plausible social and political interests which
lie behind and shape Luke–Acts.

However, once again, several critical questions need to be
asked. First, there is the fundamental question of the purpose of
Luke–Acts. Esler's interpretative method appears analogous to a
'hermeneutics of suspicion' approach to the text. Luke–Acts is
not really an account of the past in order that his benefactor,
Theophilus, may know the truth, as the author claims (cf. Lk 1.1–
4). Rather, it is a coded address to a sectarian community, providing legitimation and justification for its alternative identity and

[41] Ibid. 199.

lifestyle over against its parent body in Judaism. History is not history, but propaganda. Theology is not theology, but the ideology of an oppressed group. This may be putting the point too sharply. But the issue is an important one. It is the question of whether a social-science model intended for purposes of sociological explanation is being used illegitimately to describe things from the native's point of view. Luke thought he was doing one thing: but in fact he was doing another.

Second, there is the related question, raised earlier, of the legitimacy of interpreting the text as a mirror of the (in this case) Lucan community. This question has been asked explicitly by another Lucan scholar who has worked also on a theme of interest to Esler – namely, the subject of the poor and the rich.[42] In his essay, 'On Finding the Lukan Community: A Cautious Cautionary Tale', published in 1979,[43] Luke Johnson makes a number of useful observations. First, not even in the interpretation of Paul's letters, occasional as they are and written to specific communities about identifiable problems, has there been unqualified success in drawing inferences from the letters about the social situation of the addressees. The Letter to the Romans is a particular case in point. Johnson puts it this way:

> The study of Paul's letters reminds us that even in documents of a genuinely occasional nature, not every element in the document is determined by the place, the people, or the occasion. Some things are there because of the demands of genre, the impetus of tradition, the logic of argumentation, the inertia of scriptural citations, and the idiosyncratic perceptions of the author. Responsible exegesis takes these factors into account *before* using passages as a mirror to community problems.[44]

Turning from Paul to mirror readings of the Gospels, Johnson questions the common assumption that the pastoral and theo-logical concerns of an evangelist are determined by a situation of crisis among his readers: 'Reading everything in the Gospel narratives as immediately addressed to a contemporary crisis reduces

---

[42] See L. T. Johnson, *The Literary Function of Possessions in Luke–Acts* (Missoula: Scholars Press, 1977), and compare Esler, *Community*, ch. 7.

[43] L. T. Johnson, 'On Finding the Lukan Community: A Cautious Cautionary Tale', in P. J. Achtemeier, ed., *SBL 1979 Seminar Papers Volume I* (Missoula: Scholars Press, 1979), 87–100.

[44] Johnson, 'Tale', 89 (author's emphasis).

them to the level of cryptograms, and the evangelists to the level of tractarians.'[45] In regard to Luke–Acts in particular, he argues that the difficulties of mirror-reading are even more acute: the author's identity is unknown; the addressee is an individual not a church; due weight has to be given to the influence of the tradition and to Luke's professed intention to write a historical account; due weight has to be given also to differences between Luke's two volumes, differences which must complicate attempts to 'read off' the community from the text; and there is clear evidence of literary artifice in Luke's writing. Above all – and Johnson has applied this principle in his own study of the motif of possessions – it is the literary function of a theme or motif in the text which has to be taken most seriously: 'Given a fairly intricate and intelligible literary structure which, taken as a whole, conveys a coherent message, our *first* assumption with regard to individual parts within that structure should not be that they point to a specific community problem, but that they are in service to the larger literary goal of the author.'[46]

One or two final observations are worth making before we leave this particular case study. Although Esler's work is much more sophisticated than the essay of Scroggs, it may not avoid completely some of the same pitfalls. Is the sect-church typology so wedded to the problems of modernity that it lacks a necessary affinity with the subject matter to which it is being applied? It may be significant that the more recent collection of thirteen American essays on *The Social World of Luke–Acts: Models for Interpretation* makes no use at all of the sect model, preferring instead models primarily from the discipline of social anthropology.[47] Does the sect-church typology contain an implicit anti-Judaism, by casting Judaism as the monolithic, static, unreformed 'church' from which the Christian 'reform movement' separated and became a sect? Does it help the explanatory task to categorize the putative Lucan community as, not a thaumaturgic sect (although Luke–Acts arguably contains a stronger thaumaturgic interest than any other New Testament text), nor a revolutionary sect (although an imminent-end eschatology is not suppressed completely in Luke–Acts), but a conversionist sect where personal repentance and acceptance of the

---

[45] Ibid. 90.

[46] Ibid. 92 (author's emphasis).

[47] See J. H. Neyrey, ed., *The Social World of Luke–Acts: Models for Interpretation* (Peabody: Hendrickson, 1991).

gospel accompanied (mostly) by baptism is at the heart of things? Do not such types – general and approximate as they are – generate as many difficulties as they solve? And does their application to Luke–Acts not obscure the fact that the Greek word closest to what we mean by *sect* – namely, *hairesis* – is the word that Luke apparently chooses *not* to apply to Christianity, although well aware of its currency?[48] For Luke, the word *hodos* ('way') more aptly captures the identity and self-understanding of the new movement,[49] and *ekklesia* is the word he uses both for the local Christian community (e.g. Acts 5.11; 8.1, 3) and for all the local groups treated as a single whole (e.g. Acts 9.31; 20.28). Of course, it is inappropriate to accuse Esler of using categories for explanation which are not native and which a native would not recognize. The trouble with the category 'sect', however, is that, because of its roots in the Christian tradition, it hovers uneasily between being a native (emic) category, on the one hand, and a scientific (etic) category, on the other, so that it is difficult to be sure that it is being used in the value-neutral, scientific way claimed.

III. Conclusion

I have attempted in the foregoing case studies to give a critical assessment of three major essays which use the sociology of sects and sectarianism as a heuristic device for explaining the social dynamics of earliest Christianity. Other examples could have been chosen, if for no other reason than to demonstrate how strong is the current consensus that the sect model throws important light on Christian origins.

On Matthew, there is J. Andrew Overman's book *Matthew's Gospel and Formative Judaism*, which argues that this Gospel represents the uncompromising response of a minority messianic sect to the growing dominance of what he calls 'formative Judaism' in the post-70 period, and that the whole period in Judaism between 165 BCE

[48] Cf. Acts 5.17; 15.5; 26.5 for uses in relation to Judaism, and Acts 24.5, 14; 28.22 for its application by outsiders to Christianity. According to Barrett ('School', 104), 'It is clear from these passages that Luke is familiar with the application of *hairesis* to the Jewish groups of Pharisees, Sadducees, and Essenes, and that he does not himself choose to apply it to Christianity, though he knows that others did so.'

[49] Note Acts 9.2; 19.9, 23; 22.4; 24.14, 22; and cf. 2.28; 13.10; 16.17; 18.25, 26 – cited in Barrett, 'School', 103.

and 100 CE can be characterized as sectarian and factional.[50] On Mark, there is Howard Kee's monograph *Community of the New Age*, which argues that Mark's audience is a missionary sect whose world view is indebted to Jewish apocalyptic, and whose voluntaristic, inclusive and charismatic ethos is markedly at odds with dominant social mores.[51] On Paul, the work of Wayne Meeks is to the fore again, first in a stimulating essay on 'Group Boundaries in Pauline Christianity',[52] and most substantially in his book *The First Urban Christians*[53] – although it is noteworthy that both works eschew systematic application of any one social science model out of preference for a more eclectic, pragmatic approach.[54] Much more systematic in applying the sect model to Paul is Francis Watson's *Paul, Judaism and the Gentiles: A Sociological Approach*, published in 1986.[55] Taking the application of the sect model further, from the Pauline into the post-Pauline literature and setting, is Margaret MacDonald's *The Pauline Churches*.[56] This study uses the sociology of the sect to analyse and explain the churches' attitude to the world, and, like Esler on the Lucan community, sees the churches of Paul as a conversionist sect. According to MacDonald, the Pastoral Epistles represent the development, along Troeltschean sect–church lines, of a church-type community. Finally, but by no means exhaustively, there is J. H. Elliott's study of 1 Peter, which has been influential in sociological interpretations of the New Testament,

[50] J. A. Overman, *Matthew's Gospel and Formative Judaism: The Social World of the Matthean Community* (Minneapolis: Fortress Press, 1990). Diverse perspectives on Matthew as sectarian are taken in the essays by Gundry and White in the important volume edited by D. L. Balch, *Social History of the Matthean Community: Cross-Disciplinary Approaches* (Minneapolis: Fortress Press, 1991). Cf. also Graham Stanton's essay on 'Matthew's Gospel and the Damascus Document', in his *A Gospel for a New People: Studies in Matthew* (Edinburgh: T&T Clark, 1992), arguing that both texts are written for sectarian communities in sharp conflict with parent bodies from which they have separated recently.

[51] London: SCM Press, 1977.

[52] W. A. Meeks, '"Since then you would need to go out of the world": Group Boundaries in Pauline Christianity', in T. J. Ryan, ed., *Critical History and Biblical Faith: New Testament Perspectives* (Villanova: College Theology Society, 1979), 1–23.

[53] W. A. Meeks, *The First Urban Christians: The Social World of the Apostle Paul* (New Haven/London: Yale University Press, 1983).

[54] Cf. also Meeks's book, *The Moral World of the First Christians* (London: SPCK, 1987), 98–108.

[55] Cambridge: Cambridge University Press, 1986.

[56] M. Y. MacDonald, *The Pauline Churches: A Socio-historical Study of Institutionalization in the Pauline and Deutero-Pauline Writings* (Cambridge: Cambridge University Press, 1988).

not least in the works of Esler and MacDonald.[57] In *A Home for the Homeless* Elliott argues that the addressees of 1 Peter are marginalized 'resident aliens' (*paroikoi*) of Asia Minor whose conversion has increased the antagonism of the native residents towards them. They constitute, therefore, a conversionist sect in tension with the society at large. The strategy of the letter is to confirm the believers in their social and religious separation from outsiders and to emphasize their incorporation into an alternative family, the *oikos tou theou* ('household of God': cf. 1 Pet 2.5; 4.17).[58]

The overwhelming benefit of these studies is that they draw explicit attention to the kinds of social dynamics, factors and forces likely to have been influential in shaping the identity, self-understanding, thought-forms and behaviour of the earliest Christians. The sect model helps to explain why the New Testament texts show such persistent interest in defining and maintaining group boundaries, why priority is given to mission and conversion, why opponents are vilified, why ties of natural kinship are deprecated in favour of ties of spiritual kinship,[59] why exclusive claims are made for Jesus as 'messiah' and 'lord', why persecution and ostracism is the Christian believer's common experience, why an inner reform movement of Judaism very soon took on a separate identity, and so on.

However, while the consensus may be impressive, there are also grounds for caution. I mention two, by way of reiteration and conclusion. First, if it is possible to conclude that early Christianity of just about every hue was sectarian – Matthean as well as Marcan and Lucan, Johannine as well as Pauline and Petrine – we are forced to conclude that the category 'sect' has only relatively weak explanatory power.[60] Even with the kinds of refinements of the typology introduced by Bryan Wilson, it does not make possible the discrimination between the Christian groups – or within them – which is necessary to do justice to the evidence. Nor, it should be

---

[57] J. H. Elliott, *A Home for the Homeless: A Sociological Exegesis of I Peter* (Philadelphia: Fortress Press 1981).

[58] For a different analysis of 1 Peter, which was published in the same year as Elliott's book, but which interprets the Petrine household code as intended to promote greater *integration* into Graeco-Roman society, see D. L. Balch, *Let Wives Be Submissive: The Domestic Code in I Peter* (Chico: Scholars Press, 1981).

[59] I have explored this aspect further in *Discipleship and Family Ties in Mark and Matthew* (Cambridge: Cambridge University Press 1994).

[60] So, too, Holmberg, *Sociology*, 112–13.

added, does it do justice to the wide variety of splinter groups and movements in first-century Judaism, let alone 'the complexities of religious life in the larger Roman Empire'.[61]

Second, the sect—church typology is prone to being made captive to ideological interests of one kind or another. This is due in part to the binary structure of the typology, which makes possible an implicit or explicit opposition between a kind of group or society which is viewed positively and another which is viewed negatively. An anti-establishment, left-wing ideology is likely to use 'sect' as a term of approbation. On the other hand, an establishment ideology is likely to use the term as a way of both identifying and marginalizing the enemy. In between, others may claim that they are using 'sect' in an objective, value-neutral way. But such interpreters, in all likelihood, are supporters of a clearly identifiable liberal ideological agenda and are the heirs of Enlightenment rationality. If there is any truth in the point I am making here, then the limitations, as well as the strengths, of the sect model are even more manifest. To put it another way, use of this model confronts us more clearly than is usually the case with the inevitably political nature of the act of interpretation.[62]

---

[61] White, 'Boundaries', 14.

[62] See further, S. Hauerwas and S. Long, 'Interpreting the Bible as a Political Act', *Religion and Intellectual Life* VI (1989), 134–42. Note also the perceptive comment of White, 'Boundaries', 9: 'All too often the picture has been based on simplistic, idealized, or theologically tendentious reading of the New Testament documents, as in traditional Marxist historiography of early Christianity. It is no less in evidence elsewhere, as in the characteristic equation in Protestant historiography: first-century Judaism is seen by analogy with the medieval Catholic church, against which Jesus and the Reformers were parallel sectarian responses.'

8

Women, Jesus and the Gospels

I. Introduction

The aim of this essay is to give *a Christian theological reading* of the stories about women and Jesus in the canonical Gospels.[1] I put it this way because it is very important to clarify our starting point. First, originally a contribution to a book called *Who Needs Feminism? Men Respond to Sexism in the Church*, this essay springs from my own commitment, experience, learning and teaching within the fellowship of the church. I make no pretence at 'pure objectivity' and 'detachment': for the Christian gospel, in all its particularity, is a call to follow the way of God revealed in Jesus in the power of God's Spirit. This does *not* mean that 'anything goes' as a legitimate reading. On the contrary, it means that our concern to give a fair and responsible – even *obedient* – reading of the Gospels will be all the greater. This is what I mean by calling what follows a *Christian* reading.

Second, my primary concern is not that of the ancient historian. This is not to say that historical information is not important: just that its importance is limited. Unless the story from the past is *interpreted* in a way which shows its meaning for the present and the future, it remains stuck in the past as something of antiquarian value only. This applies also to the story of Jesus in his dealings with the women and men of his time. The narrowly historical question, 'What

---

[1] I wish to express my thanks to my Durham colleagues Ann Loades and Walter Moberly for their comments on an earlier draft of this essay; and to acknowledge the stimulus I have gained from working on feminist biblical hermeneutics with four postgraduate students in the Theology Department: Alison Brown, Musa Dube, Sister Rosemary Howarth CHN and Katie Paul.

was Jesus' attitude to women?', invites the devastating response, 'So what? What does that have to do with what's happening to us now?' There is a danger, in other words, that this narrowly historical question will *trivialize* both Jesus and women. It will trivialize Jesus by treating him as a Plato or a Seneca or a Musonius Rufus, whereas, for Christians, Jesus is the Christ of God who ushers in the kingdom of God. It will trivialize women by treating them merely as a subject of contemplation by a male figure of the past, rather than as people in their own right who share to the full in the story of redemption in Christ.

The Gospel stories about women and Jesus will *speak to us as believers* to the extent that they bear witness to God-in-Christ and to the breaking into human relations of the kingdom of God. It is theology, christology and soteriology which will be normative for the believer, not bare history taken on its own. This is why Jane Williams perceptively says:

> ... the debate about the ministry of women cannot really be carried out along the lines of a debit and credit column: 'Jesus was certainly a man, but, on the other hand, he thought women were important; Jesus did not choose women to be part of the Twelve, but, on the other hand, he *did* choose them to be the first witnesses of the resurrection,' and so on. It is not even any good to be able to demonstrate that Jesus was unusually good to women by the standards of his day ...[2]

This drives the point home strongly: and it is why I have called this essay a *theological* reading rather than a purely historical one. Nevertheless, this does not mean that there is no point in asking historical questions about Jesus and about the roles, status, etc. of women in the first century, nor historical and literary questions about the Gospels. At the very least, such questions can throw up information of a kind which functions as a basic bench-marker. For example, if it could be shown that the teaching of Jesus was irredeemably sexist, that he systematically discriminated against women *per se*, that women were able to respond to Jesus in only hostile ways, and that the qualities for leadership in the early Christian movement were specific to the male sex only, this would constitute a serious problem for those in the church today who wish discrimination against women to end. That there is little such

---

[2] Jane Williams, 'Jesus the Jew and Women', in Monica Furlong, ed., *Feminine in the Church* (London: SPCK, 1984), 86–99 at 97.

evidence is an encouragement to those in favour of women's liberation that they are on the right lines in the way they are interpreting the kingdom of God. So historical evidence can be important, even if only up to a point. It is a question of deciding, as Leslie Houlden points out, 'what arguments are good for what'.[3]

It is important, however, to claim neither too much nor too little for historical investigation. The tendency of conservatives in theology is to claim too much, to *stretch history* in such a way that the past becomes normative for the present without further ado. On this view, once we know 'the attitude of Jesus (or Paul or the author of the Pastoral Epistles) towards women', we know what is to be the place of women in church and society today. (Notoriously, the 'we' here are mostly men!) Theological liberals, on the other hand, tend to claim too little, to *so emphasize the 'gap'* between the present and the past that it becomes difficult for the past – even the past of Jesus – to speak, still, today. If the danger of the conservative approach is to make the present captive to the past, the danger of the liberal approach is to make the past captive to the present.[4]

Interestingly, this tendency to claim either too much or too little for history is a problem in some *Christian feminist writing* as well. Those who (in my view) claim too much for history have a tendency to see Jesus as a first-century 'feminist'[5] who taught and practised a 'discipleship of equals'[6] and sought to bring liberation from oppressive patriarchal structures. Problematic here is the proneness of this approach to special pleading on behalf of Jesus and earliest Christianity over against subsequent (especially post-Pauline) developments, when the patriarchal rot set in. Unfortunate also is the tendency for Judaism, and in particular the treatment of women in Judaism, to become the whipping-boy in this kind of approach, because the roots of sexism in Christianity are traced commonly to

[3] J. L. Houlden, 'The Worth of Arguments', in H. Wilson, ed., *Women Priests? Yes – Now!* (Nutfield, Surrey: Denholm House Press, 1975), 19–26 at 19.

[4] See the profound work of Robert Morgan and John Barton, *Biblical Interpretation* (Oxford: Oxford University Press, 1988).

[5] See W. Klassen, 'Musonius Rufus, Jesus and Paul: Three First-Century Feminists', in P. Richardson and J. C. Hurd, eds, *From Jesus to Paul* (Ontario: Wilfrid Laurier University Press, 1984), 185–206.

[6] The phrase comes from Elisabeth S. Fiorenza, *In Memory of Her* (London: SCM Press, 1983).

'the Jewish background'.[7] Those, on the other hand, who claim too little for history tend to see the entire Christian tradition as so androcentric as to be irredeemable and unredeeming.[8] The effect of this is to cut women (and men) off from the past, from the church, and from the biblical tradition of liberation. Paradoxically, also, it denies the experience of many women themselves.[9]

This brings me to my third, and final, point. What we need instead is a way of reading the Gospel stories about women and Jesus which sees them neither as normative history (which is to claim too much) nor as mere history (which is to claim too little), but as *Christian Scripture*.[10] This means that we take the Gospels with full religious seriousness as foundation elements of our Christian tradition which have a privileged status for us because the church has found them to express something fundamental about the character and will of God. By refering to them as Scripture, we are signalling that the Gospels are texts whose quality of 'sacred persistence'[11] means that they transcend the category 'history' and become the basis for a trustful exegesis in which theologically informed faith, reason, experience and imagination enable their fruitful interpretation and appropriation in the church today. It also suggests, precisely because we are approaching the Gospels as Scripture, that literary methods of appreciating the stories are at least as important as historical methods. This is why I have described my approach as a theological *reading* of the Gospel stories, as distinct from a kind of literary archaeological dig.

[7] This point is made by Bernadette J. Brooten, 'Jewish Women's History in the Roman Period: A Task for Christian Theology', in G. Nickelsburg and G. MacRae, eds, *Christians Among Jews and Gentiles* (Philadelphia: Fortress Press, 1986), 22–30 (esp. 24–6).

[8] See, for example, the position of Daphne Hampson, in Daphne Hampson and Rosemary R. Ruether, 'Is there a Place for Feminists in a Christian Church?', *New Blackfriars* (January, 1987), 1–16.

[9] I have found the following two evaluations of feminist theologies particularly helpful: Elizabeth Achtemeier, 'The Impossible Possibility: Evaluating the Feminist Approach to Bible and Theology', *Interpretation* 42 (1988), 45–57; and G. W. Stroup, 'Between Echo and Narcissus: The Role of the Bible in Feminist Theology', *Interpretation* 42 (1988), 19–32.

[10] I am indebted here to conversations with Walter Moberly and, through him, to the writings of Brevard Childs. Very helpful also is the essay of Nicholas Lash 'Performing the Scriptures' in his *Theology on the Way to Emmaus* (London: SCM Press, 1986), 37–46.

[11] See J. Z. Smith, 'Sacred Persistence: Towards a Redescription of Canon', in W. S. Green, ed., *Approaches to Ancient Judaism: Theory and Practice* (Missoula: Scholars Press, 1978), 11–28.

II. The witness of Matthew

Like all the Gospels, the Gospel of Matthew is a witness to the fulfilment of God's saving work in the life, death and resurrection of the Son of God, Jesus. With the coming of Jesus, 'the kingdom of heaven is at hand' (3.2; 4.17); and Matthew seeks to express what it means to be citizens of this heavenly kingdom, what it means to be God's new people, the church. Theology, christology, ecclesiology and ethics are linked inextricably together and provide the framework for understanding what Matthew has to say about the discipleship of women and men.

1. We need to emphasize from the start that for Matthew, the overriding reality is the breaking in of the kingdom *of heaven*. This is enormously important. It means that salvation has come: because to speak of heaven is to speak of God and the rule of God. It also means that judgement has come. Social, cultural, political and religious structures, human behaviour and relations between men and women, all are judged in relation to the severe and demanding standards of the kingdom of heaven. 'Heaven', for Matthew, is not 'pie in the sky when you die': it is the presence of God now and in the future in salvation and judgement. I say 'in the future' because the kingdom of heaven is an *eschatological* reality for Matthew. It concerns, not just the past and the present from the perspective of God, but the future under God, as well. This means that repentance and conversion can never be a static, once-for-all thing, and that human relations of superordination and subordination (including relations between women and men) can ever only be provisional, open always to new revelations of divine wisdom (cf. 11.25–30).

2. Jesus is of pre-eminent importance because he embodies the divine presence and the divine wisdom: '"his name shall be called Emmanuel"(which means, God with us)' (1.23; cf. 28.20). That is why he is called God's *Son*. Sonship, for Matthew (as for the New Testament writers as a whole), is a *metaphor of close relationship* taken over from the Old Testament and Judaism,[12] a relationship of a theological and moral kind, not necessarily contingent upon biological filiation at all. Jesus is God's Son because he is *obedient* to God. He shows this throughout his life and especially at the times of great testing: the temptation in the wilderness (where we note

---

[12] The evidence is collected and surveyed in J. D. G. Dunn, *Christology in the Making* (London: SCM Press, 1980), 13–22.

the repeated, 'If you are the Son of God . . .' in 4.1–11), and the
garden of Gethsemane (where Jesus prays three times, 'My Father,
. . . thy will be done'; 26.36–46). Just as God is portrayed as the
Father, so Jesus is the Son. But, again, 'Father' and 'Son' here
describe not a relationship of biological paternity and filiation, but
a relationship which is to be understood theologically. The fact
that God is *unlike* human fathers is made quite clear: God is 'Our
Father *who art in heaven*' (6.9). This is not to deny that this metaphorical language comes from a patriarchal culture and tradition.
What I would deny is the suggestion that this language can only be
understood in a way which legitimates patriarchal domination. In
fact, Matthew's Gospel provides striking evidence to the contrary,
in a saying of Jesus specifically addressing the issue of authority
relations in the Christian fellowship (23.8–12). What is so noticeable
in this saying, is the critique of patriarchal authority relations, the
encouragement of an ethos of mutual acceptance and concern, and
the pre-eminence given to an ethic of humility:

> But you are not to be called rabbi, for you have one teacher, and you
> are all brethren. And call no man your father on earth, for you have
> one Father who is in heaven. Neither be called masters, for you have
> one master, the Christ. He who is greatest among you shall be your
> servant; whoever exalts himself will be humbled, and whoever humbles
> himself will be exalted.

3. The impact of the coming of Jesus as the one who proclaims the
kingdom of heaven is evident throughout Matthew's story. Above
all, perhaps, the coming of Jesus is presented as *an act of divine grace
for all humankind.* For Jesus, the faithful Son, gives his life to atone
for the sins of the people and makes possible, thereby, the bringing
into being of God's new covenant people (26.26–29). Women,
significantly, figure in important ways in this presentation.

First, there are the four women in the genealogy (1.1–17): Tamar,
Rahab, Ruth and 'the wife of Uriah' (i.e. Bathsheba). Their presence
in the list is surprising. As Raymond Brown shows, they signify the
unexpected and gracious intervention of God through women to
overcome human obstacles and bring his purposes to fulfilment:
'It is the combination of the scandalous or irregular union and of
divine intervention through the woman that explains best Matthew's
choice in the genealogy.'[13] So they foreshadow the role of Mary. In
so far as they are all Gentiles (or, as in Bathsheba's case, the wife of

[13] R. E. Brown, *The Birth of the Messiah* (London: Geoffrey Chapman, 1977), 74.

a Gentile), they may foreshadow also the inclusion of Gentiles in the people of God which the coming of the Messiah makes possible.

Second, that women share in prominent ways in salvation history is evident also in the role of Mary. For, according to Matthew, a great miracle is worked in her (in fulfilment of biblical prophecy, 1.23); and, in a quite unique way, she is blessed with the presence of God: 'she was found to be with child of the Holy Spirit' (1.18, 20). Noteworthy too, is the way in which Mary is made to share so closely the fate of the infant Messiah: both his exaltation (2.11) and his vulnerability and persecution (2.13, 14, 20, 21). In sharing so closely in Jesus' persecution, she proves herself to be a true and exemplary heir of the kingdom of heaven (see 5.10).

Third, women as well as men constitute 'the crowds' who hear the gracious and demanding teaching from Jesus about the will of God. There is very little in the Sermon on the Mount relevant only to men, and what there is can properly be seen as intended, at points, to ameliorate oppressive man–woman relations (e.g. 5.27–30, 31–32). It is important to emphasize the fact that in a world in which piety is often graded according to gender, and societies of men cut themselves off from women as a way of safeguarding holiness or the quest for wisdom,[14] Jesus teaches in public both men and women, and includes women among his disciples (12.49–50).

Fourth, women as well as men benefit from Jesus' miracles of healing (4.23ff.; 8.14–17; 9.18–26; 9.35ff.; 11.4–5; etc.) and feeding (14.21; 15.38). Matthew's version of the healing of the Syrophoenician woman's daughter (15.21–28; par. Mk 7.24–30) is especially noteworthy. In Matthew, the woman is a 'Canaanite', an Old Testament expression denoting a Gentile. In the spirit of the Sermon on the Mount (at 5.7), she comes to Jesus seeking mercy for her daughter, and confessing Jesus to be both Lord and Son of David. In spite of rebuffs from both the disciples and Jesus, she persists with deep humility in her quest for her daughter's healing. She refuses to let traditional boundaries exclude her from grace. Her persistence is rewarded with the climactic pronouncement of Jesus: 'O woman, great is your faith! Be it done for you as you desire' (15.28). What is important here is not only the fact that Jesus

---

[14] For two superb accounts see W. A. Meeks, 'The Image of the Androgyne: Some Uses of a Symbol in Earliest Christianity', *History of Religions* 13 (1974), 165–208, esp. 167–180, on 'Woman's Place'; and Ross S. Kraemer, 'Women in the Religions of the Greco-Roman World', *Religious Studies Review* 9 (1983), 127–39.

acknowledges this Gentile woman's great faith, but also that her faith contrasts markedly with the 'little faith' of the disciples (cf. 14.30; 17.20).[15] What is more, her faith is on a par with that of the Gentile centurion of 8.5–13. Gentiles, both women and men, belong by grace to the new people of God.

Fifth, and finally, women play crucial roles at the end of Matthew's story, as at the beginning. At the Passion, there is Pilate's wife (27.19). Like Joseph and the Magi in the Infancy Narratives, she is the recipient of a revelation about Jesus in a dream (cf. 1.20; 2.12, 13, 19). And like John the Baptist at Jesus' baptism, she testifies to Jesus' righteousness (cf. 3.14–15). Just as Jesus does not need to be baptized, neither does he deserve to die. So the woman, another Gentile woman, is a witness to Jesus' exemplary obedience.

Other women are witnesses too. In 27.55–56, we are told of the 'many women' followers of Jesus, including the two Marys and the mother of James and John, who watch 'from afar' the stupendous events accompanying Jesus' death (cf. vv. 51–54). So they witness the beginning of the End; they (i.e. the two Marys) witness the deposition of Jesus in the tomb; they witness the second earthquake and the appearance of the angel who rolls away the stone; they witness the empty tomb; they are the *first* to receive a revelation of the risen Jesus; and they take their witness to the eleven.

4. Matthew's Gospel, then, is a story of women of faith as well as men of faith. It is a story of the revelation of the grace of God in the coming of God's Son to proclaim the kingdom of heaven and to bring into being a community of 'mothers', 'brothers' and 'sisters' (cf. 12.50) living in the light of the kingdom as children of the heavenly Father. It is a demanding Gospel, though, for the revelation of grace brings with it the obligation to respond in obedience. This obligation, this paradoxically 'easy' yoke and 'light' burden (11.30), is placed upon all who would follow: at heart, it is not gender specific, just as it is not race specific. There *are* two ways, according to Matthew, but the division is not between male and female, but between the few who are 'wise' and the many who are 'foolish' (cf. 7.13–14, 24–27). Jesus *does* appoint men who are to be leaders of the faithful, Peter in particular (16.17–19), but nothing is said to indicate that their maleness is a necessary or sufficient qualification

---

[15] Interestingly, Eduard Schweizer sees this story as illustrating only 'the miracle of the faith of the gentiles'. He overlooks the fact that it is a Gentile *woman* who has faith. See his *The Good News According to Matthew* (London: SPCK, 1976), 330.

either for leadership or for succession to leadership. Faith and radical moral integrity are what is called for; and the model for leadership is neither a Mary nor a Peter, but the unique Son of God, who shows the way ahead and promises his presence (28.18–20).

III. The witness of Mark

By comparison with Matthew the theology of Mark is less anthropomorphic, and the Gospel of Mark is less explicitly ecclesiological in its orientation. The picture of God as the loving heavenly Father who cares for his Son and for his children on earth as they are obedient to him in the life of the church, is much more muted in Mark. Prominent instead is an emphasis on the hidden sovereignty and transcendence of God, the mystery of the divine purpose especially in relation to suffering, and the imperative of faith and watchfulness in the midst of darkness (cf. chs 4, 13). As in Matthew, God is depicted as Father and Jesus as the Son (e.g. 1.11; 9.7; 13.32; 14.36; 15.39), while those who do God's will are identified as the spiritual family of Jesus (3.35). But the ethos of Mark is more sombre altogether. Mark has, as it were, stared tragedy more directly in the face without flinching. The Christian life, for Mark, is life on a knife-edge, life embroiled in chaos and contradiction, life and death endured even in the absence of God (15.34).[16]

1. This explains why, in Mark's story of Jesus, the events of the Passion bulk so large. Mark would have agreed fully with Paul, when he says (1 Cor 1.22–25):

> For Jews demand signs and Greeks seek wisdom, but we preach Christ crucified, a stumbling block to Jews and folly to Gentiles, but to those who are called, both Jews and Greeks, Christ is the power of God and the wisdom of God. For the foolishness of God is wiser than men, and the weakness of God is stronger than men.

Mark's Gospel is about the revelation of the mysterious love of God in the suffering, death and resurrection of his Son, Jesus. The death of Jesus is God's will (8.31; 9.31; 10.33–34), and Jesus follows 'the way' to Jerusalem and death in obedience to God (14.36). By the giving up of his life in death, he 'ransoms' many (10.45): that is, he

---

[16] See further J. L. Houlden, *Backward Into Light: The Passion and Resurrection of Jesus According to Matthew and Mark* (London: SCM Press, 1987).

sets free from the domination of Satan (cf. 3.27) those who have faith in him and who show their faith by becoming his followers on 'the way' (8.34–38).

2. This is a *subversive* gospel. It turns the world upside down. As Jesus himself says: 'For whoever would save his life will lose it; and whoever loses his life for my sake and the gospel's will save it' (8.35). God is found, no longer in the temple and the cult (15.38), but through faith in his Son crucified and risen. The people of God are defined, no longer in terms of the law and the nation of the Jews, but (again) by their faith in God's Son (15.39).[17] Sacred space is located, no longer in Jerusalem or the temple, but at the cross and wherever the risen Christ 'goes before' (14.28; 16.7).[18] Sacred time is determined no longer by the religious calendar, but by the coming of the kingdom of God and the beginning of the end-time in Jesus' death and resurrection. Power lies no longer in the hands of Satan, nor of Rome, nor of the civil and religious leaders of the Jews, nor with men, nor even with women (cf. 6.14–29), but with the God who ransoms 'many' by the giving of his Son.

3. I have said just now that the message of Mark is subversive in a quite radical way. *No one is left in a privileged position.* This includes women as well as men. Nevertheless, it is precisely because salvation, power, and the pious life are the special preserve of none, that they are open, now, to *all who have faith.* It is conspicuous and noteworthy, especially given the deeply embedded patriarchalism of Mark's day, that women in Mark exemplify this revolution.[19]

First, there is the healing of Simon's mother-in-law (1.29–31). The grace of God in Jesus is not restricted to men. Jesus heals women as well (cf. 5.21–43); and this is the *first* of the healing miracles in Mark. The response of the healed woman is to 'serve' (*diakonein*) Jesus and the others. The language of service, here, is not necessarily menial. More likely it is Markan language for being a disciple after the example of the Son of Man (10.45; 15.41).

---

[17] On faith in Mark, see C. D. Marshall, *Faith as a Theme in Mark's Narrative* (Cambridge: Cambridge University Press, 1989).

[18] See further the superb study of Elizabeth S. Malbon, *Narrative Space and Mythic Meaning in Mark* (San Francisco: Harper & Row, 1986).

[19] In what follows, I have been helped especially by D. Rhoads and D. Michie, *Mark as Story* (Philadelphia: Fortress Press 1982); Elizabeth S. Malbon, 'Fallible Followers: Women and Men in the Gospel of Mark', *SEMEIA* 28 (1983), 29–48; and A. Gill, 'Women Ministers in the Gospel of Mark', *Australian Biblical Review* 35 (1987), 14–21.

A second healing story is the striking account of the woman with a haemorrhage (5.24b–34). For Mark, this woman is a model of bold faith in Jesus, shown in action. The healing is unique in that it takes place solely at the woman's initiative. And, in response to Jesus' summons, she bears public witness to 'the whole truth' (v. 33), in contrast to the disciples who, typically, misunderstand. For so doing, Jesus acknowledges that her faith has 'saved' her and sends her on her way with the blessing of 'peace' (v. 34). Her story is an epitome of the Gospel as a whole. In a situation of chronic illness, ritual uncleanness (which will have excluded her from cultic worship), poverty and increasing hopelessness, she hears about Jesus, comes to him in faith and touches him, is healed (or 'saved'), and witnesses to the truth. Not only so. The skilful 'sandwiching'[20] of her story within the two halves of the story of the healing of Jairus's daughter (5.21–24a, 35–43), allows her to be a witness to Jairus (a ruler of the synagogue!) of the power of Jesus and of his need also for faith in Jesus (v. 36).

Another woman who shows bold, active faith is the Syrophoenician woman (7.24–30). Her story is as important for Mark as for Matthew. Crucially, it occurs between the two miraculous feedings (6.30–44; 8.1–10), the first of which is on Jewish soil and symbolizes the mission to Israel, and the second of which is in Gentile territory and symbolizes the mission to the Gentiles. Crucially also, it occurs immediately after Jesus teaches that the rules of *kashrut* (which separate Jew from Gentile as pure from defiled) are valid no longer (7.1–23). The coming of this Gentile woman to Jesus, her bold action in speaking up (with some persistence!), and Jesus' change of heart in response, expresses in a very powerful way Mark's conviction of a new order breaking in, and the turning upside down of the old order. Barriers of race and gender no longer hinder access to salvation for people of faith.

Yet another exemplary person in Mark is the anonymous woman who anoints Jesus' head (14.3–9).[21] The location of this story at the beginning of the Passion narrative gives it great prominence. What the woman does expresses the Gospel in a nutshell. In anointing the head of Jesus, she confesses symbolically her faith in Jesus as

---

[20] On which see further B. van Iersel, *Reading Mark* (Edinburgh: T&T Clark, 1989), 99–101.

[21] For a more detailed study of this story, see my article 'Mark as Narrative: The Story of the Anointing Woman (Mk 14.3–9)', *Expository Times* 102/8 (1991), 230–4.

Messiah ('anointed one'). It is an action which contrasts vividly with the actions of leading men, descriptions of which frame this story. On the one side, the chief priests and scribes seek to kill him (14.1–2); and, on the other side, Judas, one of the twelve, goes to betray him (vv. 10–11). Her extravagant and costly gesture of self-giving love for the Jesus who is about to be crucified (v. 8), gains for her a response of approbation accorded no other person in Mark's Gospel: 'And truly, I say to you, wherever the gospel is preached in the whole world, what she has done will be told in memory of her' (v. 9). This is striking, indeed. The memory of this woman's loving action[22] becomes itself an integral part of the gospel proclamation to the whole world. And this is fitting. For the woman functions as a Christ figure, since the story of Jesus himself follows the same pattern: acts of self-denying service; experiences of conflict which lead to rejection and humiliation; and glorious vindication at the end.

We turn, finally, to the women at the end of Mark's story of Jesus. In a Gospel which is full of surprises and reversals, one of the greatest surprises is the sudden mention of the 'many women' from Galilee who are there to witness the momentous event of the crucifixion (15.40–41), and the three women who are the only ones to witness the empty tomb and the angelophany (16.1–8). The significance of these women for Mark can hardly be overestimated. First, they are described in the terminology of discipleship: they 'followed' Jesus (cf. 1.18; 2.14) and 'ministered' to him (cf. 1.13; 1.31; 10.45). It is not only the twelve (men) who are disciples of Jesus: something which the other stories about women have shown us already. Second, from a cultural and religious viewpoint, they are relative outsiders who, by their (even limited) identification with the one who has been made an outsider on a cross, become insiders. In this they are like another outsider at the cross, the Gentile centurion, who comes to faith (15.39). Third, these women followers replace the men. The twelve have fled long since (14.50), and Peter has denied his allegiance to Jesus three times (14.66–72). Jesus' intimate circle, Peter, James and John (cf. 13.3; 14.33), is replaced by the three named women, Mary Magdalene, Mary the mother of James and Joses, and Salome. It is the women who become witnesses to these

---

[22] In passing, it should be pointed out that her sacrificial action parallels in important ways that of *another woman* whom Jesus explicitly commends: the poor widow at the temple treasury, who surrenders 'her whole living' (12.41–44). See the excellent analysis by Elizabeth S. Malbon in 'Fallible Followers', 37–9.

crucial events of salvation, not the twelve, as we would have expected. The effect is 'to compound the surprising reality of Jesus' crucifixion with the surprising reality of women's discipleship'.[23] Fourth, the three women are the first to hear the announcement of the resurrection, and it is they who are entrusted with the responsibility of telling 'the disciples and Peter' that the risen Jesus will appear to them in Galilee (16.7).[24]

4. In Mark's Gospel, then, as in Matthew's, discipleship of Jesus and bearing witness to the grace of God in Jesus are not privileges exclusive to any one gender or race or class. They are open, in a subversive and boundary-crossing way, to whoever puts his or her faith in Jesus. But faith is not just mental assent. As the stories of women show, faith means bold action and self-denying love for the gospel's sake. As the stories of women show also, such faith is likely to be found in the most unexpected places. Any suggestion that Mark, nevertheless, confines roles of *leadership* to men, beginning with the twelve (e.g. 3.13–19), fails to recognize, not only this evangelist's deep ambivalence towards the twelve,[25] but also his thorough-going critique of the conventional (and patriarchal) leadership patterns and power relations of his day (cf. 10.35–45, esp. vv. 42–44).

IV. The witness of Luke–Acts

The theology of Luke's two volumes is dominated by a 'salvation history' perspective according to which God's plan of salvation begins with Israel, is fulfilled in the coming of Jesus – his birth, life, death, resurrection, and ascension – and is being brought to fruition in the gathering of Gentiles as well as Jews into the people of God. There is a very strong emphasis on the *continuity* of God's grace, which binds closely together Israel, Jesus and the church. There is also a very strong emphasis on the *inclusiveness* of God's grace, which

---

[23] Malbon, 'Fallible Followers', 42.

[24] The response of the women to the angelophany in 16.8 is hardly one of disobedience, as is sometimes claimed. The whole presupposition of the Gospel is that they did tell what they had seen and heard! David Catchpole has shown, furthermore, that 'trembling', 'astonishment', 'fear' and silence are not responses of disobedience, but typical reactions to a revelation of the divine (cf. 4.41; 5.15; 5.33; 6.51; 9.6; etc). See D. C. Catchpole, 'The Fearful Silence of the Women at the Tomb', *Journal of Theology for Southern Africa* 18 (1977), 3–10.

[25] On which see J. B. Tyson, 'The Blindness of the Disciples in Mark', in C. Tuckett, ed., *The Messianic Secret* (London: SPCK, 1983), 35–43.

extends the boundaries of the people of God, in a quite unprecedented way, to all who respond in faith to God-in-Christ and are baptized. Stories about women exemplify this theology, along with its implications for the life of faith.

1. For the evangelist Luke, as for all four evangelists, the coming of Jesus and of his forerunner John signifies the dawning of the new age, the time of fulfilment, the time of eschatological salvation. Luke is so convinced of this that he writes his two-volume narrative to chronicle the amazing events which bear witness to the truth of what he believes (1.1–4). Most important for Luke in establishing his claim that God's new age has dawned, is evidence of *the powerful presence of God's Spirit* in fulfilment of scriptural prophecy. It is the Spirit who makes change possible by imparting divine power; and it is the Spirit who legitimates change by making God's will known.

So it is very noteworthy that, in both volumes, God's Spirit is present in a quite evident way, and that the Spirit works through women as well as men. John 'will be filled with the Holy Spirit, even from his mother's womb' (1.15), and Elizabeth herself pronounces a beatitude upon Mary by the power of the Spirit (1.41–42). The Spirit comes upon Mary to make possible the great miracle of the conception and birth of the Son of God (1.35) and to inspire her praise of God (1.46–55). Zechariah and Simeon prophesy under the Spirit's inspiration (1.67–79; 2.25–35), as does the venerable prophetess, Anna (2.36–38). John prophesies that Jesus will baptize the people 'with the Holy Spirit and with fire' (3.16); and this is fulfilled at Pentecost (Acts 1.5). Jesus himself has the Spirit come upon him in a most literal, and therefore undeniable, way, to empower him for his own prophetic work (3.21–22; cf. 4.1, 14, 18; etc.).

Luke's second volume might be more aptly titled, 'The Acts of the Holy Spirit'. The traditional title, 'The Acts of the Apostles', draws proper attention to the leading role accorded figures like Peter, John, Philip, James and Paul, but it diverts attention away from the crucial *theological and pneumatological foundation* of these men's work, and from the important roles played by a number of women who are not apostles (according to Luke!). So, for example, Luke tells us that Mary the mother of Jesus, together with the women followers from Galilee, are part of the upper room company who are filled with the Holy Spirit and share in the powerful manifestations of the Spirit, on the Day of Pentecost (1.14; cf. 2.1ff.). The experience is interpreted by Peter in terms of a prophecy from

Joel which is strongly inclusive in scope: 'And in the last days it shall be, God declares, that I will pour out my Spirit upon all flesh, and your sons and your daughters shall prophesy, . . . yea, and on my menservants and my maidservants in those days I will pour out my Spirit; and they shall prophesy' (2.17–18). We are not surprised, then, to find women as well as men participating in the new and charismatic common life which comes into being, and sharing its problems: 'And more than ever believers were added to the Lord, multitudes both of men and women' (5.14; cf. 4.32–5.11; 6.1ff.). Prominent among the women are Tabitha/Dorcas, a 'disciple . . . full of good works and acts of charity' (9.36–42); Mary, the mother of John Mark and the host of a Christian gathering (12.12–17); Lydia, a trader in purple goods, who becomes a Christian and serves as a benefactress to Paul and Silas (16.14–15, 40); Priscilla, who, along with her husband Aquila, become co-workers and fellow-travellers with Paul, and 'expound to Apollos more accurately the way of God' (ch. 18); and, in Acts 21.8–9, we are told that Philip had 'four unmarried daughters, who prophesied'.

All this is not to deny that Luke gives overwhelming attention to the twelve apostles (especially Peter) and to leaders in the mission to the Gentiles like Philip and Paul. I would not deny either that Luke actually *plays down* the importance of women in the life of the early church.[26] These considerations would be particularly important if we were trying to use Luke–Acts as a source for the historical reconstruction of the role of women in early Christianity. But, as I made clear at the beginning, reading the Gospels *as Scripture* is a different exercise. As Scripture, I would claim that Luke's two volumes are a strong and indispensable witness to the *divine reality* of the beginning of the new age of the eschatological Spirit, and that participation (*koinōnia*) in the life of this new age is open, equally, to all. In Luke's day, it was important to emphasize that this meant the full inclusion of the Gentiles in the people of God. Today, we are much more aware that it is important to emphasize that it means the full inclusion and equal participation of women in the people of God, as well.

[26] See further J. A. Grassi, *The Hidden Heroes of the Gospels: Female Counterparts of Jesus* (Collegeville: The Liturgical Press, 1979), 85–91. Elisabeth S. Fiorenza draws particular attention to Luke's omission of a resurrection appearance to women, in contrast to Matthew and John, who both report that Mary Magdalene was the first to see the risen Christ! See her article, '"You are not to be called Father": Early Christian History in a Feminist Perspective', *Cross Currents* 39 (1979), 301–23 at 308.

That Luke understands this too, in spite of the bias just discussed, finds support in the following considerations. First, Luke devotes more space to stories about women than do the other evangelists. Second, Luke's stories about women, especially in Luke 1–2, show the influence of biblical traditions about eminent women in the life of Israel (such as Sarah, Miriam, Deborah, Hannah, Ruth, Judith and Esther). Third, Luke's writing achieves a skilful and significant pairing of stories of men with stories of women: Zechariah/Mary (1.11–12, 27–29); Simeon/Anna (2.25, 36); the mother of a dead son/the father of a dead daughter (7.12; 8.41); the scribe/the two sisters (10.25–37, 38–42); the insistent man/the insistent widow (11.5–7; 18.1–8); the woman healed on the sabbath/the man healed on the sabbath (13.10–17; 14.1–6); the daughter of Abraham/the son of Abraham (13.16; 19.9); the parable of the shepherd/the parable of the woman (15.3–7, 8–10); and so on.[27] On the basis of evidence such as this, it is hard to deny that Luke's vision of Christian community is strongly inclusive, not only of Gentiles, but of women also.

2. The evangelist Luke not only wants to establish beyond any doubt that the new age of the eschatological Spirit, open to all people, has dawned: he wants also to convey *how to live* and *what qualities of character* are appropriate, in response to what God has done.[28] Important for us is the recognition that both women and men serve as models in this respect. We may take Peter's statement in Acts 10.34–35 as a kind of bench-marker: 'Truly I perceive that God shows no partiality, but in every nation any one who fears him and does what is right is acceptable to him.' Of course, Peter is speaking of his profound discovery of God's acceptance of Gentiles, like Cornelius and his household, into the people of God. But what he says is applicable equally to other 'outsider' groups, including women.

Since Luke gives more prominence to Mary than any other evangelist, we begin with her.[29] Like any disciple, she is first and

[27] See E. Schweizer, *The Good News According to Luke* (London: SPCK, 1984), 142–3.

[28] I am indebted here to the excellent study by B. E. Beck, *The Christian Character in the Gospel of Luke* (London: Epworth Press, 1989), esp. ch. 8.

[29] See further R. E. Brown *et al.*, *Mary in the New Testament* (Philadelphia: Fortress Press 1978), ch. 6; and J. A. Fitzmyer, *Luke the Theologian: Aspects of His Teaching* (London: Geoffrey Chapman, 1989), ch. 3 (on 'Mary in Lucan Salvation History').

foremost a recipient of the divine grace, whose life is changed irreversibly as a result (1.28ff.). She is a person indwelt by God's Spirit (1.35). She is obedient to God's will, even though it involves what is impossible, humanly speaking (1.37–38). She bears witness to what God has done for her, as part of her witness to the gospel of God's grace for the poor (1.46–55). She is a person who does not get carried away by marvels, but gives herself to quiet introspection and remembering (2.19, 51). She is faithful and pious in her religious observance (2.21, 22ff., 39, 41ff.). She is a person whose commitment to God-in-Christ endures, in spite of testing (2.35), not being able fully to understand (2.48–50), having to accept the cost in terms of family ties (8.19–21; 11.27–28), and having to accept her son's humiliating death: for she is there, praying with the apostles, in Jerusalem at Pentecost (Acts 1.14). Mary, in short, is a true Israelite and a model disciple. The virtues and qualities she shows are the very qualities Luke wishes every Christian person to exhibit. They are the qualities shown by Jesus himself.

Elizabeth, likewise. With Zechariah, she is 'righteous before God, walking in all the commandments and ordinances of the Lord blameless' (1.6). Her obedience and piety are rewarded in an extraordinary manifestation of divine grace which removes her shame (1.7ff., 24–25). She too, is Spirit-filled, and bears joyful, prophetic witness to what God is doing (1.41–45, 57ff.). It is surely no coincidence that the portraits of Mary and Elizabeth in Luke 1–2 are so rich in relation to what the evangelist wants to convey about Christian character. For their stories are bound up inextricably with the dawn of the new age in the births of John and Jesus; and the dawn of the new age is, at the same time, the time when the nature of Christian character is revealed.

Anna is another case in point (2.36–38). She is depicted as a person of truly biblical virtue: a woman of the Spirit (a prophetess); a woman of venerable age, and therefore wise; a woman of constancy (having remained a widow until the symbolically significant age of eighty-four); a woman of faithful devotion to God, shown in her lifestyle ('worshipping with fasting and prayer night and day'); and a woman who has remained open to the future and who bears public witness to the gracious work of God coming to pass. Again, like Mary and Elizabeth, a true Israelite and a model Christian disciple.

Finally, though by no means exhaustively, we may mention the woman who anoints Jesus (7.36–50). We saw how important this story is in Mark, where it comes at the beginning of the Passion narrative and expresses Mark's Gospel in a nutshell. The story is no less important for Luke, and functions in a similar way. But Luke has relocated it and modified it significantly. Here, it occurs shortly after the Sermon on the Plain, when Jesus pronounces God's blessing upon 'you that weep now' (6.21b), and teaches the multitude: 'Judge not, and you will not be judged; condemn not and you will not be condemned; forgive, and you will be forgiven' (6.37f.). The woman comes to Jesus weeping (7.38) and finds blessing. She comes as a 'sinner' (7.37), and is neither judged by Jesus, nor condemned, but is forgiven. So the story of this woman in her encounter with Jesus expresses in a nutshell the salvation which God makes possible through Jesus, as taught by him in the Sermon. For Luke especially, Jesus is 'a friend of tax collectors and sinners': it is *they* who are children of the divine wisdom (7.34–35).

But it is very important for Luke to show that the grace of God is not cheap grace; and in this respect also the story of the woman has a paradigmatic quality. By her actions (for she speaks not a word), she shows true love and true repentance. Her tears are tears of penitence. Her anointing of Jesus' feet is an act of love and humility. Above all, in a Gospel where hospitality is a symbol of repentance and acceptance of the kingdom of God (cf. 19.1–10),[30] the kisses, the footwashing and the anointing by the woman, signify, in a way that words cannot, her acceptance of Jesus and the way of Jesus. So, like the penitent thief at the crucifixion (23.39–43), she finds salvation and 'peace' (7.50). Not only so, for, in a quite provocative way, her faith is contrasted explicitly with the obstinate unfaith of the Pharisee Simon (7.39–47). In the words of the Magnificat (1.52), the mighty is put down and the person of low degree is exalted.

3. We may say, then, that for Luke, salvation works from the bottom up and from the margins in. *That* is the measure of God's grace. Acceptance of this radical and novel reversal of social-religious norms is difficult for those with vested interests in the *status quo* (cf. 14.15–24). In Luke's day, as in our own, such people are mainly men, along with the women who have been socialized into accepting men's ways. Change is possible only on the basis of a

---

[30] See J. Koenig, *New Testament Hospitality* (Philadelphia: Fortress Press, 1985), ch. 4; also, H. Moxnes, *The Economy of the Kingdom: Social Conflict and Economic Relations in Luke's Gospel* (Philadelphia: Fortress Press, 1988).

thorough-going repentance (*metanoia*; cf. 3.3, 8; 5.32; 15.7; 24.47; etc.). It is significant and noteworthy, that it is women who figure so often in Luke's two volumes both as active recipients of grace, and as models of the life of Christian faith lived in response to that grace.

V. The witness of John

Central to the message of the Fourth Gospel is the revelation of Jesus as the Word of God incarnate, the unique Son of God, who comes from the Father to reveal himself to the world as the true and only Way, and who returns to the Father to prepare a dwelling-place for those who believe in him. The underlying irony of the Gospel is that those who should have believed in him do not, and that those who seem unlikely recipients of revelation believe. The main aim of the Gospel is not just to elicit faith but also to confirm believers in their faith (20.30–31), as well as to provide a basis in the story of Jesus for believers to develop their own identity and life together as God's people. As we have come now to expect from the Gospels as a whole, the message of the Fourth Gospel is addressed to women as well as to men, and women play a very important part in the story which conveys that message.

1. 'In him was life' (1.4a). *That* is the fundamental claim of John, the truth to which his Gospel, and all the characters and episodes within it, bear witness. Where the other evangelists present Jesus primarily as the proclaimer of the in-breaking kingdom of God, John presents Jesus himself as the Life (14.6) and the one who gives 'eternal life' (3.16). This means that Jesus brings *a new order of creation* into being. Just as 'in the beginning . . . all things were made through him' (1.2–3), so now he comes into the world to reveal a new dispensation, the dispensation of 'eternal life'. The implications of this christology and soteriology are immense.

Negatively, it means that the old dispensation has been displaced completely. In fact, virtually every major symbol of belonging as a Jew to the people of God – Torah, temple, festival calendar, sabbath observance, the land, the Scriptures, and the patriarchs – is displaced in a quite countercultural way by the Jesus of John. Positively, the displacement of the old order of things means that the boundaries marking out the people of God have been redrawn and life as the people of God is practised in quite new ways. Now, in a radically universal way, salvation is open to all who believe in Jesus: women as well as men, and Greek and Samaritan as well as Jew. Now, the religion of the patriarchs (cf. 4.5–6; 8.31ff.) gives way to a religion directed by the Spirit (14.16–17, 26; 16.7–15). The life of faith is to be lived according to the utterly demanding, 'new' commandment, 'love one another; even as I have loved you' (13.34). That is to say, the practice of the life of faith and the doing of God's will are open equally to women as well as to men in a way which the previous dispensation made impossible.

2. It is hardly surprising that 'eternal life', as offered by Jesus in his sign-miracles and revealed by Jesus in his discourses, provokes conflict and division among the people. The coming of a new order of things always generates resistance, especially if the identity of a people, its religion, its ways of ordering gender relations, and its ways of distinguishing insider from outsider, are put in question. In John, the division is felt very keenly indeed. It is expressed right at the beginning, in the Prologue (1.9–13):

> The true light that enlightens every one was coming into the world. He was in the world, and the world was made through him, yet the world knew him not. He came to his own home and his own people received him not. But to all who received him, who believed in his name, he gave power to become children of God; who were born, not of blood nor of the will of the flesh nor of man, but of God.

So people of the new dispensation are called 'children of God'; and this distinguishes them, as those whose Father is God and whose birth is a spiritual birth 'from above' (3.3ff.), from those who claim Abraham as their father (8.33ff.) and Moses as their guide (9.28–29). We are witnessing here a real parting of the ways. The mutual animosity is strong, too (cf. 16.1–4). But for the evangelist John, the painful separation is essential, and enormously liberating (8.31–32).

3. The stories about women express this liberating, countercultural faith very well.[31] The portrayal of the mother of Jesus is a case in point. As in Luke–Acts, she is presented in a positive light. Only this Gospel has the story of the wedding at Cana (2.1–11) and the episode at the foot of the cross (19.26–27). Strikingly, these two

---

[31] I am indebted here to R. E. Brown, *The Community of the Beloved Disciple* (London: Geoffrey Chapman, 1979), app. 2: 'Roles of Women in the Fourth Gospel'; and Grassi, *Hidden Heroes*, ch. 4.

stories, in both of which Jesus' mother figures prominently, frame the whole narrative of Jesus' ministry. They are also linked thematically. First, the 'hour' to which Jesus refers in 2.4, is the 'hour' of Jesus' glorification on the cross (12.23). Second, in both stories, Mary is never referred to by her personal name. Rather, she is accorded a representative status, being addressed by Jesus as 'Woman' (2.4; 19.26).

In the first story, replete as it is with resurrection and messianic symbolism – the 'third day', a wedding banquet, superb wine in abundance, the 'glory' of Jesus – the mother of Jesus is shown to be important, not by virtue of her natural tie with Jesus, but as a person who shows faith (however inadequate) in Jesus, and whose faith is deepened (2.4) and subsequently rewarded (2.5ff.). In the second story, she is paired with that other revered figure, the Beloved Disciple, at the foot of the cross as a witness of Jesus' 'hour'. Her presence there shows her faith in Jesus and that she has learnt the lesson of 2.4. It is this faith which is acknowledged by Jesus and rewarded: she is accepted into the family of disciples of Jesus as the 'mother' of the Beloved Disciple, who becomes her 'son'. Raymond Brown puts it well: 'If the Beloved Disciple was the ideal of discipleship, intimately involved with that disciple on an equal plane as part of Jesus' true family was a woman. A woman and a man stood at the foot of the cross as models for Jesus' "own", his true family of disciples.'[32]

We turn next to the story of the Samaritan woman (4.1–42). This story is not unrelated to the story of the wedding at Cana.[33] The messianic symbolism of new wine there is reinforced now by the metaphor of living water. The displacement of the cult symbolized there by the filling with wine of the six stone jars (*hudriai*) used for the rites of purification (2.6; cf. vv. 13–22) is reinforced now by the fact that the woman responds so positively to Jesus' words about true, spiritual worship (4.21ff.), and leaves her *hudria* behind (4.28) to go and tell her fellow citizens. And in both episodes, the story hinges on a conversation between Jesus and a woman who shows signs of active faith. By way of contrast, this Samaritan woman shows

---

[32] Brown, *Community of the Beloved Disciple*, 197. Cf. also the discussion of R. F. Collins, in 'The Representative Figures of the Fourth Gospel – II', *Downside Review* 94 (1976), 118–32 at 120–2.

[33] See R. A. Culpepper, *The Anatomy of the Fourth Gospel* (Philadelphia: Fortress Press, 1983), 192–3.

considerably more faith than Nicodemus, the 'teacher of Israel', in the immediately preceding episode (3.1–12)!

The story itself is remarkable. First, we note the pushing back of socio-religious boundaries by Jesus: he reveals saving knowledge to a Samaritan (4.9, 22), and that a woman (of some notoriety: vv. 17–18). The reaction of the returning male disciples tells all: 'They marvelled that he was talking with a woman' (4.27). Second, what Jesus offers the woman is of inestimable value: liberating knowledge about the nature of true worship and the coming of the Messiah. The first use of the revelatory *egō eimi* formula in John occurs here (4.21–26). Third, the woman becomes an evangelist and bears witness to Jesus, with the result that 'many of the Samaritans from that city believed in him because of the woman's testimony' (4.39). Her preaching achieves precisely what the preaching of the male disciples will achieve, according to 17.20. Not only so. For Jesus' words to the disciples in 4.35–38 make explicit that her sowing of the seed has prepared the way for the apostolic harvest. In other words, she herself functions in an apostolic way.[34]

Mary Magdalene is another woman in John's story who functions in an apostolic way (20.1–2, 11–18). For Paul, according to 1 Corinthians 9.1, an essential qualification for apostleship is to be able to say, 'I have seen the Lord' (*ton kurion heōraka*). It is precisely these words which Mary uses when she fulfils Jesus' commission and goes and announces the resurrection of Jesus to his (male) disciples: *heōraka ton kurion* (20.18)! The same words are used by the other disciples themselves when bearing witness to Thomas: *heōrakamen ton kurion* (20.25). This is remarkable. It is as if the evangelist John is wanting to present Mary as quite on a par with the traditional apostles.

Other aspects of the account support this suggestion. First, John focuses uniquely on Mary Magdalene by omitting mention of the other women at the tomb of whom we know from the Synoptic traditions (e.g. Mk 16.1). Second, the story of Mary frames the story of the visit to the empty tomb by Peter and the Beloved Disciple (20.3–10). Her experience at least parallels theirs, therefore, and in one crucial aspect surpasses theirs: for she is the *first* to see both the angels (20.12–13) and the risen Jesus himself (20.14–18). Third, together with the Beloved Disciple, she displaces Peter. It is they who see and believe (20.8, 18), something which is not said of Peter,

[34] So, too, Brown, *Community of the Beloved Disciple*, 188–9.

but which we are left to infer from 20.19–23. Whereas other early
tradition claims for Peter the first resurrection appearance (1 Cor
15.5; Lk 24.34), John claims this privilege for Mary Magdalene.
Fourth, Jesus addresses her by name (20.16). For Mary, this is the
delightful moment of recognition. She knows now that she is in the
presence of the Good Shepherd who 'calls his own sheep by name
and leads them out' (10.3). She is fully a member of the fold: as
fully a member as the one whom Jesus calls by the name, Cephas, in
1.42. Finally, it is to Mary that the risen Jesus gives the crucial
revelation about the nature of his resurrection life: that it is not a
matter of mere resuscitation, but of ascension to the Father (20.17).
Not without justification, then, has the tradition of the Western
church accorded this Mary the title *apostola apostolorum*: 'apostle of
the apostles'.[35]

The story of Mary, Martha and their brother Lazarus, in John
11, is another episode where a woman is given a role which other
tradition gives to Peter. In Mark's Gospel, a climactic turning point
in the narrative is the confession at Caesarea Philippi by Peter: 'You
are the Christ' (Mk 8.29). This episode, so important for all three
Synoptic evangelists, is completely remoulded in John (6.66–71);
and the precise christological confession, 'You are the Christ' is
placed, strikingly, on the lips of Martha (11.27). It is to Martha,
furthermore, that Jesus first reveals himself as 'the resurrection and
the life' (11.25).

This same story is very significant in other respects, too. We note
that Mary and Martha, as well as Lazarus, are loved by Jesus (11.3,
5, 11, 33–36). Jesus *shows* his love for them by raising Lazarus from
death: an act which costs him his own life (11.8, 45–53), and accords
with his own subsequent teaching, 'Greater love has no man than
this, that a man lay down his life for his friends' (15.13). But this
love relationship is not just one-way, from Jesus to the family trio.
It is a *reciprocal* love relationship. For Mary is introduced right at
the outset as the one 'who anointed the Lord with ointment and
wiped his feet with her hair': and this we are told, before the event
has taken place (11.2; cf. 12.1–8)! This relationship of reciprocal
love conveys the essence of what John means by 'eternal life': and it
is shared between women and men alike. As the story of the
anointing itself makes clear, such love is costly: it requires identifying with the one who is 'the resurrection and the life', in his death

---

[35] Ibid. 190 and n. 336.

(cf. 11.7, 9–11). But it is also full of life-giving fragrance by which the stench of death and of the old order of things is overcome (12.3; cf. 11.39).

3. It is quite clear, therefore, that this evangelist goes further than the others in giving equal prominence to female disciples as to male disciples, including the twelve. This is because, for John, discipleship is not about ecclesiastical authority of a patriarchal kind, as this is reflected in other parts of the New Testament (the Pastoral Epistles in particular). John would have viewed this as a backward step into the old order of things, an intolerable compromise with 'the world'. Rather, discipleship is about belonging in love to the *spiritual* family of women and men who, as 'children of God', 'abide' in Jesus the Son and trust him as 'the way' to the Father.

VI. Conclusion

It is appropriate now to draw together some of the main findings of this particular theological reading of the Gospel stories about women and Jesus. In so doing, I am very aware that there is a danger of being reductionist: of boiling everything down to a few morals in a way which does a disservice to the colour, imaginativeness, multi-dimensionality and open-endedness of the Gospel stories themselves. But in an essay of this kind, the risk has to be taken. So, I offer the following conclusions.

First, all four Gospels are witnesses to the fundamental theological claim that the coming of Jesus inaugurates a new order of things: the kingdom of heaven (Matthew), the kingdom of God (Mark), the coming of the Spirit (Luke–Acts), eternal life (John). This new order is seen as an act of God's grace, a new covenant between God and humankind made possible by Jesus' life, death and resurrection, which brings into being a new community. The story of Jesus and the Samaritan woman in John captures this profoundly.

Second, the new community of the people of God expresses the grace of God by being radically inclusive. Gentiles are welcome, as well as Jews. Women are welcome, as well as men. A cameo of this truth is the story of the confrontation between Jesus and the Syrophoenician woman.

Third, acceptance into the people of God is accorded on the basis not of race, nor of status, nor of gender, but of repentance and faith in Jesus expressed in a life of love. This is epitomized in the Lukan version of the story of the woman who anoints Jesus.

Fourth, the change of heart, breaking of stereotypes and re-drawing of boundaries involved in becoming people of the new age generates resistance. It is a painful, costly, public business whose outcome is often far from certain. To save your life you have to lose it. That was true for Jesus. It was true also for the woman with the haemorrhage.

Fifth, the qualities required for leadership and positions of responsibility in the people of God are not gender specific. They are moral and religious qualities: gifts of God's sovereign Spirit, not accidents of birth. Hence the remarkable prominence and authority accorded women like the mother of Jesus, Mary and Martha, and Mary Magdalene, in the Gospel of John.

Finally, in so far as the Gospel stories of women and Jesus are, for us, Scripture, they cannot be confined, safely, to the sphere of history. Rather, as we have seen again and again, they express the gospel in a nutshell. Therefore, they are to be proclaimed, and they are to be lived out in practice: 'And truly, I say to you, wherever the gospel is preached in the whole world, what she has done will be told in memory of her.'

9

Christian Community in the Light of the Gospel of John

I. Introduction: the contemporary situation and the nature of the church

The history of the twentieth century is a history of calamitous failures in human neighbourliness. In consequence, there is widespread recognition today of the need to find ways of building and maintaining patterns of sociality which are life-giving. So strong are the perceived threats to human sociality that many political, social and religious leaders are turning their attention to ways of resisting the threats and making space for the renewal of society.[1]

Building communities which allow all people to attain their full humanity as children of God are central *Christian* concerns also. Indeed, the vocation of Israel according to the Old Testament and of the church according to the New is so to share in the life and love of God that it becomes the people and the place where the virtues and skills for life together among the nations are known and practised. The truthful, just and life-giving encounter between human beings in all their diversity which constitutes community is dependent upon true worship of the truthful, justifying, life-giving God. This means that true community is *a gift of divine grace*; and its quality as gift means that it is not something which we can presume upon or determine in advance. In the end, it is not a matter of human calculus or rational planning, however important these may be. Like happiness, it often occurs in its most profound forms when and where we least expect it. It occurs when heaven and earth touch.

---

[1] See, for example, Jonathan Sacks, *The Persistence of Faith: Religion, Morality and Society in a Secular Age* (London: Weidenfeld & Nicolson, 1991); and *The Politics of Hope* (London: Jonathan Cape, 1997).

Because God is one and Lord of all the earth, the gifts and skills which make life together possible are available to all through God's life-giving Spirit in creation. But it is also the case that the church is called and gifted to witness in a special way to the life together of people of every kind and condition which is the will of God. It does so *by being itself*: one, holy, catholic and apostolic. By its *unity*, the church witnesses to the oneness of God and to the possibility of humankind in all its diversity becoming one in praise of God. By its *holiness*, it witnesses to the disciplines and virtues which make community possible, ordering its life according to the character of the transcendent God. By its *catholicity*, it witnesses to its loyalty to the whole human race past, present and future, a loyalty vital for the preservation of humanity and reflecting God's covenant loyalty to the whole of creation. By its *apostolicity*, the church witnesses in word and sacrament to the source of both its own life and the life of the world. That source is the forgiveness of God through the death and resurrection of the divine Son – which reminds us that there can be no true community without atonement, and there can be no atonement without sacrifice.

That is to put the matter in credal and doctrinal terms.[2] But it is possible to put it in scriptural terms as well. Which observation brings us to the Fourth Gospel.

II. Theological interpretation: not 'the Johannine community' but 'Christian community in the light of the Fourth Gospel'

I begin with a word about method. As with any biblical text, we can read the Gospel of John in various ways depending on our identities and interests as readers.[3] In broad terms, if our interest lies in the world behind the text, we can read the Gospel with a view to reconstructing the intention of the historical author and testing the reliability of his account of the life of Jesus. This might include asking whether or not the author of the Gospel had an interest in 'community' and whether or not he wrote the Gospel for a

---

[2] See further D. W. Hardy, 'God and the Form of Society', in D. W. Hardy and P. H. Sedgwick, eds, *The Weight of Glory* (Edinburgh: T&T Clark, 1991), 131–44; also D. F. Ford and D. L. Stamps, eds, *Essentials of Christian Community* (Edinburgh: T&T Clark, 1996).

[3] Cf. R. Morgan and J. Barton, *Biblical Interpretation* (Oxford: Oxford University Press, 1988); and on John in particular, F. F. Segovia, 'The Significance of Social Location in Reading John's Gospel', *Interpretation* 49 (1995), 370–8.

community, the so-called 'Johannine community'. In fact, in
Johannine interpretation over the past thirty years, significant
scholarly work has been done in precisely this area, building upon
the development of both form and redaction criticism in the
immediately preceding generations. Now it is accepted as a commonplace that one of the reasons for the distinctiveness of John is
that it mirrors the experiences of a predominantly Jewish Christian
community radically estranged, not only from the wider society,
but also from the society of the synagogue, even perhaps from the
society of other Christian groups.[4] Hence, commentators point to
the moral and ontological dualism of the Gospel, the 'us-versus-
them' mentality, the hostility towards 'the Jews' and 'the Pharisees',
the prominence given to the theme of trial and judgement, the
christological exclusivism, and so on. So, it is said, the Johannine
community had the ethos of an 'introversionist (or, according to
some, conversionist) sect', a 'beleaguered community' turned in
on itself and isolated from the world.[5] It is argued, furthermore,
that the history of the community can be traced from one part of
the Johannine corpus (i.e. the Fourth Gospel, the Johannine
Epistles, and the Apocalypse) to another, thus giving us an insight
into one significant 'trajectory' in the history of earliest Christianity.[6]

Such an approach has undoubted value. It brings to the surface
possible hidden or overlooked social and communal factors which
may have affected the writing of the Gospel, while not necessarily
denying the powerful and creative influence of the 'towering
theologian'[7] whose reflection upon Jesus past and whose experience
of Jesus present shaped the tradition. It offers a window onto the
emergence of a distinctive strand in earliest Christianity and gives
evidence of the fraught 'parting of the ways' between Judaism and
Christianity. More generally, it contributes to reading the Gospel
with historical imagination and with the critical distance which
historical method makes possible. It is worth noting, however, that
the effect of this has been to turn traditional Christianity's high

[4] Representative of a substantial literature are J. L. Martyn, *History and Theology in the Fourth Gospel* (Nashville: Abingdon Press, 1979, 2nd edn); and R. E. Brown, *The Community of the Beloved Disciple* (London: Geoffrey Chapman, 1979).

[5] See, for example, W. A. Meeks, 'The Son of Man in Johannine Sectarianism', *Journal of Biblical Literature* 91 (1972), 44–72.

[6] As well as Martyn, *History and Theology*, and Brown, *Community*, see more recently U. C. von Wahlde, 'Community in Conflict', *Interpretation* 49 (1995), 379–89.

[7] The term is that of M. Hengel in *The Johannine Question* (London: SCM Press, 1989).

regard for John's Gospel – the 'spiritual gospel' according to
Clement of Alexandria – on its head. The Gospel which proclaims
God's universal love is presented now as barely Christian, or at least
as having a powerful 'dark side'.[8] As a product of the narrow,
extreme world of intra-Jewish polemic, a world opened up for us by
the comparative testimony of the documents from the Qumran
community, the Gospel's value for Christian faith is salvaged only
by the shift in interpretation made possible by John's inclusion in
the Christian canon. According to Wayne Meeks, for example:

> The kind of ethos that the narrative of the Fourth Gospel seems designed
> to reinforce, when taken at face value in its historical rather than its
> canonical context, is not one that many of us would happily call
> 'Christian' in a normative sense. One could argue that this Gospel has
> won its secure place in the affections of generations of readers and its
> profound influence on theological, literary, and moral sensibilities of
> Western culture only through an endless series of more or less strong
> misreadings.[9]

Now, Meeks may be right. He certainly represents a strong
consensus of experts in the field. But there are grounds for caution,
both on the level of historical method and on the level of critical
evaluation.[10] First, it is notoriously difficult to correlate a text like
a Gospel and the putative community from or for which it was
written. The problem of circularity – of constructing the Matthean,
Marcan, Lucan and Johannine 'communities' from a reading of
the respective Gospels and then of using those reconstructions to
interpret the Gospels – is inescapable. It is also complicated by
the likelihood that any one community may have known and been
influenced by more than one Gospel.[11] Even if we are helped in the
Johannine case by the evidence of the Epistles and the Apocalypse,

[8] See, for example, C. C. Black, 'Christian Ministry in Johannine Perspective',
Interpretation 44 (1990), 36–40; also, D. M. Smith, 'Theology and Ministry in John',
in E. E. Shelp and R. Sunderland, eds, *A Biblical Basis for Ministry* (Philadelphia:
Westminster Press, 1981), 213–14.

[9] W. A. Meeks, 'The Ethics of the Fourth Evangelist', in R. A. Culpepper and
C. C. Black, eds, *Exploring the Gospel of John* (Louisville: Westminster John Knox
Press, 1996), 317.

[10] See further Stephen C. Barton, 'Can We Identify the Gospel Audiences?', in
R. Bauckham, ed., *The Gospels for All Christians* (Grand Rapids: Eerdmans, 1998),
173–94.

[11] See on this R. Bauckham, 'John for Readers of Mark', in R. Bauckham ed.,
Gospels, 147–71.

the reconstruction depends still on a prior decision about the chronological sequence of the texts: whether (as with Smalley) Apocalypse–Gospel–Epistles,[12] or (as with Segovia) Epistles–Gospel–Apocalypse,[13] or (as traditionally) Gospel–Epistles–Apocalypse.[14] Second, the category 'sect', drawn as it is from studies (using a Tıoeltschian church sect typology) of religious groups primarily in the modern period, is prone to applications which are anachronistic.[15] It is also a category which tends to be 'loaded' ideologically – for example, in its use as a term of approbation among anti-establishment interpreters who want to play up the subversive, 'protest' character of John's vision over against more conservative, 'early Catholic' alternatives.[16] Third, it does not do justice to the Gospel genre. That is to say, whereas an epistolary text like 1 Corinthians is patently oriented towards the life, loves and hates of a particular community in a particular city, the Gospels, as distinctive (because kerygmatic) 'lives of Jesus', may have been intended for transmission to and between audiences of a much more mixed and plural kind, having as a primary goal, not community self-definition, so much as conversion to faith in Jesus as the Son of God.[17] In which case, the search for the putative 'Johannine community' may be misplaced, and the Gospels may need to be read much more literally (as testimonies to the life of Jesus), rather than as subtle 'allegories' of early church life.

These problems of historical method are compounded by problems of critical evaluation. In particular, there is the question of whether Meeks *et al.* are being as 'historical' as they claim when they drive a wedge between the text in its original historical context on the one hand and the *reception* of the text in early Christianity and subsequently in the life of the church.[18] The placing of the

---

[12] Cf. S. S. Smalley, *Thunder and Love: John's Revelation and John's Community* (Waco: Word, 1994), 57–69.

[13] Cf. F. F. Segovia, *Love Relationships in the Johannine Tradition* (Chico: Scholars Press, 1982).

[14] Cf. Brown, *Community*, and *The Churches the Apostles Left Behind* (New York: Paulist Press, 1984), 84–123.

[15] See on this Barton, 'Early Christianity and the Sociology of the Sect', in this volume.

[16] Cf. D. Rensberger, *Johannine Faith and Liberating Community* (Philadelphia: Westminster Press, 1988).

[17] Relevant here are the recent essays in Bauckham, ed., *Gospels*.

[18] See further the discussion of 'history and tradition' in F. Watson, *Text and Truth: Redefining Biblical Theology* (Edinburgh: T&T Clark, 1997), 45–54.

wedge is evident in the apparently harmless decision to take the
Fourth Gospel 'at face value in its historical rather than its canonical
context', a strategy bolstered by the suggestion that the history of
Johannine interpretation in the church is a history of 'an endless
series of more or less strong misreadings'.[19] There are a number of
problems here. First, Meeks conceals the fact that reading John in
its 'historical context' is more than a matter of taking the text
'at face value', and is instead a matter of scholarly *reconstruction*
often reflecting as much the 'face' of the scholar as the 'face value'
of the text. Second, there is a privileging of the original text in
its (reconstructed) historical context over readings of the text in
its canonical context and in the light of its history of reception in
the church. This represents a curious 'fundamentalism of the
originating moment' – a kind of scholarly counterpoint to popular
fundamentalisms which also like to 'get back' to the original.
Whereas in the popular case, getting back to the original is for the
purpose of showing how bad things have got since then and how
important it is to return to how things were at the start, in the
scholarly case, it is for the purpose of showing how 'strange' or
'dangerous' is the original and how 'difficult' it is to use for the
theological and moral formation of all 'right-thinking' people!

But perhaps there is an approach which avoids these mirror-
image fundamentalisms and the crippling positivism from which
they suffer. Such an approach is what I propose to offer here.[20] In
general terms, I would characterize it as *a 'readerly' or 'scriptural'*
approach rather than an 'historical critical' approach narrowly
conceived. Whereas the interest of historical criticism is restricted
to reconstructing the world behind or the world within the text,
the interest of the readerly or scriptural approach is more on
engagement with the (historical) text *as Spirit-inspired text* with a
view to individual and communal discernment, judgement and
transformation. The advantages of this approach are several. First,
it goes with the grain of the text itself which comes to us, not as a
bare 'historical document', but as part of the canon of Christian
Scripture, the regular reading of which in the context of prayer
and worship constitutes the church as a community of faith. Second,
it is *more historical* than 'historical criticism', since, while engaging

[19] Meeks, 'Ethics', 317.
[20] See also my earlier essay 'Living as Families in the Light of the New Testament'
in this volume.

with the text in ways that are philologically and historically informed, it refuses to play off the (original) historical context of the text against its canonical context and the history of its reception. This allows both for the possibility that the text bears unique and indispensable witness to the truth about God's ways with the world, *and* for the possibility that the witness of the text to the truth is partial and fragmented, and therefore that its location in the canon – with the other three Gospels, the Johannine Epistles, and so on – is an aid to the disclosure of the truth rather than an obstacle. Third, it is an approach which takes seriously the critical relation between canonical text *and community*: that reading John for its witness to the truth is something we do as readers whose skills in discerning the truth have been learnt in Christian sacramental communities which are themselves Scripture-shaped.[21]

In talking here about the witness of the text (John's Gospel) to the truth, I am advocating, therefore, the practice of a form of critical reason which is *theological and ecclesial.* On this view, the text is more than an historical source. It is (unique, but also partial and fragmentary) testimony to the life of the triune God. This means that what we say about Christian community in the light of John has to be measured against the *greater reality* of the life of the Trinity experienced in worship and service.[22] It is not a matter of reproducing, in some flat, wooden way, 'what John says about community'. For a start, John doesn't say anything about 'community'! Not, 'In the beginning was community', but, 'In the beginning was the Word'! So what we are after is *Spirit-inspired, creative fidelity* to the witness of John to the Word-made-flesh in the ways we order our common life. To put it another way, Christianity is not a personal or social *morality*,[23] but a *participation* in the love-life of God the Holy Trinity, at the heart of which is gift, sacrifice and doxology.

Such an approach has a number of corollaries. It means, for example, that not only do we need to hear the Gospel of John in

---

[21] See on this S. E. Fowl and L. G. Jones, *Reading in Communion: Scripture and Ethics in Christian Life* (London: SPCK, 1991). Relevant also is my essay 'New Testament Interpretation as Performance' in this volume.

[22] See further Francis Watson, 'Trinity and Community: A Reading of John 17', *International Journal of Systematic Theology* 1/2 (1999), 168–84. I am grateful to Professor Watson for drawing his essay to my attention and for his comments on my own essay.

[23] Cf. J. Milbank, 'Can Morality be Christian?', in his *The Word Made Strange* (Oxford: Blackwell, 1998), 219–32.

relation to the rest of the New Testament, but also that we have to hear it *in relation to the Old Testament*. Both Testaments together tell the story of God (who comes subsequently to be known as triune), and both Testaments together tell the story of the people of God (as Israel and the church). Another corollary is that we cannot talk about 'community' without first talking about *what it means to be the church*. This is so, not only because the church mediates Scripture to us by means of authoritative 'performance' past and present, but also because the church is itself the sacramental community which brings us into contact with God's triune life – and therefore (so long as it is faithful to its calling) shows us what true community is about. A final corollary is that our reflection on community in the light of John will have *a strong eschatological dimension*. It will be oriented, like the Gospel itself, on what God's Spirit calls us to be and to do in the present as an anticipation of a new, heavenly reality yet to be revealed; and, as a reading oriented on hope in a future that is in God's hand, it will demand of us as readers and hearers an openness to ongoing judgement and transformation, both individually and in our life together.

III. Community as communication: the salvation and judgement of the world by the Word

Having cleared the way for a reading of John which is historically sensitive and at the same time theologically open, I want to draw attention to an aspect of the Gospel whose relevance to reflection on the nature of Christian community is, I think, quite profound. In broad terms, my suggestion is that John's Gospel provides seminal ground for considering ways in which Christian existence, both individual and communal, is *constituted* (*and threatened*) *by communicative activity* of one kind or another.[24] To put it another way, whereas Rudolf Bultmann placed *revelation* at the centre of Johannine concerns,[25] I want to say that revelation is itself part of a wider concern related, not just to the enlightenment of the individual – note how Bultmann's existentialism surfaces here –

[24] After I came to this conclusion, I discovered that David Ford had made a very similar observation in relation to the Epistle to the Ephesians, in his recent *Self and Salvation: Being Transformed* (Cambridge: Cambridge University Press, 1999), 107–36.

[25] See, for example, R. Bultmann, *Theology of the New Testament* (London: SCM Press, 1955), 49–69.

but also to the constitution and reconstitution of the people of God. That wider concern is *the salvation of Israel and the nations made possible by God's self-communication to the world through the Word-made-flesh* bringing into being a people called to live in the truth and witness to the truth.

I begin by listing ten items of data relevant to my claim about the significant 'communicative' dimension of John's Gospel.

(*a*) The God of the Fourth Gospel is one who communicates with the world in love by the 'sending' or 'giving' of his Son (3.16) and, through the Son, seeking true worshippers to worship him in spirit and truth (4.23). Critically, for the narrative as a whole, this divine self-communication through the Son bypasses in certain ways previously taken for granted instruments of divine communication such as Torah (1.17–18; 5.9b–18, 39–47) and temple (2.13–22; 4.21–24; 7.28).

(*b*) Jesus is identified as the divine *Logos* who, as God's Son, reveals or 'makes known' the Father (1.14–18). The symbols used in John to display Jesus' identity and role are weighted heavily towards his communicative activity in mediating 'life'. He is the Word, the Light, the Way, the Truth, the Life, the Good Shepherd, the True Vine, the one who gives 'living water', and so on. Important here also is the universal scope of the divine communication in Jesus. This culminates, at the end of Jesus' public ministry, in the coming of 'certain Greeks' to 'see' Jesus (12.20–22), and, on the cross, the *titulus* written in Hebrew, Latin and Greek (19.19–22).

(*c*) The role of the Spirit-Paraclete is communicative also. He is the one who teaches the disciples 'all things' by bringing to their remembrance all that Jesus has said to them (14.26). He also is the one who guides believers into 'all the truth' by speaking to them 'whatever he hears' (from the Risen Christ) (16.13–15). So the communicative activity of the Son is preserved and sustained by the Spirit.

(*d*) Just as the Son has been 'sent' by the Father in the power of the Spirit at the Gospel's beginning, so the disciples are 'sent' by the Son in the power of the Spirit at the Gospel's post-resurrection climax (20.21–22; cf. 17.18). In other words, the important theme of mission, of sending and being sent – a theme which embraces the Father, the Son, the Spirit-Paraclete and the disciples – has communication for the sake of the salvation of 'the world' at its heart.

(*e*) The theme of 'the truth' (*hē alētheia*) – of direct relevance to questions about the source, authority and reliability of God's self-communication – is all-pervasive: God the Father seeks those who will worship him 'in truth' (4.23); Jesus is the way to the truth (14.6); the Spirit is the 'Spirit of truth' (16.13); and the disciple is one whom the Spirit guides into 'all the truth' (16.13). Conversely, the Pharisees are blinded by sin to the truth about Jesus (9.40–41); Pilate is blind to the truth embodied in 'the man' before him (18.38); and the devil is characterized as 'a liar and the father of lies' (8.44).

(*f*) The associated theme of communication as 'witness' (*marturia*) is all-pervasive also: the Father witnesses to the Son, the Son to the Father, and the Spirit to the Son; John (the Baptist) witnesses to Jesus and against himself (1.19–23, 29–34; 3.26–30); the disciples – Philip and Nathanael, for example (1.43–51) – are witnesses; indeed, all the characters witness to Jesus, even those who either misunderstand him, like Nicodemus, or oppose him, like the high priest (11.49–52) or Pilate (19.5, 14, 19–22); and of course, the evangelist himself is a witness through the testimony of the Gospel (19.35; 21.24–25).

(*g*) The language and speech patterns of the Gospel as a whole betray a strong communicative interest. Jesus' 'riddling' speech (in *paroimiai*), the misunderstanding which meets it, and the irony which characterizes so much of the narrative, are parts of a strategy of communication appropriate to the essential *mystery of the hidden-and-revealed God* at the Gospel's heart. The same may be said of the great miracles identified by the evangelist as 'signs' (*sēmeia*) for the way they display the divine glory (*doxa*) present in Jesus (2.11). It is true also of the parabolic actions like the temple 'cleansing' (2.13–22) and the foot-washing (13.1–20).

(*h*) The Gospel reflects a strong interest, not only in communication from heaven to earth, but also in communication from earth to heaven. I have in mind here not only the divine descent–ascent motif so strong in the Farewell Discourse (13.1; 17.11a; cf. 3.13–14), but also the motif of prayer: both Jesus' prayers to the Father (11.41–42; 12.27–28; 17.1–26) and also his instructions to the disciples about prayer (14.13–14; 16.23–24, 26–27).

(*i*) On the 'horizontal' plain, there is an interest in impoverished or broken communication. One aspect of this is the contrast drawn between violent and peaceful communicative action: the peace-offering of the One who gives the sop and the intended violence of Judas his betrayer (13.18–30), the violence of Peter to Malchus in the garden and Jesus' renunciation of violence (18.10–11; cf. v. 36), and the offering of the blessing of peace at the end by the One who had been the object of violence himself (20.19, 21, 26; cf. 14.27; 16.33).

(*j*) Finally, there is the attention given to what makes true communication possible. This is a matter of what we may call Johannine ethos and ethics. Important here are specific qualities and practices like 'oneness' (or unity), worship 'in spirit and truth', 'believing' in Jesus, obedience to the commandments of Jesus, love and being loved (epitomized by 'the disciple *whom Jesus loved*'), following Jesus' example of humble service, 'abiding' in the Son as the Son 'abides' in the Father, the practice of forgiveness, and so on.

The evidence presented here is not exhaustive, but gives more than sufficient warrant for my claim that *communicative concerns lie at the heart of John's Gospel*. This is more than a claim that the Gospel itself has a communicative goal: for that is self-evident from the statement of purpose in 20.30–31 ('But these [signs] are written that you may believe . . .'). It is the stronger claim that divine and human existence and inter-relationship are represented in what may legitimately be called communicative terms. The profound implications of this for human sociality in general and Christian community in particular are what we turn to next, developing in greater detail one or two of the points made above.

IV. The oneness of God as the communicative ground of community

Much more than the other Gospels, the Fourth Gospel places heavy emphasis on the *oneness* of the Father and the Son and the oneness of believers.[26] It does so because oneness is important in itself and because there are forces of division which threaten to undermine it. Oneness is important in itself because in the faith of Israel reflected in the *Shema* (Deut 6.4–5) and celebrated daily in the

---

[26] For what follows, I am indebted to C. T. R. Hayward, 'The Lord is One: Some Reflections on Unity in Saint John's Gospel', an unpublished paper presented at the New Testament Postgraduate Seminar of the Department of Theology, University of Durham on 3 March 1997.

temple cult, *God is one*: 'Hear, O Israel: The Lord our God is one Lord; and you shall love the Lord your God with all your heart, and with all your soul, and with all your might.' As this confession suggests, the unity of the people is bound up integrally with the oneness of God. Anything which threatens the oneness of God – paradigmatically, the worship of idols – threatens the unity of the people. Conversely, anything which divides the people – the activity of false teachers, prophets or messiahs, for example – undermines the common witness of the people to the oneness of God. In sum, the existence of Israel was characterized by a series of mutually reinforcing unities: one true God, manifesting his presence (or 'name') in one tabernacle or temple, where he is worshipped according to one calendar by one holy people who purify themselves by the observance of one Torah.[27]

Against this background – which Hayward develops in relation to the concern with oneness and purity in the Qumran community – the Johannine emphasis on oneness is highly significant. Taken as a whole, the Gospel represents a claim that the one true God has made his presence uniquely known in the person of a Son with whom he is one, belief in whom brings a new oneness into being, an eschatological unity of people drawn from every nation. This explains the extraordinarily christocentric theology of the Gospel. It is John's way of setting out the radical idea that Jesus is the Son of God, the Word made flesh, the one who, by virtue of his oneness with the Father, manifests God's glorious presence. The affirmation of the divine presence uniquely in Jesus is displayed in many ways. For example, Jesus is the one upon whom the Spirit 'descends *and remains*' (1.32–33, twice; cf. 3.34–35). He unites earth and heaven as the heavenly Son of Man upon whom the angels ascend and descend (1.51). He is the temple (2.21) where true worshippers will worship the Father (4.23–24). And he is the one who manifests 'the name' (i.e. presence) of God to believers and keeps them united in that name (17.6–26). Paradoxically, however, this radical claim about God's unique self-disclosure in his Son not only provides the com-municative ground for the unity of a new people of God: it also provokes controversy, division and 'judgement' (*krisis*). *Unity creates separation!* This helps to explain the pain of parting that John's narrative betrays. In no other Gospel is the charge against Jesus of

---

[27] For more on this theme, see Bernd Janowski, 'Der eine Gott der beiden Testamente', *Zeitschrift für Theologie und Kirche* 95/1 (1998), 1–36.

blasphemy so prominent (cf. 5.18; 10.32–39; 19.7).[28] In no other Gospel is the shape of the narrative as a whole so dominated by juridical overtones, as characters in the narrative become in effect witnesses for and against Jesus' claim to oneness with God as his Son.[29]

We may explore all this further by way of a case study. In the discourse in John 10, Jesus for the first time makes the categorical statement: 'I and the Father are one' (*egō kai ho patēr hen esmen*) (10.30; cf. 17.11b, 22). To understand the significance of this testimony of oneness, we need to go back to the beginning of the discourse. In the preceding episode, Jesus and the man born blind have been in sharp conflict with 'the Jews' and the Pharisees (9.13–41). On account of the man's new communicative insight and ability imparted by his transforming encounter with Jesus – note that the man becomes a witness and teacher (9.17, 25–34)! – the man is *excommunicated* ('put out of the synagogue': *aposunagōgos*) (9.34; cf. v. 22; 12.42; 16.2). On hearing about this, Jesus (like a shepherd seeking out the lost) 'finds' the man, catechizes him, and leads him to true worship (9.35–38). Symbolically and socially, he passes from one sphere of communicative activity to another – if you will, from one 'community of discourse' to another.

This transition is explored and dramatized in the polemical teaching which follows, in which the Pharisees are shown (by implication) to be false shepherds in Israel (like the leaders of the nation pilloried in Ezek 34) and Jesus testifies to himself as the 'good shepherd'. In the first part (10.1–10), two metaphors are (rather confusingly) intertwined: Jesus is the one true door or gate (*thura*) to the sheepfold, *and* he is the shepherd of the sheep who enters by the gate! In other words, Jesus is both the way (cf. 14.6) and the one who leads the way. Those who attempt to get into the fold by other ways are impostors, and those apart from Jesus who try to lead the sheep are strangers and thieves whom the sheep will not follow. Whereas Jesus 'calls his own sheep by name and leads them out', the voice of other shepherds are not heeded because they are not recognized. Jesus is on intimate

---

[28] 'Jesus as New Temple: Johannine Blasphemy?' is the subject of a doctoral thesis by Jerry Truex, currently in preparation in the Department of Theology, University of Durham.

[29] See on this A. E. Harvey, *Jesus on Trial* (London: SPCK, 1976); also A. T. Lincoln, 'Trials, Plots and the Narrative of the Fourth Gospel', *Journal for the Study of the New Testament* 56 (1994), 3–30.

communicative terms with God's people; the Pharisees have lost contact.

In the next part of the discourse (10.11–21), the single metaphor of Jesus as shepherd of the sheep comes to the fore and is developed: 'I am the *good* shepherd. The *good* shepherd lays down his life for the sheep' (10.11). Three times in this section, Jesus affirms that he is the 'good shepherd' (10.11, twice, 14a); three times also he affirms that he 'lays down his life for the sheep' (10.11, 15b, 17b). The first time, a contrast is drawn with the hired hand who does not care for the sheep and runs away when danger threatens. The second time, the death of the good shepherd is presented as having a surprising consequence: the bringing in of 'other sheep not of this fold' (10.16). The third time, the death of Jesus as the good shepherd is given as the reason why he is loved by the Father (10.17–18). For our purposes, it is important to point out that *the good shepherd's willing self-sacrifice in death is a communicative act*. It communicates his relationship of care for the sheep which itself springs out of his relationship of loving obedience to the Father (10.14–15, 17–18). Furthermore, it is a communicative act which has enormous *creative power*, for it brings into being a new solidarity. The oneness of the Son with the Father in laying down his life for the sheep creates a new, single flock: 'I have other sheep that do not belong to this flock. I must bring them also, and they will listen to my voice. *So there will be one flock, one shepherd*' (10.16).

But now the paradox of oneness and separation reappears. Jesus' proclamation of a new solidarity arising out of his own solidarity with the Father creates division (*schisma*) among the Jews (10.19–21). The division is over the *identity* of Jesus, an issue which has been a point of controversy right through this central section of the Gospel (i.e. chs 7–10). Some think he is demon-possessed and therefore not to be listened to (10.20–21). Others question him, wanting to know if he is the Messiah. They do so, significantly, in the temple, the place of the divine presence (10.22–23; cf. 18.20). They want him not to keep them waiting in suspense any longer, and to communicate 'plainly' (*parrēsia*) (10.24b). But the Jesus of John knows that barriers to communication exist which take time to overcome – perhaps will never be overcome. So he replies in words of judgement designed, perhaps, to dislocate taken-for-granted communicative and symbolic norms:

I have told you, and you do not believe. The works that I do in my Father's name testify to me; but you do not believe, because you do not belong to my sheep. My sheep hear my voice. I know them, and they follow me. I give them eternal life, and they will never perish. No one will snatch them out of my hand. What my Father has given me is greater than all else, and no one can snatch it out of the Father's hand. The Father and I are one (10.25–30).

Here is the oneness of sheep and shepherd and of Father and Son. The two are integrally related, and cause offence: 'The Jews took up stones again to stone him . . . "It is not for a good work that we are going to stone you, but for blasphemy, because you, though only a human being, are making yourself God"' (10.31, 33). And, of course, they are right: Jesus is making himself God (cf. 10.34–38; also 1.1; 5.18; 20.28), but in a way they do not comprehend, for they are not of Jesus' sheep.

The point, I hope, is clear. In Johannine perspective, as in the faith of Israel, there is a profound connection between *who God is and what it means to be a member of the people of God*. In particular, the oneness of God is the communicative ground of the oneness of his people. But for John, the oneness of God has been revealed as *a more complex unity*, a unity between the Father and the Son made known by the Spirit. This unity has a communicative dimension. It is a unity of presence, of love, of will, of work, of gift, of Spirit. Furthermore, it provides the grounds for the *transformation of the people of God into a new unity*. By laying down his life in death, in obedience to the Father, the Son (as the Good Shepherd) opens up the way for an eschatological people made up of Gentiles as well as Jews: the 'one flock' led by the 'one shepherd' (cf. 10.16b). But tragically, this new, eschatological unity is itself a cause of offence and separation. The oneness of God communicated as gift and sacrifice is *not coercive*. As in the *Shema*, it is a summons to respond freely in wholehearted love (cf. 13.1, 34–35; 14.21, 23, 24; 15.9, 10, 12, 13, 17; 17.23–24, 26).

V. Worship 'in spirit and truth': the doxological community

If there is a profound connection in John between the oneness of God and what it means to be the people of God, that connection is made not just a matter of belief, even if right belief (itself the expression of a concomitant interpersonal trust) is central. It is made also a matter of practice: in particular, *the practice of worship.*[30] Perhaps one of the reasons for the common tendency to play up the so-called 'individualism' of the Fourth Gospel is that salvation has been seen as a matter primarily of private ratiocination and individual illumination. Certainly, the evangelist's own statement of purpose in writing is 'that you [plural!] may *believe* [*hina pisteu(s)ēte*] that Jesus is the Christ, the Son of God' (20.31). Certainly also, John's narrative is punctuated by extraordinarily dramatic one-to-one encounters with Jesus. Nevertheless, there is reason to see John differently. For example, the one-to-one encounters are encounters between Jesus and individual figures who have a very significant *representative* status: Nicodemus is a Pharisee and 'a leader of the Jews' (3.1), the woman at the well is a representative Samaritan (cf. 4.9), Pilate represents Roman authority, and so on. So these individuals are not to be taken individualistically! Even the statement of purpose in 20.30–31 does not just focus on the importance of 'believing'. It goes further: believing makes possible '*life* in his name'. This 'life', or 'eternal life', is more than a matter of right belief. It is the gift of God made possible through the death of his Son and imparted by the Spirit (cf. 4.14; 5.26; 6.27, 35, 53–58, 63; 7.38–39; etc.). What I want to show now is that, in Johannine perspective, this 'eternal life' which comes from God as gift finds expression in true worship, and that true worship, as a fundamental communicative act whereby heaven and earth touch, lies at the heart of true community.

The obvious texts which display John's concern with true worship are those to do with the temple: in particular, the Cleansing of the Temple (2.13–22) and the encounter between Jesus and the Woman of Samaria (4.1–26). Texts relating to the temple are important because the temple is where God's presence or 'name' or 'glory' (*shekina/doxa*) dwells, and therefore it is the focal point of the life of Israel.[31] True communication between God and the people of God in worship constitutes the very essence of the people's common life: its priestly polity, its economy of tithes and sacrifices, its calendar

[30] For what follows I am indebted to M. M. Thompson, 'Reflections on Worship in the Gospel of John', *The Princeton Seminary Bulletin* 19 (1998), 259–78. On the 'doxological' dimension of Christian faith in general, see D. W. Hardy and D. F. Ford, *Jubilate: Theology in Praise* (London: Darton, Longman & Todd, 1984).

[31] See now C. T. R. Hayward, *The Jewish Temple: A Non-Biblical Sourcebook* (London: Routledge, 1996); also, Bernd Janowski's discussion of Israel's exilic '*Shekina*-Theology' in his *Gottes Gegenwart in Israel* (Neukirchener: Neukirchen-Vluyn, 1993), 19–147.

of festivals and pilgrimages, its ritual practices, and its holiness worked out in rules of purity. Because John's Gospel proclaims *God's presence in Jesus* and, after his ascension, in the Spirit-Paraclete, it is not surprising that the question of true worship becomes of paramount concern, and that the temple, the festivals, the purity rules, the high priesthood, and other aspects of the cult, are a focus of attention.

Apart from the two crucial episodes mentioned, the following data reflect this attention also:

(*a*) The Prologue proclaims that 'the Word became flesh and *tabernacled* [*eskēnōsen*] among us, full of grace and truth; we have beheld his *glory* [*doxan*], glory as of the only Son from the Father' (1.14). The allusions here to the presence of the *shekina* in the tabernacle of the people of Israel are unmistakable. But now, of course, God manifests his presence in Jesus (1.17b).

(*b*) When the blind man comes to understand that Jesus is none other than the Son of Man (from heaven), he confesses his belief by word ('Lord, I believe') and by worship ('and he worshipped [*prosekunēsen*] him') (9.38). The word of confession and the practice of worship are presented here, cameo-style, as inextricably linked. Earlier in the same episode, the blind man turns teacher and, with true insight, speaks of the importance of God-fearing piety for being in good communication with God: '[I]f anyone is a worshipper of God [*theosebēs*] and does his will, God listens to him' (9.31). The interest in worship comes through again.

(*c*) The Greeks who come to Philip with a request to 'see Jesus' (itself an expression of openness to revelation), are described as being among those 'who went up [to the temple mount] to worship [*proskunēsōsin*] at the feast' (12.20). Again, faith and worship are made inseparable.

(*d*) Jesus' teaching in the Farewell Discourse about the hostility and persecution which the disciples are to expect from 'the world' (15.18 – 16.4) reaches a powerful climax with the warning that 'the hour is coming when whoever kills you will think he is offering service to God' (16.2). The word for service here is *latreia*, and its connotation is cultic. So the NRSV rightly translates it as 'worship'. We may infer from this warning that opposition to the proclamation of Christ (as one with the Father) is seen as a threat to true worship. Not just belief, but matters of liturgy and life are central concerns *on both sides*.

(*e*) To a degree unparalleled in the Synoptic Gospels, the Jesus of John times his ministry by the calendar and the festivals – Passover (2.13, 23; 6.4; 11.55; 12.1; 13.1; 18.28, 39; 19.14), Tabernacles (7.2), Dedication (10.22) – and locates his ministry in or in relation to the temple. Typical of the latter is Jesus' reply to the high priest in the high priest's courtyard: 'I have spoken openly to the world; I have always taught in synagogues *and in the temple* [*kai en tō hierō*], where all Jews come together' (18.20; cf. 7.14, 28; 8.20; 11.56). This testimony towards the Gospel's climax corresponds with the testimony from Scripture cited at the outset of Jesus' ministry: 'Zeal for *thy house* will consume me' (2.17; cf. Ps 69.10).

The question all this data raises is: Does the Fourth Evangelist display this enormous interest in worship and the temple cult only to show that it has been superseded because the presence of God has now been manifested eschatologically in the Son? Certainly, 'low church' (mainly Protestant) interpreters have tended to take it that way! However, could it be the case that worship in relation to the cult and the temple is now seen in a more complex light? Whatever our answer to this question, the prior point has been confirmed: the practice of true worship is as central a concern in John's Gospel as the confession of right belief. So, from a Johannine perspective, *the communicative acts which constitute community would have to have worship at their heart.* A statement of Jesus to the Samaritan woman (to which we shall return) makes this clear: 'But the hour is coming, and now is, when the true worshippers will worship the Father in spirit and truth, *for such the Father seeks to worship him.*' (4.23).

The episode of the Cleansing of the Temple in 2.13–22 is given enormous prominence in John. As is commonly pointed out, unlike the Synoptics, the Fourth Evangelist places this episode at the beginning of Jesus' public ministry, rather than after the Entry into Jerusalem. It is Jesus' first act on the occasion of his first (of three) visits to Jerusalem. Having revealed himself at the Cana wedding as the embodiment of God's presence or 'glory' (2.11), he now goes to the temple in Jerusalem, the place where God's glory was presumed to dwell. There, in a communicative action of prophetic symbolism whose violence is unparalleled elsewhere in the Gospel, Jesus drives out the traders and the sacrificial livestock from the temple with a whip: 'Take these things out of here; you shall not make my Father's house a house of trade' (2.16). As elsewhere in John, the action of Jesus is then explored for its significance. The tell-tale sign in the text is the repeated reference to what the disciples of Jesus 'remembered' – presumably under the inspiration of the Holy Spirit (cf. 14.26) – after the event: specifically, after Jesus' resurrection (2.17a, 22a). This interpretative 'remembering' takes two forms (cf. 2.22b). The first is scriptural. In the light of Psalm 69.10, and taking *kataphagetai* as a double-entendre meaning both 'consume' and 'destroy', Jesus' action in the temple is seen as a fulfilment of the (enscripted) will of God for the preservation of the honour of God's house, and as a contributory factor in Jesus' death. The second 'remembering' is dialogical. The Jews ask for a 'sign' legitimizing Jesus' action in the *hieron* ('temple'), and in a typically riddling response which takes the communication to a different level, Jesus answers with reference to a *different* shrine, the temple (*naos*) of his own body: 'Destroy this temple [*ton naon touton*], and in three days I will raise it up' (2.19). Typically, again, the Jews misunderstand: so the narrator provides the interpretation: 'But he spoke of the temple of his body' (2.21).

What is the evangelist seeking to communicate through the communicative acts and words of Jesus in this episode? Surely, that *Jesus' body – specifically, his crucified and risen body – is the eschatological temple of God*, the place where the glory (*doxa*) of God dwells and where true worship takes place. Some see this as the *replacement* of the Jerusalem temple and therefore of cultic worship. But that is not what the text says. Arguably, Jesus' action has as its goal, not the end of the temple, but its reformation and purification. An alternative reading, therefore would be to interpret the evangelist as talking of *another, far superior* temple which, by analogy with the eschatological abundance of the water-turned-to-wine in the previous episode (2.1–11), signifies the time and place of eschatological 'fullness' (cf. *plēroma* in 1.16) present in the person of Jesus the Messiah.[32] In which case, the temple and cult in Jerusalem, once purified, serve as 'signs' which, *while they last*, point beyond themselves to God's presence (for the salvation of Israel and the nations) in his Son. But the fundamental point remains: the Fourth Evangelist cannot conceive of the life of the people of God apart from the reciprocal communicative acts between God and his people which we call worship; and that reciprocal communicative action is bound up now with the incarnate Logos crucified and risen.

---

[32] So Thompson, 'Reflections', 10–12.

The story of Jesus and the Samaritan Woman in John 4 develops this theme further. Taking the form, well known from the patriarchal narratives, of a wooing at a well, the narrative shows Jesus the eschatological bridegroom (cf. 3.29) encountering a Samaritan woman at the well of the patriarch Jacob. Extraordinarily, the one who can turn water into gallons of wine, is tired and thirsty: so he asks the woman for a drink. But soon the conversation gets into very deep water indeed (!), for, of course, Jesus is talking at a different level. By yet more riddling speech, he is wooing the woman to accept from him '*living* water' (4.10, 11), 'a spring of water welling up to eternal life' (4.14). As we know from biblical texts (e.g. Isa 55.1; Zech 14.8; cf. Ezek 47.1–12) and from later in John's Gospel itself (7.37–39), water is a symbol of eschatological salvation generally and of the gift of the Spirit in particular.[33] But the woman has some way to go before Jesus can make this clear. First, there is a brief 'to and fro' about her marital status. This allows Jesus to reveal that he knows that the woman has had five husbands and that her present relationship is adulterous (4.16–18). In turn, this leads the woman to acknowledge that Jesus is a 'prophet' (4.19; cf. 9.17b). Curiously, she then proceeds directly to talk about Samaritan *worship*: 'Our fathers worshipped [*prosekunēsan*] on this mountain; and you say that in Jerusalem is the place where men ought to worship [*proskunein*]' (4.20). The link with the revelations about her marital status are quite opaque until we recognize that the 'five husbands' along with her current adulterous relation are probably symbolic of idolatrous worship (cf. 2 Kgs 17.13–34), having the biblical overtones of 'going after' other gods as a kind of promiscuity (cf. Hos 2.2).[34] So the dialogue is not as incoherent as it at first appears. It is about *the true worship that comes from receiving from Jesus the gift of 'living water' which is the Spirit.*

Jesus' climactic revelation, in which the word for 'worship' (*proskunein, proskunētēs*) occurs six times, makes this clear: 'Woman, believe me, the hour is coming when neither on this mountain nor in Jerusalem will you worship the Father. You worship what you do not know; we worship what we know, for salvation is from the Jews. But the hour is coming and now is, when the true worshippers will

---

[33] See M. Turner, *The Holy Spirit and Spiritual Gifts Then and Now* (Carlisle: Paternoster Press, 1996), 61.

[34] See on this S. M. Schneiders, *The Revelatory Text* (San Francisco: HarperCollins, 1991), 190–1.

worship the Father *in Spirit* [*en pneumati*] and truth, for such the Father seeks to worship him. God is Spirit, and those who worship him must worship *in Spirit* [*en pneumati*] and truth' (4.22–24). Several comments are called for here. First, Jesus acknowledges the salvation-historical primacy of Israel: 'salvation is from the Jews' (4.22b). So there is continuity with the life and worship of Israel as well as discontinuity. Second, Marianne Meye Thompson is right, I think, when she says that worship of the Father 'in Spirit and truth' constitutes 'neither a polemic against external ritual and forms of worship, nor an argument in favor of the interiorization of worship, nor a criticism of the idea of "sacred space" *per se*'.[35] The point at issue is primarily *pneumatological and eschatological* – 'the hour is coming *and now is*' (4.23a) – rather than sacerdotal. Third, the reference to 'true' worshippers and worship 'in Spirit *and truth*' is noteworthy. Implicit here is a recognition of the ever-present possibility of worship as communicative activity which is distorted and therefore idolatrous – a failure to align the worship of God with the character of God as Spirit (4.24a) and truth. Finally, there is the extraordinary theological testimony that the Father 'seeks' (*zētai*) true worshippers to worship him truly (4.23b). This is testimony to the reciprocity of divine love: God gives his Son in love (cf. 3.16) so that his people might respond doxologically.

VI. Conclusion

My concern in the preceding has not been to give a historical reconstruction of 'the Johannine community' according to the prevailing norms of historical criticism. That is an exercise of the historical imagination which others are engaged in, often with very interesting results; and the present essay is indebted to that work in many ways. But I have been attempting something different: not historical reconstruction but *theological interpretation historically informed*. My goal has been to engage in a reading of the Fourth Gospel as Scripture with a view to discerning how it might speak today about the nature of Christian community, with the implications that might have for human sociality in general.

My reading – and of course, it is a provisional, incomplete reading – has led me to three substantive conclusions. First, in so far as the Gospel of John is shot through with motifs that can properly be

---

[35] Thompson, 'Reflections', 13.

called 'communicative', it seems legitimate to make the theological inference that, seen in Johannine terms, Christian community is *constituted by communicative activity* of various kinds. The most important communicative activity is between heaven and earth, and earth and heaven. Christian community happens when heaven and earth meet. Therefore, it is an eschatological and pneumatic reality which has the nature of gift.

Second, Christian community is predicated on *the oneness of God* – the oneness of the communicative activity of the Father and the Son in the Spirit – who, by the same Spirit, brings into being a new oneness of the people of God on earth. Implicit in this oneness is a *critique of idolatry*, for idolatry, as the worship of that which is 'not God', consists in communicative activity which is fundamentally distorted, confused or misdirected. If this is so, then the unity of the community depends upon confession of the truth that God is one – a unity (so Christians believe) of Father, Son and Holy Spirit whose love all humanity is invited to share.

Third, and related, Christian community has at its heart a particular form of communicative activity: that of *worship of God 'in Spirit and truth'*. Such worship is what constitutes community – or, better still, *communion* – with God and with our fellow creatures. It is also what forms and shapes us as individuals and in our common life. It does so because it has a *particular* locus: the 'temple' of Jesus' body. It does so because it involves *particular* communicative acts: eating Jesus' flesh and drinking his blood (cf. 6.53–58). That creates identity and community. But it also creates division: 'After this many of his disciples drew back and no longer went about with him' (6.66). The gift of love which is the way to eternal life is *not coercive*, it does not *force* people to belong: otherwise it would not be gift.

10

Christian Community in the Light of 1 Corinthians

I. Introduction

In his encyclical recalling Christians to a life of greater moral seriousness, Pope John Paul II uses as the cornerstone of his argument the
dialogue between Jesus and the rich young man in Matthew 19.16–
26.[1] This is an effective strategy, not least because the text lends
itself so readily to a call to spiritual conversion and moral
transformation in accordance with both the Ten Commandments
and the teaching of Jesus.

In considering the nature of Christian community, if we were to
ask after the biblical text which lends itself most naturally to *our*
task, then Paul's First Letter to the Corinthians would be a popular
and wise choice. First, because (unlike the Gospels) it is a letter to
an identifiable early Christian community in a pluralistic, urban
setting; second, because the main focus of its concerns is to do with
how to live together in unity as people who have been 'baptized
into Christ'; third, because it is here that the metaphor of the church
as 'the body of Christ' is expounded at greatest length; fourth,
because 1 Corinthians addresses with considerable sophistication
the question of the relation between the church and the world;
and finally, because in the letter, Paul's apostolic autobiography is
related to his moral exhortation in a way which is instructive,
especially for questions of leadership and authority.

In addition, many readers of 1 Corinthians will testify to the
fact that here is a text which speaks across the centuries to our

---

[1] Pope John Paul II, *Veritatis Splendor* (London: Catholic Truth Society, 1993),
12ff. Worth noting is Walter Moberly's response 'The Use of Scripture', in C. Yeats,
ed., *Veritatis Splendor – A Response* (Norwich: Canterbury Press, 1994), 8–24.

contemporary concerns in a way that appears remarkably prescient
– as if we are all Corinthians![2] What Paul says resonates, for example,
with the concerns addressed by Jonathan Sacks in his Reith Lectures
for 1990, in which he highlights a number of serious threats to
our social fabric: economic individualism, moral pluralism and
the privatization of values, the loss of institutions which sustain
communities of memory and character, the shift from a traditional
duty-based ethic to a secular rights-based ethic, the tendency of the
religions to polarize into extremes of liberalism or conservatism,
and so on.[3] In the light of such threats, Sacks calls for the renewal
of community, both at the local level of families, churches and
voluntary associations, and at the national level of society now
reconceived (although rather too vaguely)[4] as a 'community of
communities'. Towards the end of his final lecture, he says:

> We have run up against the limits of a certain view of human society:
> one that believed that progress was open-ended, that there was no limit
> to economic growth, that conflict always had a political solution, and
> that all solutions lay with either the individual or the state. We will search,
> as we have already begun to do, for an ethical vocabulary of duties as
> well as rights; for a new language of environmental restraint; for
> communities of shared responsibility and support; for relationships
> more enduring than those of temporary compatibility; and for that
> sense, that lies at the heart of the religious experience, that human life
> has meaning beyond the self.[5]

In the sentence which follows, he adds: 'These are themes central
to the great religious traditions, and we will not have to re-invent
them.' Quite so. Indeed, within the Christian scriptural tradition,
many of these themes come together and are addressed, at least by
implication or analogy, in 1 Corinthians, as we shall see.

II. The word of the cross and the transformation of community

Paul's letter to the Corinthians is written with a view to restoring
order and unity in a community seriously threatened by division

---

[2] Cf. Fred B. Craddock, 'Preaching to Corinthians', *Interpretation* 44 (1990), 158–68.

[3] Jonathan Sacks, *The Persistence of Faith: Religion, Morality and Society in a Secular Age* (London: Weidenfeld & Nicolson, 1991), esp. 84–94. Cf. also his *Faith in the Future* (London: Darton, Longman & Todd, 1995), 55–8.

[4] Cf. Stanley Hauerwas, 'What Could it Mean for the Church to be Christ's Body?', *SJT* 48 (1995), 1–21 at 12.

[5] Sacks, *Persistence*, 92.

and factionalism. This concern surfaces at the beginning of the letter (1 Cor 1.10ff.) and, as Margaret Mitchell has shown, unites the letter as a whole.[6] It is not the case that chapters 1–4 deal with the problem of religiously motivated party strife and chapters 5–16 with a conglomeration of loosely related pastoral and theological challenges facing the church. Rather, the common denominator which ties all the issues together is that they all contribute to centrifugal forces which threaten the unity, identity and therefore also the very existence of the church.

Fundamental to Paul's response is the strategy of (what we might call, irrespective of its associations in current British politics) 'back to basics'. Most notably, where the baptismal ritual of entry into church membership appears to have been open to subversion into a ritual of entry to a particular church *faction*, Paul counters by reminding the Corinthians of the power of God made available to them by the preaching of 'the cross of Christ': 'For Christ did not send me to baptize but to preach the gospel, and not with eloquent wisdom, lest the cross of Christ be emptied of its power' (1 Cor 1.17). This recalls the Corinthians to the inaugurating word of revelation which they share in common. It also recalls them to Paul himself as the apostle who came as the messenger of revelation and to whom, therefore, they owe common allegiance as their spiritual 'father' (1 Cor 4.14–21). Gospel word and gospel messenger belong together, the implication being that to depart from one is to depart from the other also.

But Paul's words are a reminder of something else as well. They are a reminder of the basic *transformation of life* which the revelation of the power of God in the cross of Christ makes possible: 'but to those who are called, both Jews and Greeks, Christ the power of God and the wisdom of God' (1 Cor 1.24). That short phrase, 'both Jews and Greeks' (*Ioudaiois te kai Hellēsin*), speaks volumes. It expresses the universal scope of the saving revelation and the call to embody that in a transformed pattern of common life where the lines of purity are drawn no longer according to ethnicity (cf. 1 Cor 10.32; 12.11), and where the lines of human worth are drawn no longer in relation to rank and status in the world at large (1 Cor 1.26–29). Instead, God has acted in sovereign, creative love and brought into being a new, eschatological humanity:

[6] Margaret M. Mitchell, *Paul and the Rhetoric of Reconciliation* (Louisville: Westminster John Knox Press, 1993).

'[God] is the source of your life in Christ Jesus, whom God made our wisdom, our righteousness and sanctification and redemption' (1 Cor 1.30). What has such potential for creating divisions old and new – conflicting notions of wisdom (*sophia*), divergence over what constitutes righteousness (*dikaiosunē*), and so on – are focused back again on the revelation of God in Christ and his cross.

What all this implies is that for Paul Christian community is both *a response to, and a participation in, divine grace*. This grace has a particularity about it – it is a heavenly 'secret' (*mustērion*) now made known – and that particularity defines the identity of both the apostle who imparts it and the community who receives it. Thus, because God's revelation is cruciform, the life of the apostle and the ethos and identity of the community are to be cruciform also. The authority of the apostle and the unity of the church arise out of their faithfulness, in the power of God's Spirit, to this revelation in all its particularity. What undermines apostolic authority and threatens church unity is summed up in the term 'to boast' (*kauchasthai*). It is 'boasting', along with the associated competition for honour, status and power, which blind humanity to the hidden wisdom of God revealed in Christ (cf. 1 Cor 2.8) and sow the seeds of an agonistic social order oriented on violence, domination and intolerance of the weak. But in Christ, a new community is called into being, and 'boasting' is transformed from violence into doxology: 'Let him who boasts, boast of the Lord' (1 Cor 1.31; cf. 3.21; 4.7).

III. The Lord's Supper and the church as a community of memory

We ought not to be surprised in reading 1 Corinthians to discover that Paul's preaching of the cross and the related practice of baptism in the name of Christ raised as many problems as it solved. The bringing to birth of a new humanity and transformed patterns of common life would not be authentic if they did not involve pain, struggle and conflict. This is the case for Paul himself: 'When reviled, we bless; when persecuted, we endure; when slandered, we try to conciliate; we have become, and are now, as the refuse (*perikatharmata*) of the world, the offscouring (*peripsēma*) of all things' (1 Cor 4.13). So why should it be different for Paul's churches? The point is made powerfully by Fred Craddock:

It is naïve to think one can function with the simple formula: People
have problems and the gospel resolves them. The fact is, the gospel
generates in individual lives and in society a new set of problems. One
has only to love impartially and hatred is threatened and stirred to
violence. One has only to speak the truth and falsehood takes the stand
with pleasing lies. Invite persons of different social and economic backgrounds around the same table and the fellowship is strained, often
breaking apart. Announce freedom in Christ Jesus and some turn a deaf
ear to the call for restraint for the sake of the weaker brother or sister.
Place in church leadership persons who have never led in any other arena
and arrogance often replaces service. Plant the cross in a room and the
upwardly mobile convert it into a ladder. Evil, by whatever name it is
called, will not sit idly by and allow the gospel to transform a community.[7]

If evil does not sit idly by when Paul preaches the cross and people
are baptized into Christ, neither does it restrain itself when people
try to embody and consolidate their new identity around a shared
table and a common meal. Now, the tendency to convert the cross
into a social ladder and baptism into a ritual of status differentiation
carries over into that most crucial of rituals of solidarity in antiquity,
table fellowship around a meal: '[W]hen you assemble as a church,
I hear that there are divisions (*schismata*) among you . . . For in
eating, each one goes ahead with his own meal (*to idion deipnon*),
and one is hungry and another is drunk. What! Do you not have
houses to eat and drink in? Or do you despise the church of God
and humiliate those who have nothing?' (1 Cor 11.20–22).

This is a revealing accusation.[8] On the positive side, it shows that
people from a wide range of social backgrounds are coming together
en ekklēsia: for some have plenty and others have nothing, some
have leisure enough to be able to arrive early and others are in
servitude and arrive late (cf. 1 Cor 11.33). On the negative side,
however, the accusation shows that, instead of functioning as a
practical and symbolic focus of life-transforming unity, the meal
bears all too many of the marks of the competition for dominance
brought into the church from the household, the voluntary association and the city state: hence the conspicuous consumption, the
eating apart, and the attempt to exercise influence by bestowing

---

[7] Craddock, 'Preaching', 167.

[8] See in general Gerd Theissen, *The Social Setting of Pauline Christianity*
(Edinburgh: T&T Clark, 1982), 145–74; Wayne A. Meeks, *The First Urban Christians*
(New Haven: Yale University Press, 1983), 157–62); and Stephen C. Barton, 'Paul's
Sense of Place: An Anthropological Approach to Community Formation in Corinth',
NTS, 32 (1986), 225–46, esp. 234–42.

honour on some and shame on others. The church was offering its own version of the imperial 'bread and circuses'.

If we ask how things could have degenerated so, we are forced to reckon with a number of considerations. First, it seems clear that the process of resocialization which began with conversion and baptism into Christ was slow and uncertain due, not least, to the power of inherited cultural mores and social reflexes and to the pervasiveness of alternative models of sociality in the wider environment.[9] Given that believers were now living *in two social worlds simultaneously*, and that Paul wants to discourage moves to withdraw from the pagan world (cf. 1 Cor 5.10; 7.12–16), the danger that the community of saints would be contaminated by the old ways remained strong. This is likely to have been the case, especially in the more 'ingrained' ritual or ceremonial areas of life like temple worship, marriage ties and sexual relations, and meals public and private.

Second – and what I want to draw particular attention to here – it also seems clear that the Christian community at Corinth was a group *short on shared narrative and corporate memory*.[10] Among other things, it appears that its members (especially the prominent ones) so exalted individual 'spiritual' experience that they neglected shared engagement with the Scriptures and the apostolic tradition, and played down the importance of the more didactic gifts of prophetic discernment and teaching (cf. 1 Cor 12.7ff., 28–30; 14.1ff.). This helps to explain why Paul, in this very act of epistolary communication, adopts the role of a father instructing his spiritual offspring (1 Cor 4.14–21). It also explains why, at crucial points, he *reminds* the Corinthians of both dominical and scriptural tradition which he has passed on to them previously but which they seem to have forgotten or misconstrued or remembered only selectively (cf. 1 Cor 15.1ff.).

The Last Supper tradition is one such point (1 Cor 11.23ff.; cf. 10.14–22). Having castigated the Corinthians for their abuse of

---

[9] Cf. James D. G. Dunn, *1 Corinthians* (Sheffield: Sheffield Academic Press, 1995), 79: 'It should occasion no surprise that a movement of such religious motivation operated within social conventions which were at odds with its primary inspiration without apparently being aware of the fact.'

[10] On the idea of memory as helping to constitute a community, see Stanley Hauerwas, *A Community of Character* (Notre Dame: University of Notre Dame Press, 1981), 53–71. On the role of remembering in relation to worship in particular, see Nicholas Wolterstorff, 'The Remembrance of Things (Not) Past: Philosophical Reflections on Christian Liturgy', in T. P. Flint, ed., *Christian Philosophy* (Notre Dame: University of Notre Dame Press, 1990), 118–61, esp. 130ff.

table fellowship, he recalls them from eating their 'own' meals to participation together in the 'Lord's meal' (*kuriakon deipnon*), informed by authoritative tradition received 'from the Lord' and 'handed on' to them by the apostle himself. What is especially striking here is the way in which, as with the ritual of baptism early on in the letter, apostolic tradition is introduced as a control and a corrective. It is as if the non-verbal communication which takes place in the ritualized behaviour of the meal is so powerfully expressive and yet also so open to a variety of construals – some of which can be destructive and divisive – that an accompanying authoritative communication of a verbal kind is required. The food for thought embodied in the meal requires for its interpretation the food for thought embodied in the apostolic tradition. If you like, word and sacrament: where the word *situates* the meal and those who eat it in a community of memory and shared narrative.

Significantly, that narrative is part of the same narrative introduced at the letter's beginning: Christ crucified. Says Paul: 'For as often as you eat this bread and drink the cup, you proclaim the Lord's death until he comes' (1 Cor 11.26). So the narrative of Christ crucified is intended by Paul to be the constant point of reference. It is what imparts the power for a new pattern of common life at the start, and it is what imparts the power for consolidating that common life as it goes on. By repeatedly drawing it to their attention and by insisting that their regular gatherings for the meal serve to proclaim it, Paul, the good teacher, is impressing indelibly on their corporate memory both what has brought them to life and what will sustain that life in harmony.[11]

IV. Holiness, discipline and the church as a community of character

If the Christian community at Corinth was short on shared narrative and corporate memory, it appears also, and as a corollary, to have been lacking in discipline – so much so that the unity and integrity of the community were at risk.[12] Paul's letter gives evidence of a

[11] On the significance of repetition, note sociologist David Martin's comment in his essay, 'Profane Habit and Sacred Usage', *Theology* 82 (1979), 83–95 at 84: 'The act of repetition is a summons to complete attention.'

[12] I have been helped to think more seriously about the nature of Christian discipline by Craig Dykstra's essay 'Disciplines: Repentance, Prayer and Service', in R. P. Hamel and K. R. Hines, eds, *Introduction to Christian Ethics: A Reader* (New York: Paulist Press, 1989), 293–307.

divisive rivalry working itself out in a number of ways: the exercise
of patronage, the practice of 'boasting' and other forms of self-
display, and the destructive distribution of honour and shame.
The letter also gives evidence of spiritual immaturity, lack of
discernment in basic areas of social intercourse, the exaltation of
individual liberty over communal responsibility, and a dangerous
naïvety about personal authority and the limits of the religious community. The relative absence of a shared narrative reiterated in
common worship and reinforced by communal discipline meant
that the resources for building a *community of character* were in short
supply.

Paul's response takes a number of forms.[13] First, he uses *a
particular kind of language*. This is the language of holiness understood as separation and discrimination, a language available to him
already from the Jewish moral tradition.[14] Noteworthy, for example,
is the designation of the addressees at the very beginning of the
letter: 'To the church of God (*ekklēsia tou theou*) which is at Corinth,
to those sanctified (*hēgiasmenois*) in Christ Jesus, called to be saints
(*klētois hagiois*), together with all those who in every place call on
the name of our Lord Jesus Christ' (1 Cor 1.2). There could be no
clearer expression of Paul's intention to refocus the Corinthians'
self-understanding on their authentic, common vocation to be God's
holy people, united under the lordship of Christ. The same could
be said of his use of the language of divine election (e.g. 1 Cor
1.26ff.), the language of servitude or indebtedness to God, Christ
or the Spirit (e.g. 1 Cor 3.5–23), and the pervasive language of fictive
kinship to designate believers as 'brothers' and 'sisters', members
together of the household of God.

Corresponding with this language of separation used of insiders
is the language used of outsiders. They are 'the pagans' (*hoi ethnoi*),
'the world' (*ho kosmos*), 'those outside' (*hoi exō*), 'the unrighteous'
(*hoi adikoi*), 'the immoral' (*hoi pornoi*), 'unbelievers' (*apistoi*) and
'idolaters' (*eidōlolatrai*) – to mention just the most prominent terms
in the lexicon of holiness upon which Paul draws (cf. 1 Cor 5–6;

---

[13] See further Wayne A. Meeks, '"Since then you would need to go out of the
world": Group Boundaries in Pauline Christianity', in T. J. Ryan, ed., *Critical History
and Biblical Faith: New Testament Perspectives* (Villanova: College Theology Society,
1979), 1–23.

[14] Cf. Christopher Rowland, 'Moses and Patmos: Reflections on the Jewish
Background of Early Christianity', in J. Davies *et al.*, eds, *Words Remembered, Texts
Renewed* (Sheffield: Sheffield Academic Press, 1995), 280–99, esp. 289–93.

7.12ff.; 10.7; etc.). Such terms are intended by Paul to reinforce the Corinthian believers' (apparently rather weak or confused) sense of belonging to a new, redeemed humanity. They offer the Corinthians a traditional, rhetorically powerful linguistic resource by means of which both to think about themselves differently and to see themselves as being different.

As well as the language of separation, there is Paul's insistence on *moral and social discipline* in the community. Thus, because the acceptance and exercise of discipline requires the acknowledgment of authority in the community, Paul asserts the legitimacy of his own apostolic authority over the community as its founder, father, nurturer and principal model. But he does not stop with that. He also imparts a countervailing 'wisdom' to that being propagated by those he views as troublemakers. He demands the renunciation of habits of speech and action which promote faction rather than unity. He introduces principles and rules for the orderly and seemly governance of members' social relations, including instructions on who to eat with and who to sleep with. Under the guiding christological metaphor of 'the body of Christ', he gives instructions on the proper conduct of Christian meetings. And, in order to maximize the possibility of unity in a community with so much potential and actual diversity, he advocates an overriding ethic of humility and other-regarding love (*agapē*). All this he does in a powerful act of theological persuasion which seeks to situate the lives of the Corinthians in an eschatological perspective: between the cross, at the letter's opening, and the resurrection, towards the letter's end. It is the cross and resurrection of Christ which have gained for the Corinthians participation in the kingdom of God; and Paul's desire is to see that participation embodied in the life of the community.

I use the word 'embodied' advisedly, because it is striking how much of Paul's instruction in communal discipline has to do with members' bodies – above all, in two areas of bodily activity: eating and issues of commensality on the one hand, and sexual intercourse and issues related to marriage and gender roles on the other.[15] From

[15] For the most recent comprehensive study, see Dale B. Martin, *The Corinthian Body* (New Haven and London: Yale University Press, 1995). Cf. also, Wayne A. Meeks, *The Origins of Christian Morality* (New Haven and London: Yale University Press, 1993), 130–49, on 'The Body as Sign and Problem'; and Jerome Neyrey, 'Body Language in 1 Corinthians: The Use of Anthropological Models for Understanding Paul and his Opponents', *SEMEIA* 35 (1986), 129–70.

a social-anthropological perspective, this is not surprising. In her well-known study *Natural Symbols* Mary Douglas has shown that 'the human body is always treated as an image of society',[16] and that concerns about the boundaries of the social body tend to be expressed in anxiety about the boundaries of its members' physical bodies. The body's orifices are a special focus of attention in this regard, especially the mouth and the sexual organs. Rules, norms and customs for ordering and guarding the orifices of individual, physical bodies are a powerful practical and symbolic way of ordering and guarding the boundaries of the social body.

So what Paul says about food and sex are not disparate concerns from a vague catalogue of problems, as if Paul is a kind of first century 'agony aunt'! Rather, there is an underlying *socio*-logic, itself related to an even more fundamental *theo*-logic. In short, Paul is talking about *three kinds of 'body'*, not just one: the believer's physical body cannot be understood independently of the social body of the *ekklēsia*, and the *ekklēsia* cannot be understood appropriately except as 'the body *of Christ*'. Acknowledging this interrelationship of three kinds of body is important. It helps us to see, for example, that Paul's sexual ethics are an integral part of his social ethics, and that his social ethics (which touch on a range of issues much wider than just sex) are an integral part of belonging to Christ under the sovereignty of God in the power of the Spirit.

To take one example. In addressing a case of *porneia*, where certain members are attending meals as guests at pagan temples and having recourse to the prostitutes there (1 Cor 6.12ff.; cf. chs 8–10), Paul insists that food, sex and the body are not immaterial to the life of freedom in the kingdom of God. On the contrary, true freedom is shown in doing what is advantageous (*sumpherein*) to others (6.12a), what demonstrates God's resurrection power in the life of the individual (6.14), what expresses being part of Christ's body, the church (6.15), and what shows the believer's new identity as a 'temple of the Holy Spirit' (6.19). Says Paul:

> The body is not meant for immorality, but for the Lord, and the Lord for the body. And God raised the Lord and will also raise us up by his power. Do you not know that your bodies are members of Christ? Shall I therefore take the members of Christ and make them members of a prostitute? Never! . . . Do you not know that your body is a temple of

[16] Mary Douglas, *Natural Symbols* (London: Barrie & Jenkins, 1973, 2nd edn), 98.

the Holy Spirit within you, which you have from God? You are not you own; you were brought with a price. So glorify God in your body. (1 Cor 6.13b–20)

Striking in Paul's argument here is the way the freedom of the individual is reinterpreted by being set firmly in a wider context of significance and obligation – in the context of a solidarity whose members are not just earthly but heavenly as well. For Paul, uniting with others is a legitimate expression of freedom *only if it is a union of the right kind.* Union with a prostitute is wrong and disorderly because it contradicts the most important union of all: with the Lord and with the Lord's people.[17] In arguing thus, it is noteworthy that allusion to the shared narrative of Christ's cross and resurrection recurs once more and that Paul's incipiently trinitarian theologic comes powerfully to the fore to provide the framework for moral discernment and action.

V. The body of Christ and the church as an alternative society

The metaphor of the church as 'the body of Christ', introduced briefly in the instructions on avoiding *porneia* just discussed (cf. 1 Cor 6.15), is developed more fully later on, not least in 1 Corinthians 12.12–31. If in 1 Corinthians 6 the body of Christ is a way of situating and controlling individual bodies in their sexual relations, and if in 1 Corinthians 10–11 it is a way of situating and controlling individual bodies in their eating practices, in 1 Corinthians 12, the body of Christ is a way of situating and controlling individual bodies in their life together as the people of God, a life given primary focus in communal worship.

If we ask what it is about the metaphor that allows it to function this way in 1 Corinthians 12, attention needs to be drawn to the fact that in ancient political literature, the body was a common metaphor

---

[17] Note Hauerwas's perceptive comment in 'What Could it Mean?', 9. 'Such a practice is necessary for a reading of the Pauline stress on the body if we are to avoid the ontology of the body so characteristic of liberal societies – i.e. that my "body" is an instrument for the expression of my "true self". That is why I suspect that nothing is more gnostic than the celebration of the "body" in liberal societies. The "body" so celebrated turns out to be the body created by the presumption that there is an "I" that *has* a body. . . . The body politics of liberalism can make no sense of passages like 1 Corinthians 6.12–20. Paul did not think that we, as baptized believers, we [*sic*] ought to view our bodies *as if* we were one with another through Christ, but rather that our bodies are quite literally not our "own" because we have been made (as well as given) a new body by the Spirit.'

for society or the state, frequently used as a rhetorical means both
to combat discord and to encourage unity in diversity.[18] This
'political' dimension of the metaphor is easily overlooked if 'the
body of Christ' is understood in purely eucharistic terms or if
what Paul says in 1 Corinthians 12 and 14 is segregated from the
underlying preoccupation of the letter as a whole by too narrow
a focus on 'early Christian worship' or on things 'charismatic'.
But once we take with full seriousness Paul's underlying preoccupation with combatting factionalism and establishing order and
unity in the church at Corinth, and once we surrender modernist
hermeneutical tendencies to separate politics from religion or
worship from everyday life, we are more likely to recognize that the
argument in these chapters represents another step in Paul's attempt
to establish the church as an *alternative society* autonomous in
essential respects from the society at large.

This is consistent with Paul's use of the language of separation
already noted. It is consistent also with his condemnation of the
practice of resolving intramural disputes (probably over marriage,
property and inheritance) in the public courts (1 Cor 6.1–11),
and of joining in meals at pagan temples presided over by demons
(1 Cor 10.1–22). Nor is it coincidental that Paul uses the metaphors
of plant, building and temple as designations of the church (e.g.
1 Cor 3.6ff., 10ff., 16–17), for these are also biblical metaphors used
of the sacred polity of Israel.[19] It is very likely that 'the body of
Christ' is yet another corporate metaphor by means of which Paul
seeks to consolidate the church as a kind of 'true Israel',[20] the
eschatological people of God, an autonomous polity bearing witness
to the kingdom of God, the lordship of Christ and the power of the
Spirit. This is indeed a 'high' view of the church. James D. G. Dunn
comes to the same conclusion:

[18] See further, Mitchell, *Paul and the Rhetoric of Reconciliation*, 157–64. Recognition
of this 'political' dimension is surprisingly absent from the analysis of E. Earle Ellis,
'*Soma* in First Corinthians', *Interpretation* 44 (1990), 132–44.

[19] Cf. Paul S. Minear, *Images of the Church in the New Testament* (Philadelphia:
Westminster Press, 1960).

[20] Note the comment of James D. G. Dunn in '"The Body of Christ" in Paul', in
M. J. Wilkins and T. Paige, eds, *Worship, Theology and Ministry in the Early Church*
(Sheffield: JSOT Press, 1992), 146–62 at 161: 'The body of Christ as part of the
solution to the problem of Israel in terms of social and corporate identity, even if
only as an eschatological hope, is an aspect of the whole theme which deserves
further study.' Cf. also, Hauerwas, 'What Could it Mean?', 19–20.

[I]t is significant that the body imagery as used for the local congregations in Corinth and Rome was derived from the imagery of the body for the state. To use just this metaphor for such, much smaller, ethnically diverse gatherings within the cities and old city states of the Roman Empire was a striking assertion of ecclesiological self-understanding. . . . Indeed, if we do not press the point too far, the sense that the church in this city or that region was the body to which believers belonged carried with it the implication that this belonging was more fundamental than any other citizenship, and perhaps also that the assembly gathered for worship should provide a model of community for the larger cities and states.[21]

As to what kind of alternative society the church body is to be: this is summed up in the designation of the body as 'the body *of Christ*': 'For just as the body is one and has many members, and all the members of the body, though many, are one body, *so it is with Christ.* For by one Spirit we were all baptized into one body – Jews or Greeks, slaves of free – and all were made to drink of one Spirit' (1 Cor 12.12–13). In other words, belonging by baptism to Christ in the power of the indwelling Spirit creates a new solidarity which transcends the old divisions. In this new solidarity, there is to be unity based on an acceptance of the diversity of each member's *charisma(ta)*; a recognition that the strength of the whole depends on the full contribution of the individual parts inspired by 'the same Spirit'; a humility finding expression in special concern for the 'weaker' members; and an acknowledgment of the need for order, since 'God has appointed in the church first apostles, second prophets, third teachers . . .' (1 Cor 12.28).[22]

Noticeable in all this is the way power indicators in the society at large (status, rank, birth, gender, education and occupation) are left behind or reinterpreted in relation to Christ and the Spirit. Noticeable also is the shift from competitive social relations to relations of mutual responsibility and interdependence where what is important is the 'building up' (*oikodomē*) of the community (1 Cor 14.12, 26b). Even the restrictions on the role of women (1 Cor 14.33b–36; cf. 11.2–16) – controversial as they were then and doubtless contributing to the baleful tradition of Christian misogyny ever since – may be understood, first and foremost, as part of Paul's

[21] '"The Body of Christ" in Paul', 160–1.
[22] See further James D. G. Dunn, *Jesus and the Spirit* (London: SCM Press, 1975), chs 8–9; and *1 Corinthians*, ch. 5.

overall attempt to restrain forces threatening the disintegration of the church: for the instructions he gives occur in the wider context of teaching about the proper ordering of worship (1 Cor 11.2 – 14.40), and represent an attempt to modify a charismatic-gnostic spirituality that knows no bounds in favour of a spirituality controlled by a concern with what makes for 'peace' (*eirēnē*) in the fellowship (1 Cor 14.33a).[23]

VI. The resurrection and the church as a community of hope

It is not coincidental that Paul's attempt to overcome the enmity and discord in the church reaches a climax with the teaching on the resurrection (1 Cor 15.1–58). Clearly, part of the reason why Paul turns to this subject is that it is yet another source of disagreement. Like the disagreement which divided his fellow Jews, separating the party of the Pharisees from that of the Sadducees (cf. Acts 23.6–10; 24.21), the claim of 'some' in the church that 'there is no resurrection of the dead' (1 Cor 15.12; cf. v. 35) was a serious threat both to the unity of the church and to its moral integrity (cf. 15.32b–34). So Paul has to deal with this matter: and whereas on a number of other issues Paul can be seen looking for compromise and accommodation, here he is quite uncompromising. For what is at stake is nothing less than the truth of the gospel itself, compromise of which would undermine the essential basis of the believers' common life.[24] As Margaret Mitchell puts it:

> The relationship of chap. 15 to Paul's overall argument against factionalism is to be seen in his overarching strategy of redefining the standards and goals in relation to which the Corinthians should make their daily life decisions. He appeals to the resurrected life to minimize the importance of the present striving to supremacy within the community, holding those insignificant gains and losses up against the great eschatological victory which all will share . . . Paul calls them to unity in their common traditions (15.1; cf 11.2, 23), and in their future eschatological destiny.[25]

[23] So too Mitchell, *Paul and the Rhetoric of Reconciliation*, 280–3, noting the reference to Livy 34.2–4 (on the speech of Marcus Porcius Cato advocating the submission of Roman women to the Oppian law for fear of their *seditio*).
[24] This is why Paul begins his argument in ch. 15, not with the resurrection *per se*, but with a reaffirmation of *the gospel*, 'which [he says] you received, in which you stand, by which you are saved' (15.1–2), followed by a reminder of the foundational apostolic tradition which begins with the cross (15.3ff.).
[25] Mitchell, *Paul and the Rhetoric of Reconciliation*, 175.

But the resurrection has to be dealt with by Paul not just because it is a source of dispute and disorder. His concerns here (and elsewhere) are not narrowly pragmatic. Rather, like his teaching about the cross at the beginning of the letter, the importance of the resurrection is that it is a message of *profound, transforming and unifying hope in God* in relation to which every manifestation of death-dealing pessimism, pride or party spirit in the church should be left behind. Karl Barth was right therefore to claim that 1 Corinthians 15 'forms not only the close and crown of the whole Epistle, but also provides the clue to its meaning, from which place light is shed onto the whole'.[26]

Thus, in the opening section (15.3–11) it is the appearance of Christ to Paul which enables Paul to testify to God's transforming grace in the life of one 'unfit to be called an apostle' (15.9). In other words, Paul's unworthiness and weakness in comparison to others in Corinth (including other apostles) is not a disadvantage. On the contrary, the manifestation of God's grace to him in the appearance of the risen Christ is a demonstration that personal and apostolic authority does not rest in human hands and is not a matter of human striving. Rather, it comes from God *as gift* (15.28, 38, 57). This *liberates* Paul from an anxious and debilitating competition for honour – so much so that (ironically) he can even claim to have worked harder than any of the others, because of the grace of God at work in him. What is important, implies Paul, is not *who* preached the resurrection in order to bring the Corinthians to faith, but that, whoever it was, it was *the resurrection* that was preached (15.11). For it is the revelation of the grace of God in the (death and) resurrection of Christ which is the eschatological reality offering new life and hope *for all alike*.

This includes the dead as well as the living (15.12–29). It embraces those, like Paul himself, for whom each day promises to be the last on account of the constant threats to his personal well-being: 'I die every day!' (15.30–32; cf. 4.9–13). It brings the eschatological hope of transformed bodies to human beings weighed down with a sense of the body's relentless vulnerability to decay, dishonour and

---

[26] Karl Barth, *The Resurrection of the Dead* (ET London: Hodder & Stoughton, 1933), 11, cited and fully discussed in Anthony Thiselton's essay 'Luther and Barth on 1 Corinthians 15: Six Theses for Theology in Relation to Recent Interpretation', in W. P. Stephens, ed., *The Bible, The Reformation and the Church* (Sheffield: Sheffield Academic Press, 1995), 258–89.

weakness (15.42–43). It offers assurance of victory in the battle with
mortal humanity's final enemy – a victory which is the gift of God
through the risen Christ (15.57). And because the ultimate victory
is the gift of God it is no person's boast. That is why the resurrection is the basis for a new morality and social ethos (cf. 15.32b–34)
– indeed, a new 'economy'. Paul's way of putting it, using building
and work metaphors, is this: 'be steadfast, immovable, always
abounding in the work of the Lord, knowing that in the Lord your
labour is not in vain' (15.58).

Lest this be taken as pious platitude, Paul goes on immediately
to say what this means in practical terms: the Corinthians are to
manifest their hope in the resurrection of the dead by contributing
to *the collection* (16.1–4).[27] The reordering of their energies away
from self-preservation and competition for honour within the
church – in the light of resurrection faith and the hope of inheriting
the kingdom of God – releases them to work with and for those
in other churches. To put it in other terms, by leaving behind
what separates them from each other (whether in life or in death),
they are able to act in ways of faith, hope and love which unite
them in a wider solidarity. Together with the churches of Galatia
and Asia (16.1, 19), the Corinthians can share in supporting their
impoverished fellow believers in Jerusalem, thereby uniting diaspora
Gentiles with Judean Jews and consolidating the partnership
between the apostle to the Gentiles and the apostolate in Jerusalem.
This represents the coming into being of a new, translocal and multi-
ethnic polity, unprecedented in antiquity. It is as if Christ's victory
over death and the believers' hope of future resurrection *transforms
the axes of human existence both individual and corporate.*[28] What matters
now is not self-preservation and grasping for glory in the face of
death, but self-donation and the praise of God in the light of the
resurrection: 'Thanks be to God who gives us the victory through
our Lord Jesus Christ' (15.57f.).

---

[27] See the useful summary of scholarly findings in Scott McKnight's essay
'Collection for the Saints', in G. F. Hawthorne *et al.*, eds, *Dictionary of Paul and his
Letters* (Downers Grove: InterVarsity Press, 1993), 143–7.
[28] Cf. Richard Hays' helpful essay 'Ecclesiology and Ethics in 1 Corinthians', *Ex
Auditu* 10 (1994), 31–43 at 40: '[The collection] functions for Paul as the great
symbolic enactment of the unity of Gentile and Jew, thus figuring forth the
eschatological character of this new messianic community that Paul is laboring to
create.'

VII. Apostolic autobiography and the nature of leadership

In Paul's use of the metaphor of the body of Christ in 1 Corinthians, there is no reflection on who is the head. This development takes place later, in Colossians and Ephesians (cf. Col 1.18; 2.19; Eph 1.22–23; 4.15–16; 5.23). But this does not mean that 1 Corinthians is lacking when it comes to the issue of authority and leadership in the community. In particular, Paul's appeal to his own apostolic autobiography provides significant material for reflection on the nature of Christian leadership.

Read superficially, it would be easy to interpret Paul's frequent self-reference in 1 Corinthians as highly egotistical – and, of course, those hostile to Paul commonly accuse him of being domineering and manipulative. But this may be a way only of protecting ourselves against the things that are uncongenial in what Paul says. A closer, more historically sensitive reading leads to a different conclusion: Paul, in common with other Graeco-Roman moralists of his day (such as Plutarch, Isocrates, Quintilian, Seneca and Epictetus), *presents himself as a paradigm* of the behaviour he seeks to commend to his addressees. The rationale is straightforward. These moralists shared the conviction 'that example was far superior to precept and logical analysis as a means of illustrating and reinforcing appeals to pursue a particular mode of life'.[29] Paul himself puts it quite succinctly and christocentrically: 'Be imitators of me, as I am of Christ' (1 Cor 11.1).

There are two points in particular where Paul refers at length to his own example in order to provide a paradigm of how he wants the Corinthians – and especially those who style themselves 'the strong' – to behave. The first comes in 1 Corinthians 9, which interrupts Paul's instructions 'concerning things sacrificed to idols' (*peri de tōn eidōlothutōn*), in 1 Corinthians 8–10. The second comes in 1 Corinthians 13, which interrupts Paul's instructions 'concerning spiritual gifts' (*peri de tōn pneumatikōn*) in 1 Corinthians 12–14. But understood from the perspective of epistolary *paraenesis* and the common practice of Graeco-Roman moralists, 1 Corinthians 9 and 13 are not interruptions or digressions at all. Rather, each passage is integrally related to its specific context, as Paul presents his own behaviour as a practical guide for the Corinthians to follow.

---

[29] Carl R. Holladay, '1 Corinthians 13: Paul as Apostolic Paradigm', in D. L. Balch *et al.*, eds, *Greeks, Romans and Christians* (Philadelphia: Fortress Press 1990), 80–98 at 84.

So, to persuade the strong to refrain from exercising their 'right' (*exousia*) to eat food sacrificed to idols – thus threatening the unity of the church by causing grave offence to the weak – Paul shifts to the first person singular to show what he himself does: 'Therefore, if food is a cause of my brother's falling, I will never eat meat, lest I cause my brother to fall' (1 Cor 8.13). He then proceeds to give an extended example from his own practice as their apostle of how, at considerable social and economic cost, he refrains from exercising his own *exousia* to receive financial support from the Corinthians so as not to place any hindrance in the way of their receiving the gospel (1 Cor 9.1–18). For Paul the apostle, true freedom is found in being able to restrict one's freedom – which means becoming like a slave (*doulos*) – for the sake of 'saving' as many people as possible: 'For though I am free from all, I have made myself a slave to all, that I might win the more. . . . I have become all things to all people, that I might by all means save some' (1 Cor 9.19–22; cf. 10.31–33).[30] This is not an easy path, as the language of enslavement suggests. It involves putting the interests of others first: for the sake of Christ, the gospel of Christ, and the brother for whom Christ died. Not surprisingly, therefore, the argument reaches a climax with yet another piece of paraenesis about the body: in this case, Paul's own body which, like that of an athlete, has to be disciplined and trained if the prize (which in Paul's case is the reward consequent upon building up the body of Christ) is to be attained (1 Cor 9.24–27).

The second instance follows the same pattern. In the middle of instruction intended to counter the threat to church unity posed, this time, by disorder and confusion (*akatastasia*: 1 Cor 14.33) in the exercise of the so-called 'spiritual gifts', Paul reverts to the first person singular in order once more to offer a concrete paradigm of the 'more excellent way' of love (*agapē*), the practice of which will make the Corinthians' worship upbuilding rather than catastrophic for the community. Carl Holladay points out that 'Commentators have long noticed Paul's use of the first person singular here [in 1 Cor 13], but it is ordinarily taken in a general rather than a strictly autobiographical sense.'[31] He argues

---

[30] See further on this Stephen C. Barton, '"All Things to All People": Paul and the Law in the Light of 1 Corinthians 9.19–23', in J. D. G. Dunn, ed., *Paul and the Law* (Tübingen: Mohr/Siebeck, 1996), 271–86.

[31] Holladay, '1 Corinthians 13', 88.

convincingly, however, that it has to be taken literally. Paul is talking about himself: his own *charismata* governed by love (13.1–3), his own understanding of the phenomenology of love (13.4–7), and his own insight into the eschatological finality of a love already present and never-ending (13.8–13). Whereas the immaturity of the Corinthian 'strong' has caused them to regard 'knowledge' (*gnōsis*) as the ultimate eschatological reality, allowing them to lord it over others, Paul presents himself as one who has 'grown up' spiritually and who can testify otherwise: not *gnōsis* but *agapē* is the ultimate eschatological reality – because, as he has pointed out earlier, 'knowledge puffs up, but love builds up' (1 Cor 8.1b). On this paradigmatic basis, Paul can then return in chapter 14 to the second person plural, prefacing his ongoing instructions about 'spiritual gifts' with the overriding command: 'Make love your aim' (1 Cor 14.1).

We need to be wary of being simplistic in trying to articulate what all this implies about Paul as a leader. Nevertheless, it seems clear that Paul did not shirk the costly role of exercising leadership and authority in the Corinthian community. It is clear also that Paul sought to lead by exemplifying in his own apostolic life the virtues and practices which he invited his fellow-believers to imitate. Finally, Paul's goal in exercising leadership was the consolidation, not of his own power and status, but of the oneness and growth of the community 'in Christ'.

VIII. Conclusion

In the light of this examination of 1 Corinthians, we may conclude with the simple observation that Paul's primary concern was not with 'community' in the abstract, but with how to respond and bear witness to the startling, new revelation of the grace of God in the

---

[32] For an argument along very similar lines but in relation to 1 Peter, see the masterly essay by Miroslav Wolf, 'Soft Difference: Theological Reflections on the Relation Between Church and Culture in 1 Peter', *Ex Auditu* 10 (1994), 15–30. Note esp. his comment on p. 27: 'It seems obvious, but in no way trite, to note that 1 Peter does not speak abstractly about the relation between gospel and culture. Much like other NT writings, the epistle does not deal explicitly with "culture" as the place of Christian presence, nor with "society" as a field of Christian responsibility. But it does provide some overarching perspectives about how particular Christians in Asia Minor at a particular time should relate to their diverse neighbors.' Cf. also Hauerwas, 'What Could it Mean?', 11–15.

cross and resurrection of Christ and the gift of the Spirit.[32] It was because this new revelation decisively burst the bounds of previous conceptions of space and time, individual and social personhood, power and authority, and life and death, that Paul and his contemporaries were obliged to think again.

To put it another way, Paul was not a sociologist before his time trying to understand what 'community' is and why people talk about it endlessly and in so many different ways![33] Rather, Paul was a Jew zealous for the law, the temple, the land and the elect people of Israel, whose life was turned upside down 'through a revelation of Jesus Christ' (Gal 1.12) and a commission to be apostle to the Gentiles (Gal 1.16).[34] In consequence, Paul's talk is not about 'community' but about how Jews and Gentiles, men and women, slaves and freeborn can embody and celebrate the eschatological life of the kingdom of God. This is not a matter of social engineering in quest of the 'ideal community'. It is a matter of participation in divine love in the power of the Spirit and testifying of that love and power to others.

As we have seen, this 'participation' (*koinōnia*) involves – first, an ongoing transformation of life in the light of Christ's cross and in hope of the resurrection; second, sacramental gatherings which unite those gathered in practices with water, bread and wine, grounded in a shared, salvific narrative; third, a holy and disciplined lifestyle embodied in every aspect of people's social relations and expressing their new identity as 'the body of Christ'; and fourth, the acceptance of leadership by those whose depth of spiritual maturity is shown by their renunciation of 'boasting' in favour of that 'more excellent way' of love (cf. 1 Cor 16.14, 24).[35]

[33] On which see Anthony P. Cohen, *The Symbolic Construction of Community* (London and New York: Tavistock Publications, 1985).

[34] See further, Alan F. Segal, *Paul the Convert: The Apostolate and Apostasy of Saul the Pharisee* (New Haven and London: Yale University Press, 1990).

[35] I am very grateful to a number of Durham colleagues who helped me with this essay: Jimmy Dunn, Sheridan Gilley, Walter Moberly, Peter Selby and Loren Stuckenbruck.

11

Paul and the Limits of Tolerance

I. Introduction

In the popular mind of Western European liberalism, Paul the Christian apostle is often regarded as an intolerant religious bigot, in contrast to Jesus who is seen as a figure of tolerance and love. This tendency to polarize Jesus and Paul and to play one off against the other is widespread. Its roots lie in various directions. Perhaps one of the most significant lies in the tendency since the Enlightenment to disparage institutional religion because of the limits religion is believed to set on personal freedom. Once Paul becomes identified as the founder of the Christian religion, a wedge is driven between Paul and Jesus in a way which preserves Jesus as the model teacher of universal love and demonizes Paul as the source of the corruption of the original ideal. Thus, if we may generalize further for a moment, we might say that whereas the Reformation drove a wedge between Scripture and church tradition, the Enlightenment shifted the wedge back a stage and drove it into Scripture itself: in this case, between Jesus and Paul. What results is another myth of the Fall, from Jesus the charismatic Galilean teacher of the fatherhood of God and brotherhood of man to Paul the founder of institutional Christianity.[1] And, except within the Lutheran and Reformed traditions of the Christian church, Paul's reputation has suffered ever since.

What I am trying to signal at the outset, therefore, is the importance of attending to the hermeneutical dimension of our theme.

---

[1] For a comprehensive survey of the (predominantly German) scholarly debate of the last century and a half, see Victor Paul Furnish, 'The Jesus–Paul Debate: From Baur to Bultmann', in A. J. M. Wedderburn, ed., *Paul and Jesus: Collected Essays* (Sheffield: Sheffield Academic Press, 1989), 17–50.

If we are putting the question about tolerance and its limits to the historical representatives of early Judaism or early Christianity, it is essential to acknowledge that the idea of toleration has a history and that we in the liberal West tend to think of tolerance and intolerance in very particular ways, often without any awareness of the history which has shaped those ideas so decisively.[2] It is essential, in other words, to question the question: What do we mean by 'tolerance' and 'the limits of tolerance'? How useful is 'tolerance' as a category of virtue for understanding the moral world of early Judaism and Christianity? Does our concept of tolerance presuppose a secular, pluralist, individualist ideology which belongs to the modern world but not to the world of antiquity? To what extent are we in danger of looking down into the well of history and finding there only the reflections of our own images while under the illusion that we have discovered the true source of values we now hold dear for quite different reasons? Is it possibly the case that our prior commitments to egalitarian social values and *laissez-faire* individualism predispose us to think of tolerance as a virtue and intolerance as a vice, and to polarize the two in this mutually exclusive way?[3]

An analogy here might be helpful. Within that branch of theology known as liberation theology, it has become common to interpret the Bible as a kind of manifesto on liberation. The story of the exodus, in particular, has become a *locus classicus*. Here more than anywhere else, God is shown to be a God who sets the oppressed free, with the result that the story of the exodus is interpreted as underpinning revolutionary political and social action by the poor on behalf of the poor. But the question needs to be asked, Is the exodus about liberation and, if so, liberation of what kind? In a recent essay which is strongly critical of several liberationist readings, Jon D. Levenson puts it this way:

> Nothing in the Bible so readily invites the term 'liberation' as the exodus of the Israelites from Egypt. The essential question, however, has not

[2] On the history of the idea of tolerance see, for example, Susan Mendus, ed., *Justifying Toleration: Conceptual and Historical Perspectives* (Cambridge: Cambridge University Press, 1988). On toleration and the liberal political tradition see Susan Mendus, *Toleration and the Limits of Liberalism* (London: Macmillan, 1989).

[3] For a recent investigation of the ethics of tolerance, see D. W. Brown, 'Tolerance: Virtue or Vice?', in David R. Bromham *et al.*, eds, *Ethics in Reproductive Medicine* (London: Springer Verlag, 1992), 201–9; also the survey essay by J. Philip Wogaman, 'Persecution and Toleration', in James F. Childress and J. Macquarrie, eds, *A New Dictionary of Christian Ethics* (London: SCM Press, 1985), 464–8.

been so readily asked: In exactly what sense ought the exodus be seen as an instance of liberation, or, to pose the same question in other words, what is the character of the liberation typified by the exodus and how is this type of liberation to be distinguished from other phenomena to which the same term is presently applied?[4]

Levenson himself shows how strong is the liberationist tendency to interpret the text in quite anachronistic ways as a story of class struggle and popular insurrection, where 'justice' is defined in terms of the essentially modern notion of individual and social equality and where 'liberation' is defined in terms of political self-determination. He then shows to the contrary that the primary focus of the text is theological, with the consequence that the kind of freedom being talked about 'is not freedom in the sense of self-determination, but *service*, the service of the loving, redeeming and delivering God of Israel, rather than the state and its proud king'.[5]

The point of the analogy is clear, I hope. If the danger of anachronism is acute when we come to the Bible and other ancient texts with categories like 'liberation', are the dangers not equally acute with an analogous category like 'tolerance'? Are we not at risk of subverting the subject of our study by operating within the terms of an agenda whose power is all the greater for being submerged and unacknowledged? Nevertheless, awareness of the danger of anachronistic misinterpretation does not mean that to talk of 'Paul and the limits of tolerance' is a futile exercise, any more than it is futile to talk about Paul's understanding of 'liberation' or 'freedom'. It means only that our analysis be carried out with historical sensitivity, hermeneutical circumspection and resistance to the tendency to moralize about what might appear at first sight to be 'lapses' into intolerance but which come subsequently to be seen as instances of a different dynamic altogether.

II. The case of Paul

In turning now to Paul, the important issue is where to start. On the basis of what I have said already, I think it would be a mistake to start with tolerance and intolerance. Better by far to start with categories native to Paul himself and central to his own self-understanding. This can be expressed variously, and there is a lively

---

[4] Jon D. Levenson, 'Exodus and Liberation' in his book *Hebrew Bible, Old Testament and Historical Criticism* (Louisville: Westminster John Knox Press, 1993), 128.
[5] Ibid. 144.

debate over what constitutes the 'centre' and what is more 'peripheral' in Paul's theology and apostolic mission.[6] But what needs to be emphasized is that Paul's categories of thought are not those of modern liberal secular pluralism. Rather, they are those of biblical monotheism transformed in the light of the knowledge of Christ crucified and risen. A bare catalogue of Pauline thought-forms would include at least the following: the kingdom of God, creation, covenant, revelation, messiah, the land, the law, righteousness, sin, judgement, atonement, justification and reconciliation, holiness, obedience, apostleship, Spirit, resurrection and new creation. This is a world away from a post-Enlightenment liberal mentality. But it may turn out to be the case that modern debates about tolerance and its limits still have something to learn from this early Christian apostle.

1. *Not even-handed tolerance but zeal for God*

The first point I would make, then, is that for Paul, tolerance is not the issue. Paul was not an egalitarian individualist committed to maximizing the possibilities of self-fulfilment at the individual level and self-determination at the social level. Rather than tolerance, we must speak in theological terms of zeal for God and for the people of God. The autobiographical statement in Philippians 3.4ff. makes this abundantly clear:

> . . . circumcised on the eighth day, of the people of Israel, of the tribe of Benjamin, a Hebrew born of Hebrews; as to the law a Pharisee, as to zeal a persecutor of the church, as to righteousness under the law blameless. But whatever gain I had I counted as loss for the sake of Christ. Indeed I count everything as loss because of the surpassing worth of knowing Christ Jesus my Lord. For his sake I have suffered the loss of all things, and count them as refuse, in order that I may gain Christ and be found in him . . .

In his 'pre-conversion' days (if we may still speak in those terms),[7] Paul's wholehearted commitment manifested itself in zeal for the

[6] See for example, E. P. Sanders, *Paul and Palestinian Judaism: A Comparison of Patterns of Religion* (London: SCM Press, 1977); J. C. Beker, *Paul the Apostle: The Triumph of God in Life and Thought* (Philadelphia: Fortress Press, 1980); C. J. A. Hickling, 'Centre and Periphery in the Thought of Paul', in E. A. Livingstone, ed., *Studia Biblica 1978*, vol. 3 (Sheffield: Sheffield Academic Press, 1980), 199–214.

[7] See further Alan F. Segal's major investigation *Paul the Convert: The Apostolate and Apostasy of Saul the Pharisee* (New Haven and London: Yale University Press, 1990), esp. ch. 2, 'Paul's Ecstasy'.

law as a Pharisee, with persecution of the church as an inevitable corollary. After his encounter with the risen Christ, it is not the case that Saul the intolerant Pharisee is transformed into Paul the tolerant apostle. On the contrary, his zeal for the law is transformed into zeal for Christ his heavenly 'Lord'. In other words, there is continuity as well as discontinuity. The continuity lies in his single-minded devotion to the cause of God and the kingdom of God. The discontinuity lies in the fact that, whereas formerly he expressed his devotion to God through zeal for the law, after his call to be God's envoy to the Gentiles it was expressed through zeal for Christ.

Now the persecutor becomes himself persecuted; and on more than one occasion in his letters Paul 'boasts' in ironic fashion of the catastrophies that have befallen him in his new calling, catastrophies which are held up as if they are the garlands of the conquering athlete for God and his Christ (see 2 Cor 4.7–12; 11.21–33; 12.1–10). What is so striking in these catalogues of suffering is that the experiences to which they point do not turn Paul into an advocate of toleration! Such a thought does not seem to occur to Paul, because tolerance and intolerance are not categories native to him. Instead, what we find is that Paul accepts the persecution and suffering meted out to him by his opponents as the inevitable consequence and the necessary proof of his faithful testimony to Christ. Even more, he interprets his experiences as the process by which his own life is being transformed into conformity with that of his crucified and risen Lord and made a channel for divine power to work. So in 1 Corinthians 4.7ff, he says: 'But we have this treasure in earthen vessels, to show that the transcendent power belongs to God and not to us. We are afflicted in every way, but not crushed; perplexed, but not driven to despair; persecuted, but not forsaken; struck down, but not destroyed; always carrying in the body the death of Jesus, so that the life of Jesus may also be manifested in our mortal bodies.'

There is no evidence that Paul sought toleration from his adversaries.[8] Indeed, Anthony Harvey has shown that Paul's claim to have received at the hands of his fellow Jews 'the forty lashes less one' on no less than five occasions (2 Cor 11.24) means that Paul

---

[8] He did, of course, seek the protection of the Roman authorities when it was available. See on this A. N. Sherwin-White, *Roman Society and Roman Law in the New Testament* (Oxford: Oxford University Press, 1963). But seeking civil and judicial protection is quite different from advocating tolerance and complaining about intolerance.

accepted these punitive disciplinary measures against him as the price of his calling to preach Christ to Jews and Gentiles alike while remaining within the orbit of his native synagogue communities.[9] What Paul sought was not their tolerance but their conversion to the truth. If their response was one of rejection and violent opposition then that only reinforced Paul's belief that the powers of darkness had blinded their hearts and that they were in danger of forfeiting their participation in the true people of God (see 2 Cor 4.3–4).

2. Not rationalistic optimism but apocalyptic hope

This leads to a second main point. The modern liberal ideal of tolerance is based upon the exaltation of independent human reason as the basis for the right ordering of human affairs. This position has as one of its corollaries a generally optimistic view of human nature and a basic trust in history as a process of gradual evolution. The associated theology of history (if there is one at all) is impersonal and deistic. Contrast, once again, the categories and lineaments of Paul's thought. For Paul, it is divine revelation, not human reason, which constitutes the basis for the right ordering of human affairs.[10] For Paul wisdom is a matter, not of the dispassionate exercise of the rational faculties, but instead a matter of spiritual discernment of the stunning paradox according to which the wisdom of God is made known in the 'foolishness' of the crucified Christ (see 1 Cor 1.18–25). For Paul also, human nature is marred on a universal scale by sin, and history is to be interpreted not in optimistic evolutionary terms, but in the cataclysmic biblical categories of salvation history and apocalyptic eschatology. No wonder, therefore, that tolerance and intolerance are not central to Paul's thought and practice. For, according to Paul, what is necessary is not tolerance of one's fellow creatures, but trust in God and obedience to the will of God, since it is only God who saves from the coming judgement through the revelation of his Son.

[9] Anthony Harvey, 'Forty Strokes Save One: Social Aspects of Judaizing and Apostasy', in A. E. Harvey, ed., *Alternative Approaches to New Testament Study* (London: SPCK, 1985), 79–96.

[10] This is to put the point too sharply, perhaps, especially in view of Stanley K. Stowers's essay 'Paul on the Use and Abuse of Reason', in D. L. Balch *et al.*, eds, *Greeks, Romans, and Christians* (Philadelphia: Augsburg/Fortress Press, 1990), pp. 253–86.

There is a specificity here which is worth noting. It is what Christian theologians have referred to as 'the scandal of particularity'. But the general doctrinal category is the biblical one of election and covenant. It is, of course, central to Paul's thought, as Galatians and Romans make plain. What it presupposes is a world view quite alien to the humanistic rationalism which idealizes tolerance and democratic egalitarianism. For the thought world of Paul is dominated by a theocratic belief in the sovereignty of God and the lordship of Christ through the Spirit, a corollary of which is a doctrine of divine grace in choosing a people to share God's glory and to mediate God's blessing and salvation to the world. Here, it is not a matter of recognizing and accepting people's differences in a spirit of toleration on the assumption that all people are equal. Rather, it is a matter of being accepted by God on the basis of God's covenanting love revealed first to the people of Israel and latterly in the death and resurrection of God's Son.

The Epistle to the Galatians is a particularly striking illustration of what I am claiming to be the great distance between Paul's apocalyptic theology and world view on the one hand and the modern liberal view of history with its idealization of tolerance and self-determination on the other.[11] For in Galatians, Paul is hardly a model of what we might call tolerance. On the contrary, he repeatedly pronounces an anathema on anyone who perverts the gospel of Christ (see 1.8, 9), recalls for his readers the occasion at Antioch when he 'opposed Cephas to his face' for his damaging act of *hupokrisis* in withdrawing from Gentile table-fellowship (2.11–14), and is quite vituperative towards his opponents (e.g. 5.12)![12]

Paul's gospel, which came to him 'by revelation' (1.12; cf. 1.16; 2.2) – quite independent, therefore, of reason and consensus – is predicated upon what we may call a crisis view of history.[13] It

---

[11] On Paul's indebtedness to apocalyptic, see further J. C. Beker, *Paul the Apostle*; also, Wayne A. Meeks, 'Social Functions of Apocalyptic Language in Pauline Christianity', in D. Hellholm, ed., *Apocalypticism in the Mediterranean World and the Near East* (Tübingen: J. C. B. Mohr, 1983), 687–705.

[12] On the latter point, it is worth observing in passing that Paul shares with other early Christian writers and with Jewish writers also a well-developed rhetoric for villifying opponents, a rhetoric which belies once again the appropriateness of attributing to Paul or his contemporaries either tolerance or intolerance. See on this Luke T. Johnson, 'The New Testament's Anti-Jewish Slander and the Conventions of Ancient Polemic', *JBL* 108 (1989), 419–41.

[13] See further Leander E. Keck, 'Paul as Thinker', *Interpretation* 47 (1993), 27–38, where stress is placed on the resurrection of the crucified Christ as the pivotal eschatological event in Paul's thought.

concerns the revelation of the one identified as 'our Lord Jesus Christ who gave himself for our sins to deliver us from the present evil age' (Gal 1.4; cf. 1 Thess 1.10). Now a new dispensation in history has been inaugurated, and this new age of the eschatological Spirit of God represents a fundamental break with all that has gone before, which now appears only as prophecy and allegory and custodian for that which has replaced it (see Gal 3–4). Hence we note the way in which Paul's argument is built around a series of what J. Louis Martyn has identified as powerful 'apocalyptic antinomies': law versus faith/Christ, flesh versus Spirit, slavery versus freedom, circumcision/uncircumcision versus new creation, and so on.[14]

A direct corollary of this crisis view of history is that it does not permit of compromise. The matter is one of the revealed 'truth of the gospel' (2.5, 14; cf. 5.7) which must be either accepted or rejected. That is why Paul puts at stake his entire personal authority as an apostle of Christ, why he pronounces divine judgement on all who turn away from the gospel, why he pleads so movingly using the maternal imagery of childbirth so that his 'children' might not apostasize (4.19), and why he accepts persecution by his opponents as an inevitable corollary of his own uncompromising stand (see 5.11; 6.17; cf. 4.13–14).

3. Not 'live and let live' but love with a view to transformation

Deliverance by Christ from 'the present evil age' which itself makes possible the inauguration of the age of the eschatological Spirit brings into being a new community, understood as sharing already in an anticipatory way in the 'new creation' (Gal 6.15; cf. 2 Cor 5.17). By what values, then, are the people of God to live? This brings me to a third main point, to do with Paul's moral teaching. Here, if anywhere, people will look for signs of an ethic of toleration and teaching about the limits of tolerance. But once again, I would argue that to talk in these terms is misleading. In a nutshell, what is important for Paul is not 'tolerance' but 'love' (*agapē*), not egalitarian acceptance but mutual 'upbuilding' (*oikodomē*), not freedom to do what you like as long as it does not cause harm to a third party but freedom to serve God as a member of 'the body of Christ'. Galatians 5.13–14 epitomizes this position: 'For you were called to

---

[14] See further J. Louis Martyn, 'Apocalyptic Antinomies in Paul's Letter to the Galatians', *NTS* 31 (1985), 410–24.

freedom, brethren; only do not use your freedom as an opportunity for the flesh, but through love be servants of one another. For the whole law is fulfilled in one word, "You shall love your neighbour as yourself".'

The point may be demonstrated in a number of ways. First, the ethos and habitual thought forms which impart to Pauline ethics its meaning and identity are theocentric, christocentric and eschatological.[15] The theocentricity is what gives it its uncompromising character as a form of what today might be called 'command ethics'. The teaching on obedience to rulers in Romans 13 is a good example of this. It begins: 'Let every person be subject to the governing authorities. For there is no authority except from God, and those that exist have been instituted by God' (13.1–2). Its christocentricity is what makes love and sacrifice for the sake of the truth the central imperatives of Pauline morality, rather than tolerance. This is evident in the advice Paul gives to 'the strong' in Romans 15.1ff: 'let each of us please his neighbour for his good, to edify him. For Christ did not please himself; but, as it is written, "The reproaches of those who reproached thee fell on me"'. Its eschatological dimension is what impels Paul to work for the transformation of the differences and diversity which create strife in society in the direction of unity and harmony, rather than impelling him to advocate a policy of indifference to diversity or passive acquiescence to the *status quo*. As he says in Romans 14.17: 'For the kingdom of God is not food and drink but righteousness and peace and joy in the Holy Spirit.'

Turning next to the lists of vices and virtues (e.g. 1 Thess 4.1–12; 1 Cor 5.9–13; 6.9–11; Gal 5.16–26),[16] what we discover is, not an analysis of universal human rights as the basis for mutual respect along the lines of 'live and let live', but instead a summons to believers in Christ to 'walk by the Spirit' as heirs of the coming kingdom of God and to shun the 'desires of the flesh' (Gal 5.16). If it is suggested that 'love, joy, peace, patience, kindness, goodness, faithfulness, gentleness, self-control' are qualities that add up in all

[15] On the notion of 'ethos', see L. E. Keck, 'Ethos and Ethics in the New Testament', in J. Gaffney, ed., *Essays in Morality and Ethics* (New York: Paulist Press, 1980), 29–49.

[16] For a useful overview, see Eduard Schweizer, 'Traditional Ethical Patterns in the Pauline and Post-Pauline Letters and Their Development', in E. Best and R. McL. Wilson, eds, *Text and Interpretation* (Cambridge: Cambridge University Press, 1977), 195–209.

but name to what we mean by tolerance, what needs to be emphasized is that the peculiarly Pauline semantic context and thought world give to these qualities a quite different nuance. For Paul, it is not a matter of learning to live with others in spite of different religious allegiances or no such allegiances at all. Rather, it is a matter of learning to live with and for others in the power of the Spirit with a view to their transformation into the likeness of Christ (cf. Gal 3.27–28). And Paul assumes a hierarchy of priorities of commitment here. He does not treat everyone the same. Rather, as he says in Galatians 6.10, 'let us do good to all men, and especially to those who are of the household of faith'.

Then there is the evidence from Paul's own teaching and practice as an apostle. Here we may take 1 Corinthians as exemplary, for the house churches at Corinth were very much Paul's foundation (cf. 1 Cor 3.5–9; 9.1–2). What is more, their unity and very viability were threatened by *schismata* of various kinds and factionalism compounded by the exercise of the traditional means of self-display or 'boasting'. The basic point that I wish to make is that Paul does not respond with tolerance, nor does he advocate tolerance as we understand it.[17] Instead, he responds in ways rather like that expected of any political leader in antiquity.[18]

Thus, using powerful rhetorical strategies he seeks to convince and confute his audience by appealing to their founding constitution as the basis for recalling them to unity and solidarity (e.g. 1.22–24; 2.2). In rather provocative fashion, he reminds the majority of his audience of their low social status outside the brotherhood (1.26–29), and does not hesitate to point out their spiritual immaturity as 'babes in Christ' in relation to whom Paul himself is their 'father', threatening even to visit them with a rod in his hand (see 2.6 – 4.21, with the 'rod' at 4.21)! Nor will Paul allow himself to submit to judgement by the Corinthians: for Paul's politics are theocratic and he is unreceptive to the judgement of those whom

[17] On Paul's use of invective in its social context, see Peter Marshall, 'Invective: Paul and His Enemies in Corinth' in E. W. Coward and E. G. Newing, eds, *Perspectives on Language and Text* (Eisenbrauns, 1987), 359–73.

[18] For this interpretation of Paul as a politician, I am indebted to a paper by R. M. Grant, 'Paul and Aristotle on Politics', presented to the New Testament Postgraduate Seminar of the Department of Theology in the University of Durham on 7 February 1994. Grant's influence is reflected also in the essay by L. L. Welborn, 'On the Discord in Corinth: 1 Corinthians 1–4 and Ancient Politics', *JBL* 106 (1987), 85–111 (with his acknowledgement at n. 20).

he has fathered in the faith. 'It is the Lord who judges me,' he says (4.4).

Having therefore reasserted his divinely ordained authority over them, Paul then proceeds to correct abuses in the Christian association. According to 1 Corinthians 5, the man guilty of *porneia* is to be expelled from the association. Other members are neither to associate with him or even eat with him: otherwise, the purity of the group as a whole will be at risk. Now, is not this intolerance on Paul's part?, we may ask. And, if so, is it praiseworthy or not? But the question is wrongly put. Tolerance and intolerance are part of a value system of a society where individual freedom of expression is placed at a premium. Antique society was not of that kind. There, group identity and group solidarity were the chief concerns, and defining and policing the boundaries were chief responsibilities of any leader.[19] Hence Paul's duty to give the lead in the exercise of discipline: and it is 'discipline' rather than 'intolerance' of which we should speak. There is no sense that the procedure Paul institutes is unusual or arbitrary or unlikely to find acceptance. Thus, in terms which remind us of another early Christian disciplinary code (in Matt 18), Paul says: 'When you are assembled, and my spirit is present, with the power of our Lord Jesus, you are to deliver this man to Satan for the destruction of the flesh, that his spirit may be saved in the day of the Lord Jesus' (5.4–5).

In the same epistle, Paul deals with other issues to do similarly with the right internal ordering of the Christian association and its relations with 'the world' outside: the use of the judicial system of the *polis* for settling disputes among the believers; rules governing sexual practice, marriage and divorce; rules governing dietary matters and table fellowship; the practice of worship, including gender-related roles and the proper exercise of *charismata*; how to respond to the anxieties generated by the deaths of group members; and so on. What is important to note in all of this is that Paul's overriding concern is to lay down rules and to encourage attitudes and practices which are consistent with the Christian association's primary, theological understanding of itself as 'the church of God' and 'the body of Christ' in Corinth.

Anything which militates in a different direction is outlawed with not the slightest twinge of the liberal pluralist conscience. Even

[19] See further B. J. Malina, *The New Testament World: Insights from Cultural Anthropology* (London: SCM Press, 1983).

individual liberty, which Paul by no means despises but rather wishes to encourage (see 1 Cor 8–10), is qualified by his even greater concern to maintain unity in the truth.[20] Hence his own willingness to forego personal prerogatives as an apostle for the sake of the common good: 'For though I am free from all men, I have made myself a slave to all, that I might win the more. . . . I have become all things to all people, that I might by all means save some' (9.19–22).[21] Hence also the value he places on athletic imagery to do with rigorous training and strenuous self-control (*enkrateia*), the clear implication being that such practice does not come easily (9.24–27). Hence, yet again, the overwhelming emphasis on the virtue of other-directed love (*agapē*), for which 1 Corinthians 13 is so justly famous. Such love has none of the neutrality and impartiality of the modern ideal of tolerance. Rather, it is love with a view to eschatological transformation, on the grounds that it is love practised in the context of 'faith' in the risen Christ and 'hope' for the coming of God's kingdom. Love does not 'abide' in splendid isolation: it 'abides' hand-in-hand with faith and hope (1 Cor 13.3).[22]

III. Conclusion

If I appear to have frozen tolerance and the limits of tolerance out of the discussion of Paul, it is not because I do not believe in certain kinds of tolerance and certain kinds of limits to tolerance as essential virtues for life together in the societies of our modern world. No one, I hope, would wish for a return to the kinds of intolerance which gave rise in the Europe of the sixteenth and seventeenth centuries to the Wars of Religion. No one, I hope, would wish for a return to the kind of intolerance which led to the Holocaust or the kind of tolerance which acquiesced in its happening.

What I am saying is that we do not do the cause of a proper tolerance and a proper intolerance any favours if we harness

---

[20] On the analogous passage in Rom 14.1 – 15.6, see J. D. G. Dunn, *Christian Liberty: A New Testament Perspective* (Carlisle: Paternoster Press, 1993), 78–105.

[21] See the definitive study of Paul's use of the terminology of slavery in self-designation: Dale B. Martin, *Slavery as Salvation: The Metaphor of Slavery in Pauline Christianity* (New Haven: Yale University Press, 1990).

[22] See further Carl R. Holladay, '1 Corinthians 13: Paul as Apostolic Paradigm', in D. L. Balch *et al.*, eds, *Greeks, Romans, and Christians* (Philadelphia, Augsburg/ Fortress Press, 1990), 80–98.

Jesus or Paul or early Christianity to the bandwaggon of post-Enlightenment secular individualism and pluralism.[23] If we allow that to happen, then we cut off the spiritual, theological and ecclesial roots upon which Christianity's ethic of neighbourly love depends — an ethic itself deeply rooted in the Bible and early Judaism. We undermine the distinctive identity and particular truth-claims of one of the major world religions which, by its very distinctiveness and particularity, has made a significant contribution to a right understanding of tolerance and to the possibility and practice of different peoples living together in harmony, a harmony based upon faith in and faithfulness to the one true God.

---

[23] See further Jon D. Levenson's brilliant essay, 'Historical Criticism and the Fate of the Enlightenment Project' in his book *Hebrew Bible*, 106–26. Pertinent also is Jacob Neusner's essay 'Shalom: Complementarity', in his book *Jews and Christians: The Myth of a Common Tradition* (London: SCM Press, 1991), 105–16, especially his comment on p. 107: 'Tolerance does not suffice. A theory of the other that concedes the outsider is right for the other but not for me invokes a meretricious relativism that religious believers cannot really mean. Religions will have to learn to think about each other, not merely to tolerate the other as an unavoidable inconvenience or an evil that cannot be eliminated. . . . [T]hey face the task of thinking, within their own theological framework and religious system, about the place within the structure of the other outside of it. And that is something no religion has ever accomplished up to this time.'

Part Three

INTERPRETATION

12

New Testament Interpretation As Performance

I. Introduction

In recent study of the nature of New Testament interpretation, considerable attention in certain circles has been given to the possibility that there is one metaphor that is particularly appropriate for articulating what New Testament interpretation involves. It is the metaphor of *performance*. The purpose of this essay is to describe and develop this proposal and to give an assessment of it. To my knowledge, this is a task in biblical hermeneutics that has only just begun.[1] If we ask why this is so, one possible answer lies in the fact that the proposal comes in the main from systematic and patristic theologians and therefore from outside the guild of biblical scholars. The consequence is that our customary division of labour inhibits us from attending with sufficient care to what our neighbours are saying even when it bears directly on our own work.[2]

I hope to show that the performance metaphor has significant potential for the revitalization of New Testament interpretation, as

---

[1] See for example Stephen E. Fowl and L. Gregory Jones, *Reading in Communion: Scripture and Ethics in Christian Life* (London: SPCK, 1991), and David Scott's excellent essay, 'Speaking to Form: Trinitarian-Performative Scripture Reading', *Anglican Theological Review* 77 (1995), 137–59; also the brief treatments of Brian Jenner, 'Music to the Sinner's Ear?', *Epworth Review* 16 (1989), 35–8; N. T. Wright, *The New Testament and the People of God* (London: SPCK, 1992), 140–3; I. H. Marshall, 'Climbing Ropes, Elipses and Symphonies: The Relation between Biblical and Systematic Theology', in P. E. Satterthwaite and D. F. Wright, eds, *A Pathway Into the Holy Scriptures* (Grand Rapids: Eerdmans, 1994), 199–220; and Richard B. Hays, *The Moral Vision of the New Testament* (San Francisco: HarperCollins, 1996), 304–6.

[2] Francis Watson makes this point also in his recent books *Text, Church and World: Biblical Interpretation in Theological Perspective* (Edinburgh: T&T Clark, 1994) and *Text and Truth* (Edinburgh: T&T Clark, 1997).

of biblical interpretation as a whole. It has this potential because it represents an invitation to *locate our work as exegetes in a wider context of divine and human action* – in particular, in those modes of action that help constitute church and society as life-giving. The underlying assumptions, as we shall see, are theological and ecclesiological, to do respectively with revelation and the building of godly patterns of sociability.

Gone, on this view, is the 'gentleman's agreement' to keep firmly apart knowledge as something public and faith as something private, meaning as something objective and truth (or meaning 'for today') as a matter of pure subjectivity. In question also is the tacit agreement to overlook our contested identities and to operate with a neutral, standardized discourse which masks and devalues the very things that make us who we are. Such agreements, however well-intentioned and understandable historically, drain the text and our task of their life-blood. They privilege the very strategies and techniques that militate against true understanding.[3] Conceiving of New Testament interpretation as performance may help to bring the body of the text, reunited with the body of society, back to life.

II. Major proponents

1. Nicholas Lash

In the last two decades there have been several major proponents of the idea that the most fruitful way to think about biblical interpretation is by analogy with what is involved in the interpretation of a musical score or a dramatic script. The first that I know of is the Cambridge Roman Catholic philosophical theologian Nicholas Lash, in his seminal essay 'Performing the Scriptures', first published in 1982.[4] Here, in answer to the question what is involved

[3] Relevant here is the recent and ongoing debate between Francis Watson and Philip Davies: see P. R. Davies, *Whose Bible is it Anyway?* (Sheffield: Sheffield Academic Press, 1995), esp. ch. 2, and Watson's reply 'Bible, Theology and the University: A Response to Philip Davies', *Journal for the Study of the Old Testament* 71 (1996), 3–16. On the 'uselessness of standardising' (although in a different realm of discourse), see Mary Midgley, 'On Not Being Afraid of Natural Sex Differences', in M. Griffiths and M. Whitford, eds, *Feminist Perspectives in Philosophy* (Bloomington and Indianapolis: Indiana University Press, 1988), 29–41 at 34–7.

[4] Originally published in *The Furrow* in 1982 and republished in his important collection *Theology on the Way to Emmaus* (London: SCM Press, 1986), 37–46; cf. also his other essay, 'What Might Martyrdom Mean?' (originally published in 1981) in *Emmaus*, 75–92.

in the interpretation of texts, Lash makes the important point that 'for different kinds of text, different kinds of activity count as the fundamental form of their interpretation'.[5] According to Lash, among the closest analogies to biblical interpretation are the interpretation of a Beethoven score or a Shakespearean tragedy, although he also appeals to other analogies, including the interpretation of legal texts and written constitutions.

Thus, argues Lash, for the interpretation of Beethoven it is not sufficient to be able to read the notes and play the instruments. Nor is it sufficient to know, with the help of the music historian, in what circumstances the music was composed or how the score has been interpreted orchestrally in the past. Nor is it sufficient even to play the notes of the score with technical accuracy. Of course, none of these things is to be gainsaid, since playing Beethoven well without them would be impossible. Nevertheless, the central act of the interpretation of a Beethoven score is the performance, a performance that, if it is to inspire or give pleasure or console, has to be a matter of more than technical accuracy, and instead a kind of *creative fidelity* that allows the musical score to come alive again in the present moment. Important also is the recognition that this is a social or communal activity involving not just conductor and orchestra, but an audience of (more or less informed) listeners and critics as well. There is a sense in which the audience is taking part in the performance as well as the orchestra, and that what Beethoven's score 'means' arises out of the convergence of creative contributions from both orchestra and audience in a particular place and time.

Or take the interpretation of Shakespeare – *King Lear* for example. Once again, textual critics will be able to assist by establishing the most authentic version of the text; historians of Elizabethan times will help interpretation by giving us a sense of the historical background of Shakespeare and his plays; and literary critics will contribute to the appreciation of the literary qualities of Shakespeare's poetry, rhetoric, characterization, plot, and so on. But the central act of the interpretation of *King Lear* comes in the performance of the play on a stage by a company of actors in the presence of an audience. Furthermore, the meaning of the play is not best conveyed in a performance that is technically correct, for such performances are usually judged 'flat', 'wooden' or 'lifeless'.

[5] Lash, 'Performing', 40.

On the contrary, true interpretation occurs when the performance is 'original', 'inspired' or 'creative' in some sense, such that we feel that we have come to understand the play in a new way and in the process have come to understand ourselves in a new way as well.

These analogies help establish Lash's main point, that 'there are at least some texts that only begin to deliver their meaning in so far as they are "brought into play" through interpretative performance'. For Lash, the Bible is one such text, and he states his main thesis thus:

> I want to suggest, first, that, although the texts of the New Testament may be read, and read with profit, by anyone interested in Western Culture and concerned for the human predicament, the fundamental form of the *Christian* interpretation of scripture is the life, activity and organization of the believing community. Secondly, that Christian practice, as interpretative action, consists in the *performance* of texts which are construed as 'rendering', bearing witness to, one whose words and deeds, discourse and suffering, 'rendered' the truth of God in human history. The performance of the New Testament enacts the conviction that these texts are most appropriately read as the story of Jesus, the story of everyone else, and the story of God.[6]

The implications of Lash's 'performance' model of interpretation are profound and worth drawing out. For what it suggests is that inquiry into the meaning of the Bible is inadequate if it is not at the same time an inquiry into its truth – that is to say, an inquiry into whether or not creative fidelity to who and what the text is about *makes human transformation possible*. Although there are promising signs of change, prompted in part by feminist and liberationist hermeneutics,[7] in part by various postliberal theologies,[8]

---

[6] Lash, 'Performing', 42 (author's emphasis).

[7] See, for example, Carlos Mesters, 'The Use of the Bible in Christian Communities of the Common People', in S. Torres and J. Eagleson, eds, *The Challenge of Basic Christian Communities* (New York: Orbis Books, 1981), 197–210; and Christopher Rowland, '"Open Thy Mouth for the Dumb": A Task for the Exegete of Holy Scripture', *Biblical Interpretation* 1 (1993), 228–45.

[8] The writings of Stanley Hauerwas bulk large here, some of which are cited below. His work is analysed critically in Hays, *Moral Vision*, 253–66. For Britain see, among others, John Milbank, *Theology and Social Theory: Beyond Secular Reason* (Oxford: Blackwell, 1990); Rowan Williams, 'The Suspicion of Suspicion: Wittgenstein and Bonhoeffer', in R. H. Bell, ed., *The Grammar of the Heart* (San Francisco: Harper & Row, 1988), 36–53; and the well-nuanced 'two cheers for liberalism' in Colin Crowder, 'Liberalism in Theology and Religious Education', in J. Astley and L. J. Francis, eds, *Christian Theology and Religious Education* (London: SPCK, 1996), 105–13.

the problem, at least with the *public rhetoric* (if less so with the actual practice) of New Testament interpretation especially in Britain and North America, is that it separates meaning and truth – separates the 'original' meaning of the text from its meaning 'for today'.

It does so on the basis of an assumption deeply rooted in the positivist epistemology and individualistic anthropology of the Enlightenment that the business of the New Testament exegete is the basically archaeological task of unearthing the original meaning of the text in a way which is objective and rational, free from the accretions of dogmatic theology or ecclesiastical politics. Once the original meaning has been determined, and if the exegete is religiously inclined, he or she can hand it on in relay-race fashion[9] to the systematician whose task is to 'translate' the meaning 'then' into a meaning 'for today' – a meaning which no one is under any obligation to heed, of course, because, whereas exegesis is 'rational' and 'scientific', theology is 'only' a matter of personal interpretation. In any case, there is hardly anyone listening any more, because the business of interpretation as a whole has become professionalized and institutionalized, isolated and estranged from that very body of people in church and society that give it authority and legitimacy in the first place.[10]

But if we follow Lash's performance analogy, then biblical interpretation is not primarily something archaeological, the business only of the relatively detached academic for whom the question of truth can be endlessly postponed. It *cannot* be primarily an 'archaeological' task if the kind of text the Bible is delivers its meaning only as it is 'played out' in patterns of human action in church and society. Rather, on the performance analogy, biblical interpretation is something practical, personal, communal and 'political': to do with changing and being changed according to the image of the triune God whose story the Bible tells.[11] This is because, as Lash points out:

---

[9] Lash develops the 'relay race' image in 'Martyrdom', 79.

[10] See further on this the acute essays of the Jewish Hebrew Bible scholar Jon Levenson, in his book *The Hebrew Bible, The Old Testament, and Historical Criticism* (Louisville: Westminster John Knox Press, 1993), esp. ch. 5, 'Historical Criticism and the Fate of the Enlightenment Project'. Relevant on the Protestant side is Colin Gunton, *Enlightenment and Alienation: An Essay Towards a Trinitarian Theology* (Basingstoke: Marshall, Morgan & Scott, 1985).

[11] For more on this see Stephen C. Barton, *Invitation to the Bible* (London: SPCK, 1997), 12–27.

[T]he *poles* of Christian interpretation are not, in the last analysis, written texts (the text of the New Testament on the one hand and, on the other, whatever appears today in manuals of theology and catechetics, papal encyclicals, pastoral letters, etc.) but patterns of human action: what was said and done and suffered, then, by Jesus and his disciples, and what is said and done and suffered, now, by those who seek to share his obedience and his hope. We talk of 'holy' scripture, and for good reason. And yet it is not, in fact, the *script* that is 'holy', but the people: the company who perform the script.[12]

On this view the textual critic, the historian and the philologist will have their roles to play, certainly – particularly in suggesting boundaries of sense and usage within which responsible interpretation can take place. But these roles now become subordinate to the larger project of *embodying* the testimony of the text to the triune God in the life of the Body of Christ and in society at large. Nor will it be the case that *academic* training is the only kind of training required to become a good interpreter. For on the performance analogy, other kinds of discipline attain prominence as well, and a whole process of *personal formation* in the skills, practices, routines and virtues of a tradition-bearing community becomes equally important, something drawn to our attention in the past few years by theological ethicists like Stanley Hauerwas and Gregory Jones[13] and by writers in Christian spirituality like Andrew Louth, Diogenes Allen and Craig Dykstra.[14]

The analogy with the performance of a Beethoven symphony or a Shakespearean tragedy needs to be supplemented at this point, however. For performing Beethoven or Shakespeare is a limited activity and the tradition-bearing community it sustains and by which it is sustained is relatively circumscribed. Lash himself seems to recognize this when he appeals, towards the end of his essay, to

[12] Lash, 'Performing', 42 (author's emphasis).
[13] See, for example, Stanley Hauerwas, *A Community of Character* (Notre Dame: University of Notre Dame Press, 1981); and L. Gregory Jones, *Embodying Forgiveness* (Grand Rapids: Eerdmans, 1995); and 'A Thirst for God or Consumer Spirituality? Cultivating Disciplined Practices of Being Engaged by God', *Modern Theology* 13/1 (1997), 3–28.
[14] See Andrew Louth, *Discerning the Mystery* (Oxford: Clarendon, 1983); Diogenes Allen, 'Intellectual Inquiry and Spiritual Formation', in D. F. Ford and D. L. Stamps, eds, *Essentials of Christian Community* (Edinburgh: T&T Clark, 1996), 253–65; and Craig L. Dykstra, 'The Formative Power of the Congregation', in J. Astley *et al.*, eds, *Theological Perspectives on Christian Formation* (Grand Rapids: Eerdmans, 1996), 252–64.

what is involved in the interpretation of the American Constitution as another approximation to what is involved in interpreting the Bible.[15] He says: 'The fundamental form of the political interpretation of the American Constitution is the life, activity and organization of American society. That society exists . . . as the *enactment* of its Constitution. Similarly, we might say that the scriptures are the "constitution" of the church.'[16]

This is an important supplement. It helps us to see, by analogy, that Christian interpretation of the Bible as in some sense the 'constitution' of the church is *a full-time affair* – in spatial terms, that the stage on which the meaning of Scripture is 'played out' is the public domain of human society, and that the actors in this drama are all of us. It reinforces the claim that interpretation of a text like the New Testament takes place in the day-to-day life of a people, not just in the study of the philologist and historian. It also helps us to go beyond the strongly *aesthetic* and possibly rather 'highbrow' connotations of the kind of performance linked with a musical score or a dramatic script, and to acknowledge a significant *moral dimension* as well. Wise interpretation of the Bible, like wise interpretation of the American Constitution, has as its goal a society ordered towards the good and the true, and requires the ongoing exercise of moral discernment by its interpreters.

In this light, 'objective interpretation' of the New Testament is an oxymoron. What is required instead, as Gadamer argued,[17] is interpretation fully informed by *prejudice* – the *legitimate* prejudice which comes, in the case of the New Testament, from participation and formation in the life and action of a people committed to truthfully embodying the divine grace to which the New Testament itself bears witness. As I said at the outset, we cannot talk about the interpretation of the New Testament without talking also about theology and ecclesiology, revelation and the common good. Locating New Testament interpretation in this larger context –

[15] More recently, and apparently independently of Lash, another Roman Catholic theologian – this time a New Testament scholar – has made good use of the same analogy. I refer to Sandra M. Schneiders, *The Revelatory Text: Interpreting the New Testament as Sacred Scripture* (San Francisco: HarperCollins, 1991), 66, 78, 82.

[16] Lash, 'Performing', 43 (author's emphasis).

[17] See the relevant sections of Gadamer's *Truth and Method* excerpted in Kurt Mueller-Vollmer, *The Hermeneutics Reader* (New York: Continuum, 1992), esp. 257–67.

indeed, restoring it to where it properly belongs – has the potential to revitalize both our practice of interpretation and our common life.[18]

In sum, Lash's work is a corrective to certain tendencies in the essentially modernist enterprise of historical criticism of the Bible: the tendency to drive a wedge between meaning as public and truth as private; the tendency to exaggerate the discontinuity – the famous 'gap' – between the world of the text and that of the interpreter, often on the unspoken assumption that the 'primitive church' was primitive; the tendency to treat the text of Scripture 'like any other text', which becomes a pretext for interpreting the text in isolation from our relationship with God and with the tradition-bearing communities that 'display' the story of God in their common life; and the tendency to render the text mute by liberal, universalizing strategies which reduce the sense of the text to something monolithic and 'theoretical' – the sense intended by the original author as reconstructed by the historian, or the sense embedded in the semiotics of the text as identified by the literary critic.

In place of the historical critic as 'consumer' providing the raw matter which the theologian can cook according to taste, in place of the critic as 'tourist' expanding his or her horizons by excursions in foreign and rather exotic literary fields,[19] Lash argues effectively for the self-involving, practical and communal nature of biblical interpretation: 'The practice of Christian faith is not, in the last resort, a matter of interpreting, in our time and place, an ancient text. It is, or seeks to be, the faithful "rendering" of those events, of those patterns of human action, decision and suffering, to which the text bears original witness.'[20]

2. Rowan Williams

Important support for the kind of position advocated by Lash has come from several others. One is the Anglican theologian and archbishop, Rowan Williams, in an essay on 'The Literal Sense of Scripture', published in *Modern Theology* in 1991.[21] This typically dense essay complements Lash's work in an interesting way in that,

---

[18] See further the important reflections on Gadamer in relation to biblical interpretation in Louth, *Discerning the Mystery*, 29–43; and Gunton, *Enlightenment and Alienation*, 128–31.

[19] Lash, 'Martyrdom', 82–7.

[20] Ibid. 90.

[21] *Modern Theology* 7/2 (1991), 121–34.

whereas Lash is offering a corrective to historical-critical approaches to New Testament interpretation, Williams is offering a corrective to allegorical, structuralist and canonical approaches that have developed partly in reaction against historical criticism. If I understand Williams correctly, such approaches are problematic to the extent that they undermine the primacy traditionally accorded the 'literal' sense of Scripture. They do so by undermining the normativity of interpretation that is *diachronic*, where the meaning of the text is worked out in time and over time in ways which are 'bound to history', in favour of interpretation that is synchronic, where the meaning of the text is conceived in more 'spatial' terms and tends to be fixed, closed off and given in advance. According to Williams,

> [T]o attend to a 'literal' sense . . . is to insist upon there being some controlling force in the fact that meaning comes to light in a process of learning to perceive; it is to challenge the idea that there could be an adequate reading of the text which ignored the time of the text itself, its own movement, with the time of the writer and the writer's world opened up to us through the movement of the text. It is to protest against any reading which elided or softened or simply ignored the tensions realised and worked through in the time of the text . . . Concern with the literal, the diachronic, is a way of resisting the premature unities and harmonies of a non-literal reading (whether allegorical, existentialist, structuralist or deconstructionist), in which the time that matters is only the present of the reader faced with the 'spatial' expanse of a text cut off from its own inner processes and the history of its production.[22]

Significantly, for the purposes of this chapter, Williams likens the non-literal synchronic approach to observing the 'surface of a picture', and the literal diachronic approach to engaging with 'a performance of drama or music'; and he insists that interpretation of Scripture according to the literal sense is necessarily 'dramatic'. In other words, Williams is impatient with approaches to interpretation that lead to a *shrinkage* both of the meaning of the text and of our '*taking of time*' with it as readers – readers who can 'follow' the text because *our* time is continuous with *its* time. And, like Lash, he finds in the metaphor of dramatic performance an apt way of expressing the necessarily active, ongoing and transformative nature of engagement with the text. To quote once more:

[22] Williams, 'Literal Sense', 123.

Christian language takes it for granted, in several different ways, that meanings are learned and produced, not given in iconic, ahistorical form. It grows out of a particular set of communal and individual histories, and its images and idioms are fundamentally shaped by this fact. And, in working through concepts like penitence, conversion and hope, in its commitment to the freedom of God and God's grace to draw historical realities into a future as yet undetermined, it resists the notion that the understanding of faith can be only a *moment* of interpretative perception with its own synchronic integrity and completeness, as opposed to a process with strong elements of risk and provisionality. Consequently, Christian interpretation is unavoidably engaged in 'dramatic' modes of reading: we are invited to identify ourselves in the story being contemplated, to reappropriate who we are now, and who we shall or can be, in terms of the story. *Its* movements, transactions, transformations, become *ours*; we take responsibility for this or that position within the narrative. . . . 'Dramatic' reading, then, belongs with the literal sense. . . . It assumes that the diachronic is a central element in the working of Christian text and interpretation, and also – very importantly – that the time of the text is recognisably continuous with my time.[23]

Important to note in all this is that the metaphor of performance or 'dramatic' reading, as used by both Lash and Williams, is not allowed to obscure the distinction between acting and *play-acting* or between enactment and *re-enactment*. Clearly, the possibility that 'performing the Scriptures' could be taken as an invitation to play-acting is a potential weakness in the metaphor, if by 'play-acting' is meant taking on a role rather than becoming transformed into a different kind of person or a different kind of community. Of course, the significance of play-acting ought not to be discounted. It is itself a serious part of the symbolic, communicative enterprise we call 'culture'; and play-acting Scripture – from the morality and passion plays of the medieval period to the bibliodramas created in recent years by Swiss missiologist Walter Hollenweger[24] – has done a lot to help many readers and listeners 'find themselves' in the biblical text.[25] But play-acting is not what Lash and Williams have in mind. As Gerard Loughlin puts it: 'the figure of play-acting . . . fails to

---

[23] Williams, 'Literal Sense', 125 (author's emphasis).

[24] See, for example, W. J. Hollenweger, *Jungermesse/Gomer: Das Gesicht des Unsichtbaren* (Munich: Kaiser, 1983); and *Das Fest der Verlorenen* (Munich: Kaiser, 1984).

[25] See in general, Bjorn Krondorfer, ed., *Body and Bible: Interpreting and Experiencing Biblical Narratives* (Philadelphia: Trinity Press International, 1992).

grasp the risk and radical contingency, the open-endedness, of the play being enacted, the performance being given.'[26]

Instead, for Lash, performative interpretation of Scripture finds its focal expression not in play-acting, but in the celebration of the eucharist and in the liturgy of the Word. In the eucharist, 'that interpretative performance in which all our life consists – all our suffering and care, compassion, celebration, struggle and obedience – is dramatically distilled, focused, concentrated, rendered explicit'.[27] And in the liturgy of the Word, 'the story is told not so that it may merely be relished or remembered, but that it may be *performed*, in the following of Christ'.[28] Rowan Williams concurs. For him, the 'dramatic' reading which most obviously mediates the time of the text for our time is 'the scriptural lectionary bound to the festal cycle', with the paschal celebration of Holy Week at its centre.[29] That is not to say that 'performing the Scriptures' is something 'narrowly' liturgical, as if parts of our lives as individuals and communities are left out of account. Rather, it is to say that the liturgy is a focal and intentionally repeated enactment and embodiment of that story of God which for its telling will take every part of our lives for the entire duration of our lives, not only individually but corporately as well.[30]

3. Frances Young

Lest it be thought that the employment of the performance metaphor in New Testament interpretation is some kind of 'Catholic' plot, I turn next to a substantial book-length treatment by the Methodist theologian and patristic scholar Frances Young in her 1990 publication *The Art of Performance*.[31] Like Nicholas Lash, but

---

[26] Gerard Loughlin, *Telling God's Story: Bible, Church and Narrative Theology* (Cambridge: Cambridge University Press, 1996), 134.

[27] Lash, 'Performing', 45–6.

[28] Ibid. 46 (author's emphasis).

[29] Williams, 'Literal Sense', 126.

[30] On the role of liturgy, see further, Nicholas Wolterstorff, 'The Remembrance of Things (Not) Past: Philosophical Reflections on Christian Liturgy', in T. P. Flint, ed., *Christian Philosophy* (Notre Dame: University of Notre Dame Press, 1990), 118–61. On the significance of repetition in liturgy, see Stephen Sykes, 'Ritual and the Sacrament of the Word', in David Brown and Ann Loades, eds, *Christ: The Sacramental Word* (London: SPCK, 1996), 157–67.

[31] Frances Young, *The Art of Performance: Towards a Theology of Holy Scripture* (London: Darton, Longman & Todd, 1990).

234 *Life Together*

writing apparently independently of him,[32] Young addresses the problem of how to appropriate the Bible in the modern world: 'How can we treat the Bible as Holy Scripture if it is to be subjected to literary or historical criticism like any other book? . . . How can we live in and worship with the Bible – how can we "perform" the Bible – in a modern world so different from the past which produced and used it?'[33] Her answer is that the way we can do so is illuminated by study of the way early Church Fathers like Irenaeus, Melito or Origen interpreted the Bible, especially if we see what they did in the light of the analogy of a musical canon and its contemporary performance.[34]

Indeed, Young suggests in the first chapter that the analogy with music illuminates, not just the art of biblical interpretation, but a theology of the Bible as Holy Scripture as well. Just as music has, as it were, 'two natures', a temporal and a timeless, so too the Bible can be thought of (along the lines of Chalcedonian christology) as having 'two natures' – the Word of God and human words historically conditioned – both of which are to be taken with full seriousness and without collapsing one into the other.[35] In my view, this is not the most helpful use of the analogy, however. On the one hand, it makes the use of the performance analogy captive to a conception of music that may be idiosyncratic or misleading. On the other, it pushes discussion of the Bible in a narrowly ontological and 'theoretical' direction, to do with questions about the 'inherent quality' of the scriptural text. In so doing, it distracts attention away from the hermeneutical and performative, from what it might mean to *receive and interpret* a text whose meaning is disclosed in patterns of human action in the life of a people. In Lash's terms, it overlooks the fundamental point that for a text like the New Testament, the poles of interpretation are to do in the end not with texts but with persons in community, with the triune life of God and the people whom God has made.[36]

More helpful, I think, is what Young says about the formation of the biblical canon: in particular, the observation that the canonical

[32] See Young, *Performance*, 21 n. 1.

[33] Ibid. 1.

[34] Ibid. 21.

[35] Ibid. 21–5. The 'two natures' analogy recurs at different points throughout the book, and finally at 176–82.

[36] Significant here, as a development of Lash in an even more theological (trinitarian) direction, is David Scott, 'Speaking to Form', esp. 139–46.

process is not a matter of the erasure of diversity.[37] The canon of Scripture, encompassing a small library of individual works whose literary genre varies widely, is best understood by analogy with a classic repertoire in music or drama. The formation of the canon within the respective communities of Israel and the church is like the rather mysterious process of sifting which brings a classic repertoire of music into being. What is included is judged as having a significance that is epoch-making, identity-forming and of more than passing worth. It is material that does not wear thin with repetition, but is able to speak beyond the circumstances in and for which it was originally composed. Furthermore, just as authentic interpretation of the repertoire has to take account of the diversity of the musical genres of which it is composed, so too biblical interpretation has to take account of the diversity of literary genres encompassed by the Bible. It is not all law or prophecy or wisdom or (the most recent proposal) narrative. Like the classic repertoire in music or drama, the Bible – in all its diversity and complexity, and with a history of interpretation that must itself be influential in judging how it ought to be interpreted – is a fundamental dimension of the life of a people. It is its score, its script, its constitution, its story. In the act of authentic performance, both in time and time after time, the canon comes to life and the community is reconstituted and transformed.

Several of Frances Young's other suggestions drawing on the metaphor of performance must be touched on more briefly. Important, for example, is what she says about the crucial role of *tradition*, of an extra-textual framework of rules, wisdom, ethos and customary practice, for true interpretation.[38] This is so for authentic artistic performance of the classic repertoire in music: and it is even more so for the interpretation of the Bible, a point which Young illustrates from the appeal of Irenaeus to the church's *regula fidei*

---

[37] Young, *Performance*, 26–44.

[38] See further Robert Wilken's essay 'Memory and the Christian Intellectual Life' in his *Remembering the Christian Past* (Grand Rapids: Eerdmans, 1995), 165–80, esp. at 170–1: 'In many fields of creative work, immersion in tradition is the presupposition for excellence and originality. Think, for example, of music. . . . [O]ne is impressed with how often a performer like folk singer Jean Redpath speaks about tradition as the necessary condition for making and singing folk music. How often we are admonished not to let the old traditions be forgotten. Why? Surely not for historical or archaeological reasons, but because musicians, like painters and writers and sculptors, know in their fingertips or vocal chords or ears that imitation is the way to excellence and originality.'

236   *Life Together*

('rule of faith') as normative, in his controversy with the Gnostics. For practitioners of a biblical criticism whose roots lie in the double questioning of tradition that we call (without irony!) the 'Reformation' and the 'Enlightenment', what Young says as a Methodist about the legacy of the Reformation is worth special note:

> The integration of scripture within tradition, so natural to Irenaeus, was torn asunder by the Reformation. . . . The unfortunate result has been that the tradition, by becoming controversial, has acquired a separate existence alongside scripture in Catholic as well as Protestant argumentation, while the Bible has had to bear authority independent of the tradition which once provided the canons of classic interpretation. The watchword *sola scriptura* has proved a very mixed blessing, eventually spawning not only fundamentalism but a protestantism which has proved inherently fissiparous as different groups have interpreted the texts differently, unaware of the fact that frameworks external to the text are inevitable, that each would be bound to develop its own tradition, its own canons of interpretation, its own framework, which owes something but not everything to scripture itself.[39]

Young also has important things to say about the recovery of typological interpretation of the Bible, given the necessity and inevitability of an extra-textual (theological and ecclesial) framework; and she rightly observes that historical-critical hostility to typological interpretation has had the serious consequence of marginalizing the reading of the Old Testament as Scripture.[40] Here, the analogy with music is with the way individual works in a repertoire take on added significance to the extent that they are related to one another in various complex ways, or with the way, in a single piece, 'repetition, recurring themes, development and recapitulation' play an important role in giving the piece its movement, sense of an ending, and so on.[41]

Then there is Young's final chapter on 'Improvisation and Inspiration'. Here she suggests that the best way to think of the process whereby the ancient biblical text is allowed to speak today as Scripture is by analogy with the cadenzas in a concerto. Individual 'performances' of Scripture in preaching and teaching are like the

[39] Young, *Performance*, 61. Compare also Stanley Hauerwas, 'The Politics of the Bible: *Sola Scriptura* as Heresy?', in his *Unleashing the Scripture* (Nashville: Abingdon Press, 1993), 15–44.
[40] See further David Steinmetz, 'The Superiority of Pre-Critical Exegesis', *Ex Auditu* 1 (1985), 74–82.
[41] Young, *Performance*, 66–87.

improvisation of the performer of the cadenza. There is the need for faithfulness to the style and themes of the concerto, but also virtuosity and inspiration in developing these in ways fitting both to the music and to the occasion:

> The orchestra is the community of the faithful, and with the soloist its members perfect the performance in rehearsal. Ultimately the audience is the world. Just playing the old classic without a cadenza is like reading the lessons without a sermon. It is true that reading well depends on good translation and interpretation, but only the preaching enables proper development of the classic themes for a new situation. It is no good simply replaying the old cadenzas, because each generation has to appropriate the themes anew, and the renewal alone can effect communication.[42]

Interestingly, but not surprisingly, where the Roman Catholic theologian finds in the eucharist the epitome of the Christian 'improvisation' on Scripture, and where the Anglican archbishop finds it in the festal cycle culminating in Holy Week, the Methodist theologian finds it in preaching! But, of course, as each of these would acknowledge readily, none of these improvisations excludes the other. On the contrary, in ecumenical perspective they go together as that 'performance' of sacramental Word and kerygmatic Sacrament by which the church seeks to respond to that divine reality to which, in the faith of Christians, the Scriptures bear authoritative testimony.

III. Further reflections

Having discussed the 'performance' model with reference to three of its main proponents, I would like now to elaborate its value and implications in a number of further reflections.

1. Going with the grain

The first is that the performance model commends itself by virtue of the fact that it goes *with the grain* both of the New Testament itself and of the Bible as a whole. For, as is recognized widely, there is a profound sense in which the New Testament is an 'open text' that invites completion in the lives of its readers and looks forward

---

[42] Ibid. 161–2.

to a future beyond its own time and place. It is parable which subverts
preconceptions – 'Who is my neighbour?'. It is testimony which
invites response – 'Do this in remembrance of me'. It is prophecy
which awaits fulfilment – 'For now we see in a mirror dimly, but
then face to face'. It is revelation which calls for ongoing discernment – '[H]e will teach you all things'.

Witness also the Gospels, their endings in particular. Matthew
ends with a resurrection appearance on an unidentified mountain
to representative disciples to whom is given an eschatological
commission to ongoing, universal mission in the company of the
risen Son of God himself (Matt 28.16–20); Mark ends with an irony
and openness which defies attempts to fix the 'secret' at the heart
of the Gospel and constitutes instead a summons to 'fearful'
following of the One who 'goes before' (Mk 16.1–8);[43] Luke ends
with a meal unfinished and with the scene set for an empowerment
for ecclesial witness yet to come (Lk 24.28–35, 44–49), while the
second volume ends on an intriguingly mundane, anti-climactic
note with the picture of Paul in custody in Rome preaching and
teaching (Acts 28.30–31); and John ends with Jesus appointing a
successor to feed his sheep, and with an implied admission that
witness to Jesus has to be ongoing because no Gospel text could
possibly bear witness to the full reality of his life (Jn 21.15–19,
24–25). All this is a way of saying that the Gospels convey something
which is true of the New Testament generally: that the reality to
which it testifies is *eschatological* and that access to this reality comes
by way of faithful 'following', a following mediated by the text as it
is brought into play in the life of the church in service of the world.

Tom Wright has argued recently in the same direction. In a brief
but significant discussion of the nature of the authority of the New

---

[43] Cf. Rowan Williams, 'Between the Cherubim: The Empty Tomb and the Empty
Throne', in G. D'Costa, ed., *Resurrection Reconsidered* (Oxford: Oneworld, 1996),
87–101 at 98: '[T]he silence with which Mark's gospel ends indicates that the speaker
of the gospel and the subject of the gospel as a narration is not himself *silenced*. It is
not just a homiletic point to say that the "missing ending" of Mark's text is the
response of the reader or community of readers rather than a textual lacuna of
some sort. The narrative of Jesus is not finished, therefore not in any sense
controlled, even by supposedly "authorized" tellers of the story; his agency continues,
now inseparable from the narrative of God's dealings with God's people, and so
his story cannot be simply and decisively told. The telling of the story of his life and
death is … a process designed to bring the believer to the point of recognition that
this is not a life exhausted in any text or ensemble of texts, in any performance or
ensemble of performances. Jesus remains subject of his history.'

Testament, he likens the task of New Testament interpretation to the improvisation of a lost fifth act of a Shakespearean play by skilled actors who have immersed themselves in the first four acts in a way that enables them to develop and conclude the play in a way which can be recognized as being 'right' and 'fitting'. The authority of the New Testament is like the authority of those extant four acts: but the improvisation, as the filling out and completion of the drama, remains essential. Indeed, Wright takes the model even further theologically, suggesting that the biblical story as a whole can be seen as consisting of four acts – Creation, Fall, Israel, and Jesus – with a fifth act incomplete and ongoing, although the contours of its shape and ending are present already in eschatological texts like Romans 8, 1 Corinthians 15 and the Apocalypse. In a comment which highlights what I judge to be the appropriate, ecclesiological context of biblical interpretation, he says:

> The church is designed, according to this model, as a stage in the completion of the creator's work of art . . . [T]he notion that the writers of the New Testament were in some senses instituting a historical movement in which subsequent Christian generations may follow gives to the task of hermeneutics an angle and emphasis quite different from any of the regular options . . . We are not searching, against the grain of the material, for timeless truths. We are looking, as the material is looking, for and at a vocation to be the people of God in the fifth act of the drama of creation. The church inherits, at the end of the story, the task of restoring to the owner the fruits of the vineyard.[44]

2. Scripture and doctrine: 'performing' the resurrection

If the 'performance' model is given added justification by being able to be seen as going with the grain – both literary and theological – of the New Testament itself, the question arises: Does it throw light on the interpretation of particular parts of the text otherwise resistant to conventional historical-critical approaches? A case in point is the resurrection of Jesus, the subject of continuous controversy and misunderstanding at both scholarly and popular levels, as we are reminded in the tabloids and broadsheets every Easter.[45]

[44] Wright, *The New Testament and the People of God*, 142.
[45] For the most recent assessment see the collection of essays edited by Stephen Davis, Daniel Kendall and Gerald O'Collins, *The Resurrection: An Interdisciplinary Symposium on the Resurrection of Jesus* (Oxford: Oxford University Press, 1997).

In a recent essay entitled 'Living in Christ: Story, Resurrection and Salvation', Gerard Loughlin[46] argues that resurrection faith does not come from the accumulation of evidence according to the canons of 'reasonable religion' naturalistically understood. As he points out: 'modern theology, which seeks to move from the world to God, finds only more of the world'.[47] Instead of coming to us in the logical, coherent form of the narratives of critical history, which deform the Gospels by going 'behind' them to construct a single, normative account of what 'really' happened, the resurrection comes in the fourfold gospel story with all its rents, gaps and indeterminacies: for only a fourfold story like this can *make space* for the imaginative reception of the central mystery of the life of God in the death and resurrection of Jesus.

Furthermore, and making a point whose concern lies at the heart of this paper, the truth of the resurrection can be perceived only by faith,[48] by becoming ourselves part of the story, performers of the story, in our common life.[49] In the liturgical celebration of Easter, says Loughlin,

> the Church not merely reads, but prays the Scripture. Before God the Church calls to mind the story of that first Easter when the women hurried to the tomb, only to find that they were already too late. As always the Lord had gone on before them. The Church not only recalls the story, but ritually enacts it in the solemn joy of vigil and

[46] In G. D'Costa, ed., *Resurrection Reconsidered*, 118–34.

[47] Loughlin, 'Living in Christ', 120.

[48] Compare William Blake's letter to Dr Trusler of 23 August 1799, in G. Keynes, ed., *The Letters of William Blake* (Oxford: Clarendon Press, 1980), 9: 'But to the Eyes of the Man of Imagination, Nature is Imagination itself. As a Man is, So he Sees. As the Eye is formed, such are its Powers. You certainly Mistake, when you say that the Visions of Fancy are not to be found in This World. To Me This World is all One continued Vision of Fancy or Imagination, & I feel Flatter'd when I am told so. . . . Why is the Bible more Entertaining & Instructive than any other book? Is it not because they are addressed to the Imagination, which is Spiritual Sensation, & but mediately to the Understanding or Reason?' I owe this reference to Christopher Rowland.

[49] Compare also what Loughlin says about the interpretation of myth in his earlier essay 'Myths, Signs and Significations', *Theology* 89 (July, 1986), 268–75 at 273: 'The signification of myth is the movement of the literal meaning which makes us participate in the latent mythological meaning, and thus assimilates us to that which is signified. Myth is not to be analysed, but consumed; its reading at once an appropriation and an enactment . . . For the proper reading of myth is the communal living of myth, not just in participative performance but in existential commitment.'

paschal light. . . . The resurrection is known in the Church's prayerful performance of Christ's story. . . . The risen life of Christ is present in the gathering of the people who recall before God the promise that they will be called again by him who has already gone on ahead and is coming to meet them . . .[50]

On this view, the resurrection is not something 'merely' historical that can be kept at arm's length and weighed dispassionately. On the contrary, it is something *eschatological, corporeal and social*: the overflowing, stronger-than-death life of God at work in Jesus and, through him, in his body, the church serving the world. The truth of the resurrection, on this view, is hostage no longer to the judgements of secular historiography and (what my colleague Colin Crowder nicely calls) 'Old Bailey' theology of the kind found in books like Morrison's *Who Moved the Stone?* or Wenham's *Easter Enigma*. It is found rather in performance and enactment, in practices which generate 'new possibilities for human life now in history'[51] – what Paul called dying and rising with Christ, and what Loughlin calls the 'non-identical repetition of Jesus' life'[52] – in the faith that the life of Jesus is *infinite*, God's life, and therefore life itself.

3. The saints as 'performers' of Scripture

The idea of non-identical repetition of Jesus' life in the life of the church brings us naturally to a consideration of *saints*.[53] I say 'naturally', but for myself as I suppose for many others trained in historical criticism of the New Testament, consideration of the saints and of the ways in which their lives might give access to the meaning and truth of the text is by no means second nature. It is certainly

[50] Loughlin, 'Living in Christ', 124–5.

[51] Scott, 'Speaking to Form', 145.

[52] Loughlin, 'Living in Christ', 128.

[53] So, too, Loughlin, 'Living in Christ', 130–2, a concluding section of his essay entitled 'Exemplary Lives', where he says *inter alia*: 'It is in the lives of the saints (which finally constitute the life of the Church), that the "event of a transformation" – which is the risen life of Christ – is "made to happen", again and again, and each time differently. In the life-story of Jesus we see the overcoming of coercive and selfish power through the refusal of violence, the practice of forgiveness and the transformation of suffering. It is this practice which the Church aims to repeat, and in so far as it does, it is inscribed and incorporated into the very life of the crucified and risen Christ' (131).

not part of any course on New Testament interpretation that I know of, nor does it appear in standard introductions to the New Testament. For our work seems almost to be hermetically sealed off from anything that might contaminate the quest for the 'purity' of the original meaning of the text or of the historical Jesus 'behind' the text. In Rowan Williams's terms, we *claim* to be engaged in diachronic reading, but the reality is that our reading *is not diachronic enough*, not materialistic enough, not attentive enough to the *embodiment* of the meaning of the New Testament in the lives of those individuals and communities who have been transformed by it both in the past and in the present.

To put it another way, our reading of the New Testament lacks a certain *ecumenicity*. On the one hand, our professionalization in secularized academies cuts us off from the sense of belonging to the 'communion of saints' in this world and in the world to come, and on the other hand, there is a tendency to ignore those more sacramental traditions – not least those of the Orthodox churches – where the truth to which Scripture testifies is mediated not just by the text itself but also by the 'rendering' of the text, of the story of God, in the lives of saints, martyrs, desert fathers and holy women.[54]

Appeal to the Orthodox tradition brings a particular example to mind: that of the Transfiguration of Christ (Mk 9.2–8 and parallels), which, for Orthodox life, liturgy and theology is paradigmatic,[55] and which John McGuckin has explored in a biblical and patristic study published in 1986.[56] For a form-critic like Bultmann, the meaning of the Transfiguration is to be found in an essentially rationalizing cross-reference to the theophany of Exodus 24 and the post-resurrection christophanies of the Gospels; and the verdict overall is that the Transfiguration is a resurrection story retrojected into the ministry of Jesus and 'taken up by Mark to serve as a heavenly ratification of Peter's confession and as a prophecy of

---

[54] See further the moving essay by Georges Florovsky 'On the Veneration of the Saints', in his collection of essays *Creation and Redemption* (Belmont: Nordland, 1976), 201–8.

[55] See, for example, Vladimir Lossky, *The Mystical Theology of the Eastern Church* (Cambridge: James Clarke, 1957), 217–35; also Andrew Louth, 'The Transfiguration in the Theology of St Maximos the Confessor', in his *Wisdom of the Byzantine Church* (Columbia: University of Missouri, 1998), 20–33.

[56] John A. McGuckin, *The Transfiguration of Christ in Scripture and Tradition* (Lewiston: Edwin Mellen, 1986).

the Resurrection in pictorial form'.[57] The consequence is that the Gospel testimony is evacuated of any sense of spiritual reality. As philosopher Donald Evans points out in his article in the Caird *Festschrift*, in interpretations like this, Kantian relativism and common-sense empiricism have won the day.[58]

Could it be, therefore, that we would do well to look elsewhere, to the lives of saints and mystics, for better access to the meaning and truth of this story? From the perspective of the Orthodox tradition, this is indeed so.[59] In particular, we might attend to the kind of 'transfiguration' experience of a saint like Seraphim of Sarov (1759–1833) as both shared and narrated by his disciple Nicolas Motovilov:

> After these words I glanced at his face, and there came over me an even greater reverent awe. Imagine in the centre of the sun, in the dazzling light of its midday rays, the face of a man talking to you. You see the movement of his lips and the changing expression of his eyes, you hear his voice, you feel someone holding your shoulders; yet you do not see his hands, you do not even see yourself or his body, but only a blinding light spreading far around for several yards and lighting up with its brilliance the snow-blanket which covers the forest glade and the snow-flakes which continue to fall unceasingly . . . 'What do you feel?', Father Seraphim asked me. 'An immeasurable well-being,' I said. 'But what sort of well-being? How exactly do you feel?' 'I feel such calm,' I answered, 'such peace in my soul that no words can express it.'[60]

But my point about saints as performers of Scripture goes further than finding in the lives of the saints analogies of a phenomeno-logical kind which may serve to widen our horizons and therefore

[57] R. Bultmann, *The History of the Synoptic Tradition* (ET Oxford: Blackwell, 1963), 260. More detailed and interesting is the essentially *religionsgeschichtlich* study by H. C. Kee, 'The Transfiguration in Mark: Epiphany or Apocalyptic Vision?', in J. Reumann, ed., *Understanding the Sacred Text* (Valley Forge: Judson, 1972), 137–52, but again the conclusion is reductionist: Mark's story is a 'literary device' intended to convey a 'message' of assurance. Only a *message*?

[58] D. Evans, 'Academic Scepticism, Spiritual Reality and Transfiguration', in L. D. Hurst and N. T. Wright, eds, *The Glory of Christ in the New Testament* (Oxford: Clarendon Press, 1987), 175–86.

[59] This was also for Reformed theologian George Caird also. As Evans notes ('Transfiguration', 181), Caird's awareness of 'the researches of Evelyn Underhill and others, who have shown that the intense devotions of saint and mystic are often accompanied by physical transformation and luminous glow', led him to the conclusion that the Transfiguration could be accepted as 'literal truth'.

[60] Quoted in Timothy Ware, *The Orthodox Church* (London: Penguin, 1993), 119. I owe this reference to my colleague Walter Moberly.

also our hermeneutical options. For what I want to suggest is that we *can* only understand what the Transfiguration might mean and whether or not it is true if the reality which the narrative displays is *mediated to us* through the passage of time in the lives and the communion of those who have themselves been touched by 'the weight of glory'. As David Matzko puts it:

> The lives of the saints are a rehearsal of God's redemptive activity, and when rehearsing *their* lives becomes the fabric of *our* lives, we gain access to the landscape of God's way with the world. . . . Redemption constitutes the body. Likewise, sainthood is constituted by God's continuing embodiment of grace. The saints are the lineage of God's redemptive activity; they are the continuing promise of grace that comes into the world enfleshed; they are the mapping out of God's blessed way.[61]

Of course, what Matzko says here is so, not only of those individuals who have been canonized or who belong to ages long past. For this century, for example, Fowl and Jones have drawn our attention to Dietrich Bonhoeffer as a 'performer of Scripture';[62] Richard Lischer has written along similar lines about Martin Luther King Jr;[63] and Ann Loades has written about the extraordinary but also ambiguous legacy of Simone Weil as the embodiment of a Christian understanding of sacrifice.[64]

Furthermore, in a more general way, what is true of individual saints past and present is true also of the church as 'the communion of saints'. Indeed, in the eye of faith, it is by no means only in the ongoing life of the church that the testimony of people we might want to call 'saints' is to be found. There are those *outside* the church who bear the weight of glory in particular ways also, and who in so doing help us to understand better the reality to which the New

[61] David Matzko, 'Christ's Body in its Fullness: Resurrection and the Lives of the Saints', in D'Costa, ed., *Resurrection Reconsidered*, 102–17 at 114, 116.

[62] Fowl and Jones, *Reading in Communion*, 135–64; compare also Jürgen Moltmann, *The Way of Jesus Christ* (London: SCM Press, 1990), 196–204, where Moltmann cites the cases of contemporary martyrs Paul Schneider and Arnulfo Romero, as well as Dietrich Bonhoeffer, as among those who share in 'the fellowship of Christ's sufferings'.

[63] Richard Lischer, 'Martin Luther King Jr: "Performing" the Scriptures', *Anglican Theological Review* 77 (1995), 160–72.

[64] Ann Loades, 'Simone Weil – Sacrifice: A Problem for Theology', in D. Jasper, ed., *Images of Belief in Literature* (London: Macmillan, 1984), 122–37.

Testament testifies. My main point, however, is that saints and 'the saints' are an irritant and a provocation to the biblical critic. They are a reminder that interpretation as performance is an essentially material, ecclesial/societal activity, the enactment of the biblical 'script' as the life of a people through time given over in love to the service of the world.[65]

4. Reconceiving 'New Testament ethics'

If what I am saying is true then, as a fourth reflection, we need to think again about what we call 'New Testament ethics'. This came home to me at the 1997 meeting of the Studiorum Novi Testamenti Societas in Birmingham. In the third session of the 'New Testament Ethics' Seminar Group, we took as a case study for group exegesis the texts from the early chapters of Acts about 'community of goods' (*hapanta koina*). As you would expect, all kinds of illuminating historical and intertextual insights were contributed: Is Theissen correct, we asked, in proposing Hellenistic influence, or Riesner and Capper in proposing Essene influence? To what extent is Luke's portrayal an attempt to present the church as the true Israel, the fulfilment of the sabbatical ideal of Deuteronomy 15.4 that 'there will be no poor among you'? How significant is it that the accounts are bracketed by testimonies to the 'signs and wonders' (*sēmeia kai terata*) done by the apostles (Acts 2.43; 5.12)? And so on.

The problem came in the last ten minutes, when someone raised the question – successfully postponed until then – about how to extrapolate 'norms and principles' from Luke's narrative. We were stuck. We could delve behind the text into the history and literature of Israel and Qumran. We could trace developments within the narrative world of the text itself. We could even venture into the world in front of the text, at least by appealing to possible analogies with the sharing of goods in so-called 'millenarian sects'. But none of us was competent to say what the 'sharing of goods' might really mean because – or so I wondered – none of us was *engaged already* in communities shaped by experiences of Spirit and practices of

---

[65] See further, Robert L. Wilken's excellent essay, 'The Lives of the Saints and the Pursuit of Virtue', in his *Remembering the Christian Past*, 121–44; and, for a liberationist perspective on the saints, see Leonardo Boff, *Saint Francis: A Model for Human Liberation* (London: SCM Press, 1985).

sacrificial solidarity with the poor.[66] In other words, because the
personal and social reality to which Luke's narrative bears witness
was not our reality also, except perhaps in attenuated ways, we were
left high and dry, like tourists stranded on a foreign shore. And the
attempt to 'translate' Luke's testimony into 'norms and principles'
appears now as a universalizing and idealizing strategy, not so much
for appropriating the text, as for *neutralizing* it.

We have to ask the hard question, therefore, whether or not this
is so of 'New Testament Ethics' as a whole. Is it a strategy for endlessly
postponing the excruciating business of allowing ourselves *to be
changed*? Do we take a wrong turn right at the start by attempting to
reconstruct, in essentially Kantian terms, the 'ethics' of the New
Testament? In so doing, are we not confining the moral authority
of the New Testament to categories which undermine it? Are we
not, at the same time, cutting *ourselves* off from the very tradition-
bearing 'communities of character' membership of which might so
shape us as to empower us to *follow* the text in ways more consistent
with the eschatological reality at its heart? And may it not be the
case that 'following the text' may be a matter, not of discovery,
translation and application, as if we were encountering the text for
the first time, but of *remembrance* – a remembrance made possible
by attending to the example of saints and martyrs who face us with
the cost of *true* understanding?[67]

There is a strong current in contemporary theological ethics,
indebted to Alasdair MacIntyre's work on 'virtue ethics' on the one
hand[68] and to Hans Frei's work on biblical narrative on the other,[69]
that would answer these questions in the affirmative. For Stanley
Hauerwas in particular, Christian ethics is not about extrapolating

[66] Compare Stanley Hauerwas' comment in 'Failure of Communication *or* a Case
of Uncomprehending Feminism', *Scottish Journal of Theology* 50/2 (1997), 228–39
at 235 n. 13: 'I was recently asked by a friend why I do not write more about the
"poor". It is a good question. The quick answer is I do not know how to do so in a
way that is serious. I do not believe it wise to write about the "poor" or the oppressed
in the abstract. . . . [W]e lack the resources . . . to remember or to be with the poor
– or even more, to imagine what it would mean for us (that is, those of us who write
articles like this) to be poor.'

[67] See further, Hauerwas, *Community of Character*, 53–71, on 'The Moral Authority
of Scripture: The Politics and Ethics of Remembering'.

[68] See, for example, Alasdair MacIntyre, *After Virtue: A Study in Moral Theory* (Notre
Dame: University of Notre Dame Press, 1981).

[69] Hans Frei, *The Eclipse of Biblical Narrative* (New Haven: Yale University Press,
1974).

norms and principles from the New Testament, since that tends only to show how problematic the New Testament is, as well as how unsuited it is to the task, given that so much of it (i.e. the Gospels) comes in the form of narrative.[70] Nor is it the case that the church can be said to 'have' an ethic, as if the ethic is something which can be abstracted from the biblical story and then 'applied' to 'modern life'. Rather, the church *is* a social ethic, constituted as such through its ongoing performance of, its creative fidelity to, the scriptural story of God in Christ.

On this view, then, the meaning of the practice of 'community of goods' in the Jerusalem church to which Luke bears witness consists in the way it testifies to the resurrection power of God and to the many and various ways down the centuries that resurrection power has been constitutive of people's common life, both within the church and outside it. As a corollary, it is those whose lives have been shaped by such practice, and who have learned thereby to 'perform' the Scriptures, who may be qualified best to testify to it. Such people and the historical and contemporary communities to which they belong will be the 'commentaries' on the text, commentaries which conventional 'New Testament Ethics' appears to ignore.[71]

IV. Conclusion: the culture of New Testament interpretation

I have been arguing for a *new paradigm* for New Testament interpretation. This paradigm is one which sets interpretation in a

---

[70] As Hauerwas puts it (in *Community of Character*, 54–5): 'Failure to appreciate how the biblical narratives have and continue to form a polity is part of the reason that the ethical significance of scripture currently seems so problematic. Indeed, many of the articles written on the relation of scripture and ethics focus on ways scripture should not be used for ethical matters. Yet if my proposal is correct, this very way of putting the issue – i.e. how should be scripture be used ethically – is already a distortion. For to put it that way assumes that we must first clarify the meaning of the text – in the sense that we understand its historical or sociological background – and only then can we ask its moral significance.'

[71] Note Scott, 'Speaking to Form', 144–5: 'Interpretation may be so institutionalized in schools and done by learned men and women that it has become over-identified with ideas and written commentaries. Interpretation is meaning, and meaning can be said. But more basically, biblical meaning is done: meaning as relationships God intends between us and himself and between ourselves in relation to God. Because those relationships are forms of human life sharing in, showing forth and being shaped by God's own "performance" as triune life, the most authentic Christian biblical interpretation is human enactments of God-informed life . . . Interpretation, then in its final form, is God-formed human practice. What we do as the people of God is our interpretation of the Bible.'

framework of divine and human action understood as 'performance'. This is a larger framework than the more parochial ones of historical criticism and literary criticism conventionally understood, because the horizon of meaning is *not restricted to the past nor to the text as text*. Now, the Bible is seen as unique testimony to the 'performance' of the triune God, and true interpretation is a matter of so embodying the text as to become part of that performance, sharing in the divine life. To use a remarkable image, it is like the prophet *ingesting* the words of the Lord written on the scroll in order to be a prophet and to do a prophet's work (Ezek 3.1–3; cf. Rev 10.8–11).[72]

This understanding of the art of biblical interpretation is a radical one. What it represents is a call for nothing less than a *change of culture* in biblical interpretation and therefore, in so far as the two are related, in society as a whole.[73] This alternative culture will be a culture critically open to *faith and conversion* (but in ways free from coercion) because that is what is involved in allowing the text-inscribed story of God to become our story, its time to become our time, its space to become the space we inhabit also. To put it another way, the 'hermeneutics of suspicion' will be seen as not suspicious enough, as foreclosing prematurely on the meaning and truth of the text by failing to attend *with love* to what lies, sharply etched, on the surface,[74] the story of God in Christ reconciling the world to himself.

It will be a culture also characterized by *risk, struggle and new-found freedom*, because there is no scientific method to guarantee assured results when the goal in view is human transformation by authentic performance. Here, historical and literary criticism will play an important, but limited, part in contributing to close readings of the text historically informed.[75] And to be 'historically informed' will demand patient and disciplined attention to the *full history* of the text – the history of its formation and the history of its 'effects' both in generations past and up to the present.[76]

[72] Compare Loughlin, *Telling God's Story*, where Part One is entitled 'Consuming Text', and Chapter 8 'Eating the Word'.
[73] Profound on this is David S. Yeago's essay 'Messiah's People: The Culture of the Church in the Midst of the Nations', *Pro Ecclesia* 6/1 (1997), 146–71.
[74] See further, Williams, 'The Suspicion of Suspicion'.
[75] See further, Gerard Loughlin, 'Following to the Letter: The Literal Use of Scripture', *Literature and Theology* 9/4 (1995), 370–82.
[76] Relevant here is Anthony Thiselton, 'Knowledge, Myth and Corporate Memory', in *Believing in the Church: The Corporate Nature of Faith. A Report by the Doctrine Commission of the Church of England* (London: SPCK, 1981), 45–78.

This involves risk and struggle, not only because the 'security' of scientific method is not an option, and not only because our own identities as interpreters are on the line, but also because attention to the full history of the text confronts us with performances which are depraved and appalling, as liberation and feminist theologies have helped us to see.[77] The struggle comes in fighting as courageously as we can against cynicism, in accepting in humility that appalling performances past and present are also in some sense ours, and in believing that by God's grace and inspiration more authentic performances are possible.

This will involve, in turn, a culture of interpretation critically open to the witness and worship of the church and other faith communities, an *ecclesial and ecumenical* culture in which the virtuoso performances of saints (and sinners!) within the church and outside it, and the creative fidelity of the communion of saints past and present, will serve as guides to true performance. The resources here are enormous, but our occluded vision obscures them from view, and our lack of practice in the virtues and skills of a truly ecclesial and ecumenical existence open to the Spirit is a serious handicap.[78]

Finally, the *institutional and paedogogical* implications of the performance model are significant, for what the performance model implies is a major reconfiguration of the relation between Berlin and Athens, between *Wissenschaft* and *paideia*, as David Kelsey has shown.[79] At a more mundane level, what I am suggesting is a world away from the packaging of information about the Bible in modules chosen cafeteria-style by autonomous individuals ('customers'!) acting, supposedly, with 'free' choice. The performance model is

---

[77] For well-nuanced comment on liberation and feminist hermeneutics, see Scott, 'Speaking to Form', 149–51. Relevant also is the exchange between Gloria Albrecht and Stanley Hauerwas in *Scottish Journal of Theology* 50/2 (1997), 219–41.

[78] For encouragement in this direction from the Orthodox tradition, see further Vigen Guroian, *Ethics After Christendom: Toward an Ecclesial Christian Ethic* (Grand Rapids: Eerdmans, 1994), 53–80 (on 'The Bible in Orthodox Ethics: A Liturgical Reading').

[79] See David Kelsey's two works *To Understand God Truly: What's Theological About a Theological School?* (Louisville: Westminster John Knox Press, 1992) and *Between Athens and Berlin: The Theological Education Debate* (Grand Rapids: Eerdmans, 1993). A useful discussion and evaluation of the issues from this side of the Atlantic is an unpublished paper by Mark D. Chapman of Ripon College entitled, 'Scripture, Tradition and Criticism: A Brief Proposal for Theological Education'.

not about the marketing of intellectual goods for consumption by those who can afford it. Rather, as readers of the novels of Rabbi Chaim Potok will know,[80] it is about *becoming apprentices* to masters found trustworthy in the discipline of performing the Scriptures, an apprenticeship which involves critical immersion in the life of Scripture-shaped communities.[81]

Of course, this is where a change of culture of New Testament interpretation may not stop at the doors of departments of theology, seminaries and churches. If we are willing to consider things in terms of the performance model, the change is one to be asked of ourselves personally and professionally, and of an education system bending over backwards to make itself 'relevant' in a culture of consumption. More widely still, it is a change to be asked of society as a whole.[82] Learning authentic performance of Christian Scripture and sharing thereby in the story-inscribed life of God is no less radical than that.

---

[80] I have in mind here Potok's novels *The Chosen, The Promise, In the Beginning, My Name is Asher Lev* and *The Gift of Asher Lev*, all published by Penguin. *In the Beginning*, in particular, explores both the promise and perils of 'higher criticism' for performing the Scriptures in the context of Hasidic Judaism.

[81] See further on 'apprenticeship' Stanley Hauerwas, *After Christendom?* (Sydney: Anzea, 1991), 101–11; also Wilken, *Remembering the Christian Past*, 171–5.

[82] Very helpful on this from an Orthodox Jewish perspective are the recent writings of Chief Rabbi Jonathan Sacks, esp. *Faith in the Future* (London: Darton, Longman & Todd, 1995) and *The Politics of Hope* (London: Jonathan Cape, 1997).

Index of Modern Authors